Managed Care Success

Reducing Risk While Increasing Patient Satisfaction

James W. Saxton, Esquire
Chairman, Health Care Litigation Group
Stevens and Lee, P.C.
Lancaster, Pennsylvania

Thomas L. Leaman, MD
The Milton S. Hershey Medical Center
The Pennsylvania State University
Hershey, Pennsylvania

AN ASPEN PUBLICATION®
Aspen Publishers, Inc.
Gaithersburg, Maryland
1998

Library of Congress Cataloging-in-Publication Data

Saxton, James W.
Managed care success : reducing risk while increasing patient satisfaction / James W. Saxton, Thomas L. Leaman.
p. cm.
Includes bibliographical references and index.
ISBN 0-8342-1023-1 (hardcover)
1. Managed care plans (Medical care) 2. Patient satisfaction.
3. Risk Management. 4. Tort liability of managed care plans.
I. Leaman, Thomas L. II. Title.
[DNLM: 1. Managed Care Programs—organization & administration—United States. 2. Risk Management. 3. Malpractice—United States.
4. Liability, Legal. W 130 AA1 S27m 1998]
RA413.S327 1998
362.1'04258—dc21
DNLM/DLC
for Library of Congress 98-9985
CIP

Orders: (800) 638-8437
Customer Service: (800) 234-1660

Editorial Resources: Bill Fogle
Library of Congress Catalog Card Number: 98-9985
ISBN: 0-8342-1023-1

Printed in the United States of America

1 2 3 4 5

This book is dedicated to two people. The first is Dr. Smith, who is both a real person as well as an amalgam of all the physicians stuck during the transitional period of time in health care trying to figure out the new rules. Dr. Smith never asked for the changes, he never voted on the new systems to be introduced—they simply appeared. To his credit, he is trying now to adapt. He is, and always has been, the backbone of the American health care system. To lose him would be tragic. It is also dedicated to Dr. Phoebe Smith, who represents the doctors and other health care providers literally being brought up in this system who understand that the delivery of health care is changing, and are willing to work to influence those changes, and enjoy the practice of medicine.

CONTENTS

Introduction

Health care, at least since the advent of scientific medicine, during this century, has been changing and progressing. The changes have been dramatic: control of many infectious diseases and eradication of some, use of fiberoptics and lasers, imaging techniques, the ability to eliminate dental caries, transplantation surgery, microsurgical techniques, electronic communication, genetic engineering, designer drugs—and this is only a partial list. While all of these changes have occurred within a practice lifetime, the rate of change has been relatively slow and deliberate, at least in comparison to the changes in the health care delivery system within the past decade.

The exciting changes in the science of medicine have all been driven by technological advances. The effects of each change have been studied in detail, and each has been subjected to professional scrutiny and to long established governmental regulations. During this same time span there have been some changes in the health care environment in practice styles and practice arrangements: single specialty groups, multiple specialty groups, and networks. These were often driven by the entrepreneurial spirit of a few physicians.

We have now entered a new era. The health care environment of today is vastly different from that of a decade ago. There is absolutely no sign that this is a mere phase, or swing of the pendulum, and that we will soon be returning to the previous way of doing business. Industry and the federal government want both a continued reduction in health care costs or at the very least a slowing of health care inflation and both perceive managed care as doing so with some substantiation. Forces that began this effort would not permit a return. Nor would the great superstructure of health care administration that we have constructed, employing tens of thousands of people, permit it. The only thing that seems certain at this point is that the health care environment of ten years from now will be vastly different from the health care environment of today.

These practice changes are not driven by technology, nor by the entrepreneurial spirit of a few physicians. They are driven by even more powerful forces, the very essence of our capitalistic system, the marketplace. The marketplace, in terms of the paying patient, the employers who pay health care costs, and the federal government, is demanding more cost effective health care. They want more value, as proven by carefully conducted cost analyses and outcome measurements, not by mere proclamations.

The issue for each of us as individuals is not whether these changes are good or bad, but that here and now we must determine how best to move within the new health care environment. What is best for our patients, our families, and ourselves?

If one were to try to place a point in time when the recent changes began to accelerate, perhaps the focus would be in 1993 when President and Mrs. Clinton introduced the Health Security Act. This proposal consisted of 1,352 pages of legislation which attempted to reform, among other issues, certain aspects of our tort system, welfare, insurance, taxes, anti-trust regulations, medical education financing, and the way in which health services would be both purchased and delivered. Although this legislation failed as a package, it instigated great activity throughout the country. We began to see the formation of the "alphabet soup" of health care integration. These include the PHO, IPA, IPO, MCO, MSO, PO, PHCO, GPWW, PSO, and an OWA.* All of these vehicles of integration were, in part, an effort to make sure that providers were included in managing care, or, perhaps better, managing health. These are all vehicles through which contracting or other types of collaboration could occur.

The managed care market has evolved and matured at different rates in different places in the country. The only constant has been continued growth. The precise definition of managed care is elusive. In its simplest form, managed care is a finance and delivery arrangement for health services. It attempts to align incentives in such a fashion that costs can be reduced and yet still strive to maintain patient satisfaction and good

*Actually found in the literature, indicating "other weird arrangements."

health outcomes. In its mature forms it can have many worthwhile, even lofty, goals: better coordination of services, health education, preventive services, and patient and physician satisfaction. However, there are also many potential dangers. Utilization controls may block access to needed, or desired, diagnostic or therapeutic procedures. Reducing choices may add to patient skepticism and dissatisfaction. Financial incentives can lead to, or have led to, a breakdown in trust between the patient and the doctor.

Describing managed care is like painting a sunset, by the time you identify the shapes and colors, they have changed. You negotiate a contract with one managed care organization, only to find out soon afterward that it has been sold to another group, which has, in turn, just merged with another company. With each there is a change in personal contacts and a change in the contract.* Considering the fundamental purposes of managed care, the clearest conclusion is that to be successful in the future, providers will need to deliver health care differently, using fewer resources, yet maintaining good health outcomes and patient satisfaction. To accomplish this, providers are beginning to change what may be referred to as the three Ws; **w**here care is provided, by **w**hom, and **w**hat care is provided. To deliver services differently and maintain the same high standards of satisfaction and outcomes, physicians clearly face new liability challenges. Risk management, in the classic sense, will be changed forever. Some of the fundamental principles will still apply, but the way in which they are applied will need to change. Defensive medicine, in the sense of doing procedures to protect the provider, will no longer work. Utilization controls will penalize the physician, and, ultimately, limit the physician's practice, an unacceptable outcome.

This book is intended not only for physicians and dentists, but for all members of the health care team who are facing the challenge of delivering services in this new environment. It is written by a physician with experience in private, group, and academic practice, medical education, and as an expert witness in malpractice litigation; and by an attorney whose entire practice has revolved around working with health care providers, including physicians and managed care organizations, on risk

*From year to year it seems the products managed care organizations want to offer members change, and the way they want to reimburse providers may change. Their emphasis on one type of delivery of service may change.

management issues and is facing these issues, literally, in the courtroom on behalf of physicians and other providers.

We will review, briefly, the evolution of managed care generally, then bring it into the physician's office, describing many of the expected changes. We will describe the costs of being sued for malpractice, which are now higher than ever before and distinctly different. The issues of why people sue and who is most likely to sue will be addressed. We will then discuss the increased risks, and new risks, that develop in your practice. Not only have the risks changed, but the tools you have available to meet those risks have also changed. The principle and the process of informed consent will also be revisited, as they apply in this new setting. We will then present the principles, and practical applications, of malpractice litigation prevention in this radically changed milieu. With the help of risk managers and professional liability insurers nationwide, we will spotlight recurring dilemmas from which claims seem to be growing, and give some guidance for risk reduction.

It will be shown that these strategies can, and must, with our patients as partners, meet the managed care goals of good health outcomes and patient satisfaction, which also can lead to profitability.

This book is not meant to be a substitute for an experienced practice attorney, but to raise an awareness of these issues and as a practical guide to address them. The changes, consolidations, mergers, and integration are occurring quickly. It is time to examine what these changes are doing to your own liability picture, so that you can deal with them most effectively. We hope that you enjoy this book and are able to use it effectively.

ACKNOWLEDGMENTS

This work would not have been possible without the ideas, information, and support of many people. Our conclusions are based on the careful research and reporting of several thousand investigators, and we appreciate their efforts. We are also grateful to the law firm of Barley, Snyder, Senft & Cohen, LLC, for their continuing encouragement and the use of their facilities and research capabilities. We are delighted with the art work of Sally Saxton, who has so accurately depicted the exasperating, but endearing, Dr. Smith. We are also appreciative of the superb secretarial skills and persistence of Nancy Davis, the investigative inquisitiveness of Washington College of Law, American University law student Cindy Nicholson, and the extraordinary and perceptive organizational skills of doctoral student Michaele O'Brien. We also want to note our deep sense of gratitude to Rebecca Pratt, literary consultant, for all she has taught us about writing books.

Most especially, however, we want to express our appreciation, for their unflagging support and confidence in us, to Sally and Jeanne, our wives and very patient partners.

PART I

The Concerns

CHAPTER 1

Dr. Smith Meets Managed Care

"All I wanted to do was to take good care of my patients."
Dr. Smith

Source: Copyright © 1997, SC Saxton.

Dr. Smith sits slumped in a chair in my office. He has two serious malpractice cases pending, and that is the least of his problems. He is a good, conscientious doctor. How did he get to this point? It isn't a long story, but it is a common one:

Meet Dr. Smith. Dr. Smith has been a family practitioner in the same community for 25 years. He and his wife moved there when he first entered practice. He is board-certified in family practice and has successfully completed three re-certifying examinations. He has a typical family practice, caring for patients from birth through many of the difficult life decisions they face, often involving his counsel. His practice, in some cases, spans more than one generation. For example, he delivered Susan Scott, helped her grow up, then delivered her first baby. He stopped doing deliveries about five years ago.

Most of this time he had been a solo practitioner. Twice he had an associate, but after several years of work with Dr. Smith, both associates started their own practices. Both times this was with Dr. Smith's encouragement—he did not have a noncompete clause in his contracts. He liked the fact that he could serve as a mentor for these younger doctors; the community was growing, so there was never a shortage of patients. Dr. Smith was involved in his community and had been the chairman of the local community hospital board and president of the medical staff at one time. He had also served on the Quality Review Committee and kept very involved in the hospital's continuing education programs, many of which he actually coordinated.

Dr. Smith prided himself on how well he knew his patients, and the relationship he had with them. He said that he really knew how to be "comforting" to his patients. He confided once that in years past he had made a few mistakes, or errors in judgment, about which he felt badly. However, in these situations, he showed his true concern, was open and supportive, and never really had a serious disagreement with a patient. In fact, he had never had a lawsuit or claim, although he admitted he had outcomes that were not expected or desirable and at times thought for sure his patients would sue. Close relationships and good and open communication had apparently worked. Dr. Smith thought the people in his town knew he was doing the best he could. His practice was thriving, and, most importantly, he was enjoying his work.

About three years ago, the dominant employer in Dr. Smith's community signed on with a managed care organization for employee health care benefits. This was an arrangement that he had only read about and heard about at the hospital. There had been a program at the hospital explaining some of the varieties of managed care organizations and giving advice as to negotiating managed care contracts. This concept was something quite foreign to him, and he hadn't really absorbed all of the information. He understood that employers could get more comprehensive benefits for their employees, the quality of care would be very high, and the cost would be much less. This was a high priority for a company in view of the highly competitive business environment and rapidly rising health care costs. Dr. Smith saw how the combination seemed very attractive. However, from the physician's perspective, it looked like the physician agreed to have lower fees, or worse yet, not charge at all and just accept a monthly per-member fee. It didn't make sense to him and he did not need any additional patients. Dr. Smith thought that his community would never embrace managed care and wondered whether this would be just a fad. He thought this capitation arrangement might put him in a conflict situation with his patients.* He understood there were some good principles, too: preventive medicine, pushing healthy habits, acting as a coordinator of care—but he did most of that now. On balance, this did not seem to be much of a change for him or his patients, and he would rather not get involved in it.

Dr. Smith did not believe there would be much of a change in his patient base because he knew that the employer had also chosen some sort of point of service agreement. In other words, the employees could choose a provider outside of the network, although it might cost them a little more. He was confident that most of his patients would not sign up for the managed care plan, and even if they did, would pay the little extra money to retain his services. For this reason he decided not to be on the panel. It wasn't hard to get on the panel, but he wanted nothing to do with this health maintenance organization (HMO) as they called it. He thought it might be a passing fad. There was big talk at the hospital among doctors that no one would sign up, but in the end, most of his colleagues did. Nevertheless, it wasn't for him.

Unfortunately, however, in the first year he saw that the "little extra money" did make a big difference to many of his patients, and his patient base began to drop. Many patients did sign up for the plan and would "stay in the network." This bothered Dr. Smith, not so much because of financial concerns, although that was part of it, but many of his longtime patients had gone somewhere else. Further, when he saw some of these patients, they asked why he did not sign up. He felt like asking, "Why don't you pay a little extra and come and see me?" but that wasn't like him.

In the second year, Dr. Smith decided he needed to sign up on the panel and therefore submitted to the credentialing process. He expected no difficulty since he had an excellent reputation in the community; however, he had a lengthy application to complete. Further, when the managed care organization reviewers did an audit of his office, they made several pointed suggestions for changes, particularly in the medical records system. Dr. Smith thought these were a bit cum-

---

*Capitation is a set fee based on a prearranged agreement, not the actual costs of care for an individual patient. This fee, or the CAP rate, is usually expressed in units, or PMPM, meaning per member per month. This amount is paid to the physician at a set time each month for all enrolled employees.

bersome but felt, in all likelihood, they were probably for the good. He also had to provide far more information than he did for hospital credentialing. When he asked about it he was told that the HMO took provider credentialing very seriously and that it even marketed its plan, in part, on the basis of its excellent panel of physicians. There were also liability concerns, he was told. He was informed that the HMO was hoping to be accredited by a large national accrediting agency so all sorts of requirements had to be met. He guessed that this, on balance, was good, after all, since he would not want to be on a panel with physicians who were not high quality providers. He was given a large book that explained his different responsibilities, along with a full set of policies and procedures. He gave it to his office manager/head nurse/receptionist, Gladys, to review, but never really went through it very carefully himself. Gladys told him with a wink that she would review all those rules right away, as she put it in the storage closet. It was a huge amount of material and included many practice guidelines, which Dr. Smith thought was amusing. Why would a doctor need a practice guideline? There was also information on his capitation rate, what his responsibilities were, when he would be paid, utilization review procedures, and committee structure, just to name a few sections. He signed the provider agreement without closely reviewing it. It was his understanding that the agreement was the agreement, and there wasn't going to be much he could do to "negotiate" this. He was in a solo practice after all, what clout would he have?

During the first year after he signed up, he began to notice changes which were subtle at first, and then became more and more pronounced. During that year other employers also began to move into the managed care market. Soon, about 30% of his practice was capitated; that is, Dr. Smith received a certain amount per month per patient regardless of the care he provided. He was also required to follow certain rules or policies concerning referrals for consultations or even tests. There were only certain specialists he could refer to and only certain laboratories he could use. Many of these policies he did not completely understand.

Dr. Smith began to see new patients, which he had not realized was going to occur. Many of these new patients had complex medical problems and hadn't had appropriate or comprehensive health care for years, requiring a lot of extra (uncompensated) time. It wasn't that he did not get paid for these patients, but he did not get paid for the amount of care he provided. He couldn't shortchange the patients, these were needed services; however, he wondered why someone hadn't provided them before. He also noted that he was seeing his patients at more frequent intervals. Patients needed to come in prior to referral or even to obtain prescriptions. His waiting room seemed to stay full. Even before he signed up with the plan, his patients usually had to wait. It was just how his practice was; sometimes a patient would take longer or there was an unexpected emergency. Usually Gladys would explain the problem to the patients and it would be all right. However, now these patients seemed to expect a great deal more. The wait was longer and the patients were less patient! Gladys was getting stressed—after several patients told her the HMO informed them that they could be seen within two to three days for a nonemergent visit, Gladys retorted, "we are not your HMO!" Patients began to grumble about the wait to get on the schedule and the wait in the reception area. Gladys really did not have the time or inclination to "chat" with patients. Dr. Smith's hours began to expand to absorb the new volume. The staff became resentful of these managed care patients and felt that they were taking advantage of Dr. Smith's and their own time. Patients also began questioning both Dr. Smith and Gladys about the new rules. Why couldn't they go to the orthopedic surgeon they wanted? Why did they have to travel further to get an x-ray? Dr. Smith was ill-prepared for these questions, but tried to smooth things over. Gladys was not so tactful, saying, "you're the one who signed up for the HMO." The staff was becoming frustrated. This frustration began spilling over into the patient care and was damaging the close relationship with their patients that they had always cherished.

After the first year with the plan, Dr. Smith was informed by the medical director of the managed care organization, Dr. Wright, that his utilization was out of line with that of his peers. Dr. Wright explained that utilization meant the number of referrals Dr. Smith made, the number of imaging procedures he ordered, and the laboratory use. He also explained to Dr. Smith that he was the gatekeeper of these resources and it was important to conserve them—not denying appropriate care, but trying to use judgment as to when they were really needed. Dr. Wright was actually very complimentary, saying that with his experience, Dr. Smith himself could do many of the things for which he was referring patients. Dr. Smith suggested that perhaps his peers were not utilizing resources appropriately, but it was quickly explained that he was the "outlier" with utilization outside of the "norm." He needed to analyze clinical situations more carefully before referrals were made or tests were ordered. He should do a little cost benefit analysis—he should not simply send patients for a specialist consultation without determining whether it was needed at that point in time, or whether it was something which he could handle himself. Dr. Wright had a surprising amount of data on graphs demonstrating this information. It was hard to argue the point.

Dr. Smith was also told that his staff needed to be more professional and cordial to patients since the organization had received a number of complaints. This was shocking to Dr. Smith—working with patients and pleasing them had always been his strong suit. He knew the HMO was doing surveys, and had assumed he would finish at the top. Dr. Wright shared with Dr. Smith some of the survey results and clearly there were a number of complaints. Telephone calls were not answered promptly enough, it took too long to get an appointment, the wait in the reception area was too long, and there were specific complaints about the staff and about himself. Patients felt he did not provide enough information. They thought the receptionist was short with them and that he appeared rushed. This really surprised him. Dr. Wright also raised an issue about being more tactful in answering questions raised by patients about the new system. Dr. Wright's notes contained quotes that must have come from Gladys about the HMO. Some of them were not flattering. What could he do? Gladys held strong opinions and liked to voice them. Dr. Smith could certainly see they were bothersome to Dr. Wright—they were all highlighted in his comments.

Dr. Smith was upset and frustrated by this, but tried to address all of these concerns. He realized that he could not simply do without the managed care organization. It now represented too large a part of his practice. First, he spoke to his staff and they were quite incensed that, given all the hard work they were asked to do to take care of these new patients, instead of appreciation they were being reprimanded. The staff had been working harder than ever, there were more patients, more visits, more telephone calls, more coordination, more complaints, and yet they had received their smallest pay increase in recent years. Now they were being asked to do a little more and work a little harder. Gladys was talking about retiring and his other two part-timers said they wanted to quit. Dr. Smith consoled all of them, telling them it was going to get better. However, he was not sure how, since his capitation rate was not going up and his expenses were.

Dr. Smith became extremely careful about his utilization patterns because he realized that his economic survival depended on staying within the "norm." He did a lot of soul searching. He certainly did not want to limit access to care. He had read horror stories about this. However, he knew the other doctors that Dr. Wright referred to, and most of them were very good; he wondered how they did it. He determined there must be a balance that could be struck and he would have to be more conscientious about this. Although this was easier said than done; he began to second guess himself; maybe he was an "overutilizer" and maybe he had been practicing "defensive medicine." He was committed to get placed with the rest of them on those charts and graphs!

He went after it furiously for the next two years. He changed his practice style and pushed his staff even harder. Unfortunately, Gladys retired, which saddened him. She had been with him for many years. He hired a young woman fresh out of school who seemed very eager. This was going to help economically. He was able to hire someone at half of Gladys' salary since it had built up over 20 years. The staff was still stressed though, and it seemed like it wasn't getting easier. His capitation rate was not increasing and although he was pushing preventive services and healthy lifestyles, his patients still seemed to have a lot of health needs. Dr. Smith wondered about the benefits of these health promotion and preventive services, since he provided them often; but many patients changed plans or doctors. He wondered when these efforts would pay off. More of his practice was based on capitation and he really couldn't see pushing himself or his staff any harder. His front desk was still not handling complaints well. The long patient waiting time continued and he was becoming increasingly uncomfortable with this new practice style.

Now Dr. Smith faces two serious pending malpractice cases. The first involves a 42-year-old man whose wife had called Dr. Smith at home one night, explaining that her husband was having some upper abdominal pain. She also said he was belching and sweating, and thought it could have been the "all-you-can-eat" fried fish dinner he had a few hours earlier. Dr. Smith spent a great deal of time with her on the telephone and, because the symptoms really did sound gastrointestinal in nature and because the man did not have any real cardiac risk factors, he advised them that the man could use an antacid and to come into the office in the morning. Of course, if he felt worse or anything changed, they should call him immediately. The patient had asked whether he should make a trip to the emergency department and explained that he had seen such prompting on various commercials by a local emergency department. But Dr. Smith assured them that seeing him in the morning would, in all likelihood, be fine. He was acutely mindful that the emergency department is one of the most expensive modes of treating a patient. However, it was the fact that it really just didn't appear necessary that drove his decision. Unfortunately, clinically the patient deteriorated rapidly and died of a myocardial infarction on the way to the emergency department very early the next morning. Dr. Smith was devastated. He, of course, did not have the patient's chart at home and was not able to document this until the next day. He didn't write a note at home, either. The dictation he did the next day, explaining why he felt the emergency department visit was not necessary, would later in litigation be described as "after-the-fact and self-serving."

The second patient is a 45-year-old woman in whom he had thought he felt a thickening in the upper outer quadrant of her right breast. He ordered a mammogram which showed diffuse changes that were consistent with her known fibrocystic disease. He advised her to cut down on caffeine intake and to return for a recheck in four months. He had contemplated sending her for a surgical consultation, but it just seemed premature. But the patient never came back for a follow-up, and a year went by. It turns out she does have a carcinoma and unfortunately, it has spread to her nodes. Her attorney is saying an earlier diagnosis would have made all the difference. She is claiming that she should have been referred for an immediate biopsy. Dr. Smith knew he had emphasized with her that she needed a follow-up, a point the patient denied. Unfortunately, there was nothing in the notes. The patient said that Dr. Smith downplayed the need for a follow-up and now she wondered if it was because he had certain financial incentives. She had read about this type of situation in the newspaper. Her attorney wanted to see all of the statistics about his referral patterns, as well as his contract with the HMO. He subpoenaed all of the HMO's records. Dr. Smith thought back to those graphs.

He had improved a great deal, at least in the view of Dr. Wright's company. Would a jury be able to see the graphs? He didn't improve his utilization record at the expense of the patient's health. Would the jury understand his perspective?

Dr. Smith admits in all candor, that in years past, he might have made both of these referrals earlier, but that is not the way that medicine is practiced now. It is not his fault, it is the system, he believes. Neither of these cases were bad medicine, they just looked bad. Maybe his documentation wasn't what it should be, but he had become so busy. He did not know these patients that well, they were relatively new. H remembered that one had a run-in with Gladys—the patient had mixed up his appointment date or maybe he was running late again. Dr. Smith also remembered that the patient with breast cancer had been a problem and was always complaining about something. Regardless, he was very concerned about these cases, and when he looked at the charts he was unhappy about the lack of documentation. More importantly, he didn't like the picture that was being painted of him in the formal complaints in these lawsuits. It was as if he had withheld care for economic reasons, which wasn't the case at all, but he could see how someone could come to that conclusion. In years past he would be happy to go in front of a jury of his peers, people of his community, and explain, but not now; the public is upset about all of this and, Dr. Smith added, "I don't blame them!"

To add to his troubles, Dr. Wright had informed him that patient complaints had continued and, if anything, were worse. One patient complained that Dr. Smith was actually withholding care. Dr. Smith had, years previously, quickly referred this patient to a dermatologist to remove a skin tag, but now he insisted that he could do it himself and would not authorize a referral to a specialist. Dr. Smith tried to explain to Dr. Wright that the patient had completely misunderstood him and Dr. Wright agreed. However, the patient had also complained to the State Bureau of Professional Occupational Affairs, who now wanted to do an investigation of Dr. Smith's office. Dr. Wright explained that there was nothing they could do about that but that the patient's actions seemed unreasonable. They could not pay for the defense of that claim and unfortunately it was a negative for him in the recredentialing process. That brought up another point.

Because of the volume of patient complaints, and the fact that he was still outside utilization parameters, although doing much better, the managed care organization decided to terminate his contract. Dr. Wright explained it was a hard decision but that the liability picture for managed care organizations was heating up. Some states had enacted laws so patients could even sue the managed care organization. They had to tighten up their credentialing. He had two suits now, a complaint with the state, many patient complaints, and there was really nothing he could do. Dr. Wright explained that they would try to avoid National Practitioner Data Bank implications, but Dr. Smith did not even understand what that was. A managed care organization that deselects a physician for quality reasons must arguably make a report to the National Practitioners Data Bank. However, if the deselection is made without course, perhaps because a large employer customer left the health plan and not as many physicians are needed, no report is necessary.

Dr. Wright had a problem, too. He believed fervently in his organization. It provided a necessary service to the community. Before his company came to this area, many families were not receiving adequate health care. They did, of course, have emergency care available, but as for preventive services, or even regular care for chronic ailments that were not too symptomatic, like hypertension or mild diabetes mellitus, they just did without. The costs were too high. Dr. Wright was proud of the panel of physicians they had been able to recruit. Every one of them was well qualified—good credentials, excellent references, and, of course, board certified. He was also keenly aware—the office reminded him almost daily—that costs must be controlled rigorously in order to meet the competition and to stay in business. If they could not compete successfully they could not provide a service.

Dr. Wright had data that showed 90% of his fine physician panel was able to stay within the utilization parameters that the company had established. In order to control expenses, there were two obvious choices available to him. The utilization norms could be reduced; i.e., they could tighten the restrictions on the use of imaging procedures, laboratory testing, and consultations. This would entail some hazards, however, because health outcomes might be adversely affected, there would most certainly be more than the normal patient complaints, and there would certainly be increased malpractice liability. The other alternative, which carried none of these hazards, was to control, or eliminate, the "outliers." Outliers were described as those providers whose practice statistics were consistently beyond the norm. Perhaps in the future because of increased competition, it would take some of both.

Dr. Wright liked Dr. Smith. He had an excellent reputation in the community and seemed to be a very caring physician. He was earnest and conscientious, and had really tried to follow the company's policies. Dr. Wright knew that one of the organization's original goals in recruiting Dr. Smith was to attract his patients into their health plan, and they had been phenomenally successful. Dr. Wright also knew from past experience that if Dr. Smith left the panel, only a few of his patients would follow him. What would he do?

Reviewing the data and his notes on their meetings, Dr. Wright felt that they had given Dr. Smith every opportunity to conform, but he was just not capable of practicing medicine in a competitive environment. And now he had two malpractice claims against him, a professional licensing complaint, and his patient surveys were very unfavorable. In the best interests of the organization and of the community they served, Dr. Smith would have to go.

This really hurt Dr. Smith and his practice. He had never been professionally criticized before. He lost patients, but more importantly he lost his zeal for what he had done for the last quarter of a century. He was frustrated and wondered how he was going to deal with these new organizations and this new way to practice. Although, he was soon approached by a large for-profit company that really seemed sound. It wasn't managed by physicians but by businessmen with experience at running physician practices, they said. They could deal with managed care. Dr. Smith would have to sell his practice and he would get one-third of the amount of the sale's price in cash, one-third in a promissory note, and one-third in stock. A certain percentage of his revenues would then go to the company. Apparently the notes were unsecured and he would have to hope the company did well. He could not sell his stock for several years; the company had not even gone public yet, but he hoped the stock value would increase or at least have some value. More importantly to Dr. Smith, he no longer had to run his practice—he no longer had a practice to run.

What could have happened? Dr. Smith emphatically insists that he is the same physician he had been for the last 25 years. "All I wanted to do was take good care of my patients." He had not changed, why is all of this happening to him now?

In part, it is because Dr. Smith is the same doctor that he has been for the last 25 years. Everything else in the health care environment has changed—change is basic and fundamental—but Dr. Smith never really evolved or changed with it. He then tried to jump into it all at once and was not prepared. He tried to keep up by joining the panel, but he did not learn enough about the new rules and failed to appreciate the very fundamental changes that managed care brought to his practice. The hallmark of his practice in years past was the close relationship that he had with patients and how good he made them feel. This was his description of "comforting patients" even when an error in judgment or mistake was made. He failed to prevent the rapid deterioration of these relationships when the system changed, and he failed to realize what these changes would mean to his practice and his staff. He did not educate himself or his staff. His staff became resentful. He did not learn the new importance of documentation or to have documentation systems in place to act as a safety net. He fell into a trap from which he could not climb out.

The health care landscape has changed too much for a physician to remain static. It is no longer enough to keep abreast of clinical research and enjoying one's practice; it also depends on keeping up to date on the structure of medical practice. One cannot simply jump into managed care without understanding what it means and what changes it brings to the practice. One needs to establish systems to help prevent some of the problems that Dr. Smith incurred.

NEW RISKS

Practicing in a managed care environment adds new risks at many different levels and increases some of the old risks. Some of these are issues which, if unresolved, lead to conflicts of interest, in turn leading to real dilemmas, some of which are discussed in Chapter 10.

Gatekeeper Risks

In primary care, with the expanded role of the "gatekeeper" function, new responsibilities are added. The primary care physician, or other physician if given that role, is now responsible for health maintenance, health promotion, and overall coordination of care for the patient. This is a prime principle of HMOs and is the thrust of managing care, or better said, managing health. As more responsibilities are added, more pressures are also placed on the provider to use resources carefully. This is referred to as utilization or monitoring utilization. At first blush, it seems like an inherent conflict. How can a health care provider do more with less? This is the squeeze play that providers first feel when they become involved in managing care. It is a narrow path: provide excellent health care and patient satisfaction, and at the same time conserve resources and meet appropriate managed care goals. However, it is possible, recognizing that there are both risks and potential for abuses.

A primary care physician first entering into capitation arrangements may find that there are many new patients with complex problems. Some of these patients may not have received comprehensive care in the past. Such patients are always an interesting challenge and do require a disproportionate amount of time, which is not immediately compensated.

Patients may also come to their doctor's office more often. Literature that they receive from their managed care organization or the benefits department of their employer may encourage them to do so. They may seek help earlier in the disease process, especially if there is no financial disincentive to do so. For all of these reasons, there is usually an increase in number and complexity of visits. Providers should make sure that in their provider agreement there is an understanding about how many new patients must be accepted,[1] in order to keep from being overwhelmed, especially when just starting. They should make sure that the agreement is read carefully and have it reviewed with someone knowledgeable about these issues, preferably the practice attorney. Many medical societies provide guidance and there are handbooks or articles concerning this issue.[2,3]

Utilization Controls

The provider, because of utilization parameters, may be expected to keep treating patients for all the problems which are within the scope of that physician's capabilities. In private practice, many primary care physicians treat patients with minor trauma, such as simple fractures and superficial lacerations, when they have time available, but refer such patients when busy. However, in a managed care environment this can again become the rule. Providing care to the full extent of one's skills also adds volume to the practice. All of this promotes extra stress for both physician and staff, at a time when they must make intense efforts to maintain their most valuable asset, the close patient relationships. Physicians also have to make sure their skills are well honed in those areas. Good communication with patients is the key so patients understand the process and do not jump to the conclusion that there is economic motivation. Sometimes physicians will complain to patients, or in response to questions from patients, about the need to do more procedures themselves, instead of referring the patient elsewhere, explaining that they are just following a "managed care rule." This puts the physician in a bad light as well. A little education of the patient in this area can go a long way, noting that the physician is well-qualified and experienced in this area and that it was more convenient for the patient, as well as being more efficient from the managed care standpoint. Remember, most patients are uninformed about managed care, and what they do know or think they know they may not like. From a practical point of view, although so-called "gag rules" have become disfavored,[4,5] it is really not appropriate to bash, blame, or defame the managed care organization. However, it is clear that physicians have a duty to advocate on behalf of patients, but there is an appropriate way to do so.[6] Most managed care organizations have a grievance procedure for patients to seek a review of an adverse utilizations decision. This is an area of great concern and one in which our attention needs to be directed. Physicians should be prepared to provide input and to support these appeals. In fact, a physician or dentist can be held liable for not advocating, in some fashion, a position for a patient when there is a disagreement among the physician and managed care organization as to what care needs to be provided.[7–9]

When a patient requests referral and is refused, the patient may very easily assume that the reason is some perverse financial incentive. Much depends on how the refusal process is handled. Do patients really understand the system they have chosen? Was there a thorough explanation by the physician of why the request was refused or postponed? The physician might say, "Let's wait until I can determine if your backache is a bone problem before we send you off to an orthopedic surgeon. Perhaps it is related to a pelvic problem, tension, or a gastroenterological disorder. We don't want to put you through any unnecessary tests, procedures, or x-rays. As soon as we have narrowed down the possibilities, if it's not within my own area of expertise, I will refer you promptly to an expert in that area." Many of the potential problems with patients can be handled by better communication. Spending a little time thinking through these explanations and planning how to communicate on these issues can be very helpful. Additional patient educational material can help as well, perhaps explaining about the consultant's role in the managed care organization.

The term "gatekeeper" does not provide an accurate description of the role of a primary care physician or any provider assuming that role. Keeping the patient from what? Does the provider hold the key to care? A better term would be a "care coordinator" or "coach," someone who heads the health care team, who is responsible for the patient's care on a long term basis, not merely for the crisis of the moment. Another term, perhaps even more descriptive, could be "shepherd": one who provides continuing holistic health services and cares for the patient as a person. Being the primary care physician means being responsible to ensure systems are in place so the patient does not slip through the cracks. It means making sure that patients know the importance of follow-up tests and that it is their responsibility to obtain them, and then having a recall system to assure this happens. It means making sure there is a comprehensive history form for patients to complete and a system whereby they update it. It means having a health screen completed, and providing educational materials for healthy habits, including diet, exercise, nutrition, and smoking. It means doing screening for diseases such as diabetes, cancer, or cardiovascular disease. Much of this may be required by various accreditation agencies in the future.[10] When one is the coordinator of care, additional responsibilities come with it. Patients and jurors will hold that person accountable if these systems break down. In the future these coordinators of care could be not only family doctors, internists, or pediatricians, but other specialists also, if they are appropriately trained.[11]

In a recent case involving several providers, this point was driven home. The case involved an alleged misdiagnosis of a breast carcinoma of a 46-year-old woman. The patient had obtained a screening mammogram that was interpreted by a radiologist as showing some abnormality; the radiologist recommended a follow-up within four months. The primary care physician, receiving the report, recommended the same. An obstetrician/gynecologist who was involved also felt it was important. The patient had a different story and indicated that she felt her obstetrician/gynecologist had downplayed the need for the follow-up mammogram. As time went on, she was able to feel a definite mass in her breast, but did not want to follow up with it for fear of what she may find out. Within the discovery process, during the deposition or question and answer period, the patient all but admitted that she thought there was a real problem. The cancer was diagnosed six months after it could have been had the patient followed up as advised. The plaintiff's expert said the delay could have made a difference. The defense had strong experts on the standard of care for all the defendants, the radiologist, the family doctor, and the obstetrician/gynecologist. The defendants also felt comforted that many fine nationally renowned experts testified that the delay had little to do with the unfortunate death of the patient, given the biological life of the cancer and the particular type of cancer.

The end of the story, though, is not comforting. The jury found against the family doctor who really had the least involvement. He got the mammogram report and told the patient to follow up with the recommendation. The jury disregarded all of the causation testimony and entered an extremely large verdict, approaching one million dollars. The jury made some of their thinking public after the fact. They felt the family was due some award. They felt, among other things, the family doctor could have done more to impress upon the patient the need to follow up. The jury assumed that by definition the family doctor was the "coordinator of care." It is interesting that this case had nothing to do with managed care nor was the doctor an appointed "gatekeeper." The term was never even used during the trial. Apparently, it was just the jury's perception. Whether you choose to be a "gatekeeper" or not, others may assume this role for you.

Telephone Call Volume

Another change causing risk will be the increase in the volume of telephone calls. Patients will call in with questions about health concerns, medications, or insurance. These telephone calls will cause some practical problems in a physician's office for which one needs to be prepared. The first problem is the sheer volume. Who is going to handle these calls? Will it be the already busy front desk? Will that then detract from the welcome for patients coming through the door?[12] Will it cause a level of stress and distraction so that neither the welcome nor the telephone call will be handled well? Both are very important in a managed care setting. Second, when clinical discussions take place, does the individual involved have enough clinical experience? Is this person following protocols? Do patients have easy access to clinical information from a nurse, advanced practice provider, or physician when necessary? Telemedicine has become a major factor in practice, especially in primary care.[13–16] This is not only the sophisticated telemedicine found in radiology, pathology, psychiatry, and other specialty areas, but the telemedicine that goes on everyday in an office.

Patient Expectations

Patients' expectations have risen over the last few decades, and that change has accelerated rapidly in the past several years. Patients have seen great changes and advances in medicine and now want those changes and advances to be used for them. They want to be diagnosed, fixed, restored to health; they want their care given without complication, conveniently, quietly, successfully, and, of course, inexpensively. Their expectations are high, and when expectations go unmet, there is a greater likelihood that patients are going to look for an attorney to have their care scrutinized. In the geographical areas in which managed care is well-established, the competition is intense. Managed care organizations compete fiercely, boasting their quality. Their commercials and billboards portray prompt, high quality care in a comfortable fashion. The commercials portray everything running smoothly and on time, and show a doctor with plenty of opportunity to converse with each patient. It is no wonder that people are disappointed when the actual office is overflowing with patients, and their visit seems to be hurried because the doctor has fallen quite far behind, again.

The Civil Justice System

We are headed toward a collision course because contemporary utilization demands are out of synchronization with expectations of patients. To compound the problem, our civil justice system is economically blind. When physicians are summoned to the courtroom, they find that there is no validity to the argument that a certain test would have been of only marginal benefit and therefore the expense not justified. When, in retrospect, that particular test could have made all the difference to a patient, it is very difficult for a jury to accept that it only had a "marginal benefit." It is hard for jurors to understand why a physician is now qualified to perform certain procedures when he/she wasn't in the past. Why did the ambulance drive past one neonatal intensive care unit to another that was further away just because there was a contract with the one that was further away?

When economics appear in the courtroom, an explosion often occurs.[17,18] For example, in Dr. Smith's cases, the plaintiff's attorneys were able to obtain, through discovery, all the graphs and internal memos from Dr. Wright to Dr. Smith. They painted a picture that Dr. Smith had been a higher utilizer, which meant he obtained too many referrals and tests. He then was told he needed to "get in line with his peers." Over the next two years the graphs showed that he did decrease utilization and, in fact, he received a bonus because his utilization improved. The conclusion the plaintiff's attorney was drawing, as set forth in his demand for payment letter, was that this change in utilization was at the direct expense of his client! Would a jury see it that way? Would they wonder if their doctor had a similar agreement? Would they be angry or just scared that this could happen to them or a family member? Would it affect the jury's deliberations?

One of the greatest challenges to managed care and to the physicians practicing in a fully developed managed care market is rebuilding the image and showing the public that their health still comes first. There has been so much public outcry that legislation has now been introduced in most states as well as at the federal level.[19] Managed care organizations are aware of the need to rebuild their image and are attempting to do so. Physicians practicing in these systems will inevitably be affected by that image also. It is important to emphasize the good and appropriate principles of managing health care and the negative principles need to be revised, replaced, or abandoned. Much of this can be done at the provider level. This will be discussed in greater detail when we cover actual managed care delivery in Chapter 10.

Specific Risks

There are specific risks which are inherent to the managed care system. When a physician sees a greater number of patients for a greater number of problems, in a more strictly limited time frame, there is a greater likelihood of a misdiagnosis or late diagnosis. These types of claims are on the rise and seem to be related to maturing managed care environments. These are the most commonly stated clinical causes for medical negligence actions. There is also an increasing number of suits for failure to refer or failure to order specific tests.[20] Constant awareness of the danger is the first step in prevention. Having recall systems in place and following clinical protocols or guidelines could help lower this risk.

Advanced Practice Providers

Physicians may also rely more on the use of advanced practice providers (this is an inclusive title for people with certified clinical training as nurse clinicians, physician assistants, midwives, nurse anesthesiologists, and similar professionals) who can provide great benefits to both physicians and patients.[21–24] However, this also creates another level of risk. Patients may be quick to jump to the conclusion that the advanced practice provider somehow "missed" the diagnosis

Figure 1–1 Dr. Smith's latest utilization review. *Source:* Copyright © 1997, SC Saxton.

that the doctor would have made. There are no data that would indicate that this would be the case, but the patient's perception may drive the initiation of a lawsuit under those circumstances. When advanced practice providers join a practice, careful planning and both patient and staff education are essential; physicians must know that all of the various supervisory statutes are being followed and that the advanced practice provider is properly credentialed and continues to receive all appropriate continuing education. Failure to do so could lead to a claim of negligent credentialing or even corporate negligence in some circumstances. This means that an independent claim could be made against the physician's corporation for failing to have necessary policies and procedures in place to handle the hiring, supervision, and ongoing monitoring of the advanced practice provider. A consultant or specialty practice has many of these same issues. Even if a consultant is not yet capitated it does not mean that the same type of stresses that one finds in a managed care environment should be taken any less seriously. An excess of specialists in many areas creates even greater levels of competition to be placed on panels. Often this creates a need to be even more innovative in the way a physician delivers services, which brings many new risks. Further, specialists could find that they are treating various illnesses or injuries at a later point in time, which can also bring challenges. The family doctor may treat an injured shoulder longer and send the patient to an orthopedic surgeon much later in time. If there is a shoulder dislocation this could be problematic.

A withhold or risk pool is when a portion of payments for services rendered is placed within a pool as a source for any subsequent claims that exceed projections for a defined group of patients or product which is defined by size or geographic location. Funds that remain in the pool after a specified term are paid out to providers, thereby creating an incentive for lower utilization. The potential for "up-side" payout from risk pools is the basis for providers to convert managed care style of practice from fee-for-service (FFS), because although the reimbursements are compressed as managed care becomes more mature within the region, the provider is capable of seeing larger populations of patients for less cost per patient.[25]

Resources are shrinking, but patients will still expect more. When tests are not ordered or a certain therapy not employed, apprehension may be aroused in the patient's mind that costs are the determining factor. The same type of problems associated with shrinking staff, different use of staff, and telemedicine, apply in a consultant's office and the same type of preparation is necessary.

DEFENSIVE MEDICINE

Defensive medicine is no longer acceptable. It is too costly and it deliberately builds a wall between the patient and health care team. Further, it is inconsistent with the careful use of resources necessary with managed care. Some wonder whether defensive medicine actually exists. In the January 27, 1997 issue of *Forbes Magazine,* Peter Huber suggests it does. He further suggests it is time for a "radical lawyerectomy." This "medical procedure" would cure the Medicare crisis by "amputating lawyers." Legislators have performed partial "amputations" which have saved millions of dollars through reforms protecting community health care centers from malpractice. Huber suggests that more cuts such as cap awards, abolishment of punitive damages, and financial limits on medical malpractice suits as forms of tort reform could "save the country as a whole well over $50 billion a year." The theory that supports Huber's philosophy is that "unlimited liability gets you more medicine, not better." In other words, "defensive medicine" means that more money is being allocated for medicine and for more procedures, but the quality of medicine is not improving.[26]

Many of Huber's concerns had also been addressed in a 1996 article in the *Quarterly Journal of Economics.* The authors, Daniel Kessler and Mark McClellan, examined the impact of "defensive medicine" on cardiologists' methods of treating patients as a result of liability threats. The study concluded that malpractice reforms would reduce medical costs by 5 to 9% and have a positive "substantial effect on mortality or medical complications."[27] Therefore, it is argued that state or federal legislation, either directly or indirectly limiting liability, could have a positive effect on the practice of medicine. One can conclude from such studies that defensive medicine does occur, in part because of the threat of litigation, but it is both expensive and not in the patients' best interest. In a managed care environment utilization parameters won't permit it. But did it provide the doctors with some protection? If so, that protection is gone. What protection will they have now without significant tort reform? Exposure will increase and doctors will need to seek other ways of protecting themselves. Further, even in states where there is tort reform, plaintiff's lawyers have found ways to assert claims that fall outside the tort reforms and even avoid malpractice caps. For example, as will be discussed further in Chapter 10, plaintiff's lawyers are beginning to claim that when physicians withhold financial information or incentives from patients, they are breaching a fiduciary duty to those patients. The lawyers argue that these claims are not limited by the medical malpractice caps, so the potential of large awards looms over the physician.

RISK MANAGEMENT

Risk management principles, which have worked in the past to prevent claims, need to be incorporated into the new environment, but not as defensive medicine. They need to be incorporated with great emphasis—"Making patients feel good" always worked for Dr. Smith, and it is still helpful, but with a new look. Making patients feel good must now be provided by the entire health care team, and the patient needs to be totally involved. Dr. Smith should have concurrently been looking at his practice, knowing what changes to expect and the new risks they entailed, and putting into effect systems that would reduce those risks. However, Dr. Smith did not know what was going to happen, and he fell into the trap. This is easy to do since physicians are often so busy and so involved in patient care that it is hard for them to think of planning drastic changes. This is one of the reasons for this book: to let the Dr. Smiths know some of the changes and to offer advice on some steps to reduce the attendant liabilities. Another reason is to assist all those who have made the successful transition to managed care, in reducing their malpractice liability, by sharing the experience of others.

CREATING OPPORTUNITIES

Instead of only looking at managed care as creating new risks, it also needs to be recognized as creating new opportunities. Within the managed care organization there are opportunities and resources for additional patient education in prevention, health maintenance, disease management, and the way that services are provided. That is one of the hallmarks of managing care. Involving the patient, informing the patient, and recognizing the patient as partner, has great benefits for all. We need to begin to realize that the patient is one of the most underutilized resources in the physician's office. Physicians need to take advantage of these opportunities. Managed care has to do a better job of making opportunities available and work harder on being a resource for physicians.

Another example of an opportunity is advanced practice providers. Although they can add a different type of liability exposure, they can add an entirely new dimension to the health care team. Many patients may not need, or even want, to see a physician on every visit. As long as advanced practice providers are seen as an extension of the relationship, and not as an obstruction to that relationship, they can create added value. They usually have more time and often more abilities in educating patients. Dr. Smith, for example, with such assistance, could have seen patients at a more appropriate pace without appearing hurried or rushed. Being successful, however, requires planning and effort, not just adding an advanced practice provider to the staff. Dr. Smith would have had to announce the arrival of the advanced practice provider, prepare his patients, and educate his staff on what this individual could do (and, in fact, find out himself). He would have first needed to inquire about that person's training, experience, and the scope of his or her practice so he could have a comfort level in the person's abilities.

Advanced practice providers can add tremendous value to a practice, both in primary and in secondary care.

Physicians need to consider how they are delivering care in this new setting: is it at the right level, is it by the right person, is it in the right environment or location? Determining different ways to deliver services, using fewer resources and at the same time incorporating risk management principles into the new process, can prevent claims. It can also meet appropriate managed care goals of increasing patient satisfaction and improving outcomes. New ways need to be developed to involve the patient as a health care partner. With these considerations in mind, the following is the advice we gave Dr. Smith:

1. **The managed care contract and related documents.** Dr. Smith needed to read his contract carefully. He needed to discuss it with his practice attorney, so that he could understand what the contract meant. The contract is an important agreement. and there are parts of the contract that can be negotiated. It is also important to review the attachments to the contract or other documents, such as policies and procedures. Have those policies and procedures been provided? Are there necessary carve-outs to the contract?* What level of care will he be expected to provide? Is there an indemnity provision which would mean that he could be responsible if the managed care organization were sued? Does his insurance carrier cover such liability? Is there an understanding on whether or not he needs to accept new patients and, if so, to what extent? How is he going to be paid? Are there withholds or risk pools? Does he understand what this means? Is there a conflict of interest with his patients because of financial incentives? Should there be some type of disclosure to his patients? How should that be packaged? How inclusive is the consultant panel? Where will patients need to go to get x-rays, lab tests, emergency department visits? Does he have any rights if he is invited off the panel? What is the definition of medical necessity? What is the appeals process? A lot of this information will probably be found in the policy and procedure manual—it was the one Gladys put in the storage closet. These are all questions that need to be answered. He should also find out what information is being sent or provided to the members of the managed care organization. He might get the clearest picture of what his patients' expectations are by seeing what they are being told.[28]

*"A carve-out is a category of health care not covered as a benefit within the contract (thus, carved-out of the pricing structure), usually an area of high cost or requiring special expertise, such as behavioral, sub-acute, podiatry, chiropractic, x-ray, transplants, that is not subject to discretionary utilization and not included within the capitation rate." Richard Rognenhaugh, *The Managed Health Care Directory* (Gaithersburg: Aspen Publishers, Inc., 1996).

2. **Educating himself and his staff.** Dr. Smith did not understand what managing care meant.* He needed to take the time to learn more about it. His hospital certainly had information available[29] and there are several short books available to explain managed care contracts and the principles of managed care itself.[30] After Dr. Smith had an understanding, he needed to educate his staff, or have someone come in and help him do so. The staff is a pivotal part of the team in any managed care setting. The staff took this lead from Dr. Smith. When he was frustrated with the managed care organization so were they and it was reflected in how they interacted with the patients. Staff need these tools to help with this transition. The first tool is education.
3. **Be prepared for initial changes.** Dr. Smith, after learning more about what happens in a managed care environment with a capitated arrangement, would know that he is going to see increases in patient volume. He should get prepared for that, and also prepare his staff. He should consider extending his hours and know what this would mean to his practice economically. He should be thinking about whether or not he will need an advanced practice provider to help with these volume increases. He should understand that telephone calls are going to increase enormously, and that he will need a backup system. While he may not be able to do this all initially, the planning process should begin. The staff should understand this and understand how important it is to coordinate those telephone calls and the new documentation systems. Dr. Smith should have been thinking about some simple protocols for how the telephone calls are answered and how they should be documented. He should be looking at the economic impact so he does not end up having his resources overly squeezed, causing inappropriate shortcuts or cutting corners.
4. **Taking care of complaints.** Most patients do not know much about managed care, so there are bound to be complaints, as there were in Dr. Smith's practice. There needs to be some thought about how these complaints are going to be handled. What information should be provided to patients? How should they be informed on how to use the managed care system? This can be coordinated with the organization that certainly has an equal interest in the process. Patient satisfaction is paramount. Complaints about the managed care organization should be taken through appropriate channels. No one benefits from allowing the managed care organization to be bashed without making an effort to address the criticisms. This certainly doesn't mean succumbing to inappropriate goals, but having open dialogue with patients about one's limitations or the plan's limitations is important. Some

*An excellent source for physician education is "Managed Health and You," a newsletter specifically created to help physicians be successful in a managed care environment.

of this can be helped by making it clear to patients at the beginning of the relationship, packaged in an appropriate way, what it means to manage their health (more about this in Chapter 6).

5. **Consultants.** Dr. Smith needed to refer to the specialists who were on the panel. In his planning, he could have found out more about these specialists and their qualifications. Did he recognize any of the providers on the panel? He should speak with his peers. He could ask the managed care organization about the panel selection process. Are there red flags or areas of concern? He can talk to one of the consultants. Then, when making a referral, he could do so with comfort and confidence. Relationships can be built with consultants and protocols or methods can be developed for a smooth transition of care. He could have avoided the bouncing ball syndrome whereby the patient is caught between a primary care physician making a referral and a specialist who is subcapitated not thinking the referral was necessary.
6. **Documentation systems.** This will be considered in greater detail in Chapter 7. Dr. Smith had absolutely no documentation systems to deal with this new arrangement. He did not have a practice brochure or a comprehensive health history form or a method to get basic information about each patient. He was not prepared to document telephone calls, he did not document conversations with utilization officers within the managed care organization, he did not have a documentation system for recalls, he did not understand how important documentation was. Better documentation may have fended off the lawsuits that plagued Dr. Smith. Some of the forms of documentation could have also served to educate and involve his patients more, which may have helped in his ratings on his patient satisfaction surveys.

Dr. Smith had a good practice and he did not need these capitated arrangements. Managed care organizations came into his community and soon that was where his patient base migrated. He went into these arrangements grudgingly without his eyes open. He tried to work within the system, but really did not have the tools or the understanding to do so. He got caught in a transitional model. In this transitional period, the gray areas of when to refer, when not to, or when to obtain the test, get fuzzier. There have always been gray areas in medicine and physicians will always have to use their own good clinical judgment. Using good clinical judgment to refrain from ordering a certain test or requiring a certain referral, in retrospect, could be made to look as though financial incentives were what drove the decision, not good clinical judgment, unless the reasoning is properly documented. The justice system must rely on documents, and in the courtroom, perceptions are everything.

It is difficult to develop these new systems, to educate oneself and one's staff, and develop the understanding of what you need to do, when you're busier than ever, having just entered a managed care environment. However, the alternative is not acceptable. What Dr. Smith needed to do was to understand the changes better, prepare more and take the necessary time for this learning process. This time will be well spent since the changes which managed care brings are just beginning.

REFERENCES

1. H.L. Jensen, MD, "The Impact of Managed Care on Physicians," *American College of Medical Quality* 6 (1991): 111.
2. W. Knight, *Managed Care Contracting: A Guide for Health Care Professionals*, (Gaithersburg: Aspen Publishers, Inc., 1997).
3. "Managing Managed Care," *American Medical News* 9 (1996): 7.
4. S. Boschert, "Gag Orders Pose a Catch-22 for Physicians," *Family Practice News*, 15 February 1996, 56.
5. D.R. Branch, "Capitation Plus Gag Equals Conflict of Interest," *Family Practice News,* 15 March 1997, 60.
6. "Right to Know Bills Might Release Secrets, Says Industry," *CCH Monitor* 4.8 (1996): 10.
7. Wickline v. State of California, 192 Cal. App. 3d 1630, 239 Cal. Rptr. 810 (1986).
8. Wilson v. State of California, 222 Cal. App. 3d 660, 271 Cal. Rptr. 876 (1990).
9. R.C.W. Hall, MD, "Legal Precedent Affecting Managed Care," *Psychosomatics* 35.2 (1994): 105.
10. T.A. Dorros and T.H. Stone, "Implications of Negligent Selection and Retention of Physicians in the Age of ERISA," *American Journal of Law and Medicine* 21.4 (1995): 387-88. Also consider NCQA and Joint Commission requirements in Chapter 9.
11. L.O. Prager, "Gatekeepers on Trial: Primary Care Liability Risks Are Rising With Growth of Managed Care," *American Medical News* 39.6 (1996): 1.
12. F. Davis, "Give Your HMO a Checkup: Evaluating a Health Insurance Plan," *Working Women*, (July 1996): 61.
13. R.P. Carlson, "Can Telemedicine Deliver What It Promises?" *Family Practice Management* (March 1996): 36.
14. Physician Insurers Association of America, *Telemedicine* (1996); Online: http://www.hrsa.dhhs.gov/telemeds.htm.
15. J. Morrissey, "On Call," *Modern Healthcare*, 25 August, 1997, 72.
16. C. Siskos, "Is There a Doctor on the Line?" *Finance Magazine*, (July 1997): 12.
17. Prager, *American Medical News*, 27.
18. "Malpractice Plaintiffs Hit Big," *Hospitals and Health Networks* 5 (March 1996):14. The three biggest lawsuits ended in awards of $98.5 million, $45.3 million, and $42 million.
19. L. Scott "HMOs Tighten Own Rein," *Modern Healthcare* 14 (July 1997): 54.
20. G. Aston and J. Johnsson, "Making Managed Care Share Malpractice Risk," *American Medical News*: 3.

21. L. Muir, “Disease Management,” *Hospitals and Health Networks* 5 (June 1997): 24.
22. D.L. Olmstead and M.L. Williams, “Billing for CRNP Services,” *Pennsylvania Medicine* (December 1996): 26.
23. C. DeAngelis, “Nurse Practitioner Redux,” *Journal of the American Medical Association* 271 (March 1994): 868.
24. T. Leaman, MD and J.W. Saxton, “The Mid-level Practitioner; Friend or Foe to the New Physician?” *Young Physicians*, (May, 1997): 20–23.
25. R. Rognenhaugh, *The Managed Health Care Directory* (Gaithersburg: Aspen Publishers, Inc., 1996).
26. P. Huber, “Rx: Radical Lawyerectomy,” *Forbes Magazine* 27 (January, 1997): 112.
27. D. Kessler and M. McClellan, “Do Doctors Practice Defensive Medicine?” *The Quarterly Journal of Economics* 111.2 (1996): 353.
28. W. Knight, “Managed Care Contracting,” see generally Chapter 3.
29. A.J. Azzara, “Managed Care Referrals and Malpractice Law: Are You at Risk?” *Family Practice Management* (February, 1995): 32.
30. D.S. Mayes, Managed Dental Care: A Guide to HMOs. (Brookfield, International Foundation of Employee Benefit Plans, Inc., 1993).

CHAPTER 2

Managed Care in a Nutshell

"All is flux, nothing stays still."
Heraclitus, c.540 – c.480 B.C.

By now, textbooks and entire courses of study have been developed describing the evolution of managed care in both medicine and dentistry. Such a task is outside the calling of this book, but a brief look at the roots of managed care and a description of its development over the years may be helpful in gaining insight as to where we find ourselves today and where we may be headed in the future. Managed care is not a discrete entity but a spectrum of activities carried out in a multitude of organizational structures. It continues to evolve: by changing the clinical practice of medicine; by spawning new structures for the delivery of care; and by responding to the ever changing demands of the marketplace. It is a phenomenon that is occurring not only in this country; despite many differences, some similarities in practice arrangements have been noted between the United States and Great Britain.[1] One area that is attracting interest in Europe is the concept of disease management, which is an important aspect of managed care, especially in well-developed markets.[2] David Woods, president of Healthcare Media International, Inc., a Philadelphia-based publishing and communication company, authored a major research report on managed care for The Economist Intelligence Unit, published in December, 1997. This report describes managed care as having components that are easily exportable and attractive to other countries, including utilization and disease management.[3]

HISTORICAL PERSPECTIVE

It may be helpful to know that managed care is not a concept that has developed overnight or even over the last decade. In this country, it had its beginnings in organizations that, half a century ago, were looking for ways to provide greater levels of health care coverage for a larger number of individuals at a better price; in some ways, not dissimilar to what is being tried today. It has now become big business with over 55 million HMO enrollees and hundreds of organizations, both non-profit and publicly traded companies which are listed on the New York Stock Exchange.[4] Managed care, of course, comes in many different sizes, shapes, and colors. Many organizations, not traditionally envisioned as managed care organizations, have embraced managed care concepts, including financial incentives, wellness and patient education, as well as utilization control and disease management.

What is clear is that managed care is no longer a glitch in the market or an alternative to the mainstream. It is becoming the predominant way to finance and deliver health care; it is estimated that by the year 2000, up to 80% of all employees who are in employer-paid-for health plans will be in a managed care organization. A recent survey by William M. Mercer, Inc., indicates that 40% of these employees presently are members of HMOs.[5] As the Medicare and Medicaid population moves into managed care, the numbers will quickly increase.

The roots of managed care can be followed at least back to 1910 to the Western Clinic in Tacoma, WA. In that year, the Western Clinic charged a premium per member per month to provide certain services to its members. Other such organizations began to develop. In the late 1920s doctors in Oklahoma and Los Angeles set up health plans for local workers on a prepaid basis. In the 1930s premiums were said to be as low as $12.00 a year with no limit. Doctors operating on this type of budget were forced to develop certain standards so as to conserve resources. In 1929 Baylor Hospital in Texas provided approximately 1,600 teachers with prepaid health care through its hospital facilities.

This concept continued to evolve, especially on the West Coast, then traveled east to evolve into the Blue Shield plans. In the 1930s the American Medical Association (AMA) disfavored prepaid medical practices, but nevertheless, they continued to grow. Most notably among them was the Kaiser Foundation Health Plans. These were initiated in 1937 by Sidney Garfield, MD, originally to finance medical care for workers and families who were building an aqueduct in the southern California desert to transport water from the Colorado River to Los Angeles. It is doubtful that those who began the Kaiser Foundation Plan in the late 1930s could have predicted it would have nearly eight million members by 1996.

Other large plans have been developed including the Group Health Association (GHA), which was started in Washington, D.C. in 1937. This organization provided insurance for homeowners in an attempt to help reduce the number of home mortgage defaults that resulted from large medical expenses. With all of these early plans there was great opposition from organized medicine, but the groups flourished, and by 1994 GHA had over 130,000 members. The GHA was then purchased in 1994 by Humana Health Plans, a for-profit publicly traded corporation.

These managed care organizations were relatively small in the 1930s and 1940s, usually put together to fill a need, often by a single employer, group of employers, or industry. Even though they were thought of as a threat by organized medicine, there were some markets, particularly in Washington and California where they began to grow more quickly. However, even by 1970 the total numbers of HMOs was still less than 40.[6]

The Seventies

The industry got a push in 1973 by the enactment of the 1973 Federal HMO Act.[7] Paul Ellwood, MD, a pediatrician who is often considered to be the father of managed care, had many discussions with leaders of the U.S. Department of Health, Education and Welfare and had been involved in designing the Health Planning Act of 1966. He coined the term Health Maintenance Organization, to be used instead of prepaid plans, and developed its basic concepts. Under the 1973 HMO Act, grants and loans were made available for start-up phases and restrictive state laws were under certain circumstances overridden. There was a provision requiring employers of more than 25 employees who offered indemnity coverage to also offer federally qualified HMOs with closed panels, staff model, or open panels. The Act did not serve to boost HMO development, at least initially; however, through the 1970s there was steady growth and soon thereafter the growth accelerated. By the mid-1980s there were still only 300 HMOs, mostly quite small, and in 1985 just under 19 million people were covered by an HMO. It is estimated that as much as $190 million was provided through federal grants and loans for the development of HMOs.

As managed care in the form of HMOs began to grow, so did other types of health care delivery vehicles. Preferred Provider Organizations (PPOs) became popular. A PPO is generally thought of as an entity through which an employer's health benefit plan can contract for covered services with a select group of providers, including physicians and hospitals. There is utilization management and discounted fees for service. Unlike a typical HMO, in a PPO, members can go outside of the service plan, but they would have to pay a larger deductible or coinsurance. This variation is referred to as a POS or Point of Service preference. PPO growth in the 1970s and 1980s also accelerated.[8]

During this same period of time, when HMOs and PPOs were experiencing a great deal of growth, there was an increasing dissatisfaction with traditional health insurers on the part of the business community. In the mid- to late-1970s, employers became unhappy with the relationship with the insurance industry, feeling that they were paying large fees just to process hospital and physician claims for their covered employees. Some businesses began to self-insure and soon others were discontinuing their reliance on commercial insurance. Many for-profit carriers, apparently to protect their profitable niche in the expanding health insurance market, failed to follow the managed care trend.[9]

The Eighties

By the early 1980s the HMO industry, even though still small, gained a great deal of influence and began to take on a leadership role. Essentially there were three types of health care insurance arrangements at that time—although the second and the third really blend together. First, in the early 1980s, the vast majority of working Americans and their dependents were covered by conventional indemnity health insurance plans, purchased by employers as a benefit. Employees were free to choose any provider, and health care providers had little constraints on practice. The insurance provider acted principally as a vehicle for passing the compensation between the employer and health care provider. Bills were submitted on a fee-for-service basis and paid. Second was the prepaid HMO, which covered only 5% of American workers in 1980. The majority of these workers received care from a group model HMO and the remainder were in open panel HMOs. The third type of health insurance arrangement, developed by the end of the 1980s, was the new financing and delivery arrangement, which has now become known as classical managed care. There was a focus on utilization, cost reduction, risk sharing, and risk pools. This innovation exploded so that by the end of the 1980s, 50% of employees were receiving services through managed care organizations.[10] These new organizations were able to drop costs and bring savings to employers. Managed care plans sought to purchase the services they needed from hospitals and physicians for the lowest possible price, but with an interest in maintaining an acceptable level of quality of care and patient satisfaction. These plans included HMOs, PPOs, a POS arrangement, and hybrid arrangements.

The Nineties

As a result of efforts to decrease costs, physician income showed a decline for the first time in 1994.[11] In 1996–1997, however, some managed care organization profits have also dropped, and the easy savings squeezed out by obtaining discounts and pushing the excess out of the system, have ceased. As the managed care market becomes fully developed, organizations will no longer be able to compete on the basis of cost alone, but will need to compete on the basis of quality.[12]

Managed care came under tremendous attack in the 1990s. Many people felt that quality was being sacrificed and that the consumer did not receive the same high quality care under managed care plans as in fee-for-service. A four-year study in the Boston, Chicago, and Los Angeles areas, of chronically ill patients, mostly the elderly and poor who were managed by HMOs, determined that they did not fare as well as their counterparts who were treated by fee-for-service physicians.[13,14] Of the 822 patients in the study who were 65 years old or more, 54% of the 346 enrolled in an HMO had a deterioration in health as compared to 28% of the 476 in a fee-for-service environment.[15]

Further, there has been quite a public outcry against HMOs. In the mid-1990s there was almost daily criticism of managed care in the popular press. *Time* magazine's cover story of January 22, 1996, entitled "What Your Doctor Can't Tell You," presents an example of public attitudes towards managed care.[16] In October of 1995, *Newsweek* ran a similar story entitled "Beware Your HMO."[17] In August of 1995, an article in *Business Week,* "The Lethal Side Effects of Managed Care" also described a similar study.[18]

LEGISLATION

There has been much state legislation in recent years aimed at regulating the managed care industry. In 1996, 1,000 bills at the state level have been proposed in 35 different states regarding different types of reform.[19] This legislation includes attempts to limit the ability of managed care plans to direct the flow of patients to specific providers and to allow patients direct access to specialists without a referral (these are commonly referred to as direct access laws). There is also legislation mandating minimum duration of hospital stay for births and other procedures.[20] Bills were also enacted that would prohibit contracts between managed care plans and providers that established exclusive arrangements; in other words, contracts that did permit providers to sign agreements with other managed care plans. There was also proposed legislation aimed toward mandating that any provider willing to meet the price terms of a health plan must be accepted into the network (these are referred to as any willing provider laws). Other laws concerning disclosure of the financial incentives that a managed care plan and a provider may have were also proposed. The managed care industry believes that such legislation can hurt the formation of effective and cost efficient networks and that self regulation, which is also taking place in some areas, will be much more desirable.[21,22] In 1996 alone no fewer than 12 states enacted pieces of legislation aimed at, one way or another, curbing what was felt to be abuses in managed care.[23]

In 1997 the trend continued with many states such as New Jersey passing rather comprehensible legislation regulating managed care organizations. Federal legislation is also under consideration which would include two bills introduced by Rep. Charles Norwood, titled "Patient Access to Responsible Care Act" (H.R.1415) and "Responsibility in Managed Care Act of 1997" (H.R. 2960).[24,25]

Enter the Doctor Smiths

What did this all mean for the physician? What was happening during this evolution? In some parts of the country physicians were starting to see a different mix of patients in their practices. Not only was there fee-for-service and indemnity coverage to provide fee-for-service, but now a portion of their practice was a negotiated per-member-per-month fee for certain covered services. Doctors were being encouraged to dabble in what would become managed care. The basic concept that drove managed care—providing coverage at a reduced cost—was being embraced by all insurers. In the 1980s there was encouragement for second opinions, coordination of services for expensive conditions, employer wellness programs, screening for hypertension and diabetes, stress reduction, and all forms of utilization review. In the 1980s it was pretty clear that health care spending was fast becoming a major issue. It was, and is, very hard for physicians to dabble in different types of plans with different types of requirements and rules. The proper logistics are bewildering and require entire new systems to monitor these varied arrangements.

POLITICAL ASPECTS

In the late 1980s managed care continued to grow with the federal government programs, Medicare and Medicaid, becoming involved (see Figure 2–1). New vehicles through which managed care could be incorporated were being developed. Physician Hospital Organizations (PHOs), independent practice associations (IPAs), physician organizations (POs), insurance physician organizations (IPOs), and many others were developed as vehicles through which managed care contracting could take place. However, the growth was still, relatively speaking, insignificant, and health care spending was continuing to increase. By the early 1990s, it found its place on the national agenda.

During the 1992 presidential election campaign, health care, providing for the 37 million uninsured, and reducing health care spending, became national issues. A week did not go by without a health issue in the headlines. President Clinton made it a campaign issue.[26–30]

After the election a task force was assembled to study the issue comprehensively. After the expenditure of multiple millions of dollars and countless hours of hearings and debates, the result was the Health Security Act.[31] This Act, which contained 1,351 pages of proposed legislation, would have changed the way health care was bought, how health systems were created, how health care was delivered, the mix of health care providers, tort reform, tax reform, insurance reform, welfare reform, and anti-trust reform. Many predicted it was doomed to fail, and of course it did eventually. However, it caused a flurry of activity by providers who now wanted to plan change and look for innovative ways to provide

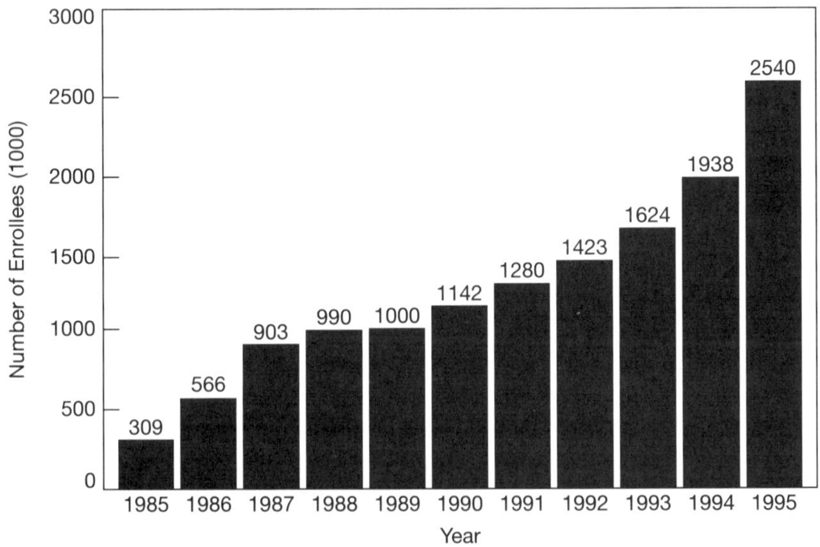

Figure 2–1 Medicare risk enrollees (month of April). *Source:* Data from *Managed Care Contract Reports,* Health Care Financing Administration. Baltimore, Maryland.

services within a different type of managed care environment. They wanted to maintain quality of care, yet reduce costs. The phenomenal growth, in some areas of the country, did not allow much time for transition. From the provider's perspective it became difficult to balance the different plans within one's practice when a part of the practice was in a capitated arrangement and yet a significant portion of the practice was still fee-for-service. The systems needed to address each of these are often quite different. Physicians and practice managers would say that the quality of care is no different, but different strategies have had to be developed in the physician's practice to provide the care, and the incentives are different.

By the mid-1990s it was acknowledged that managed care was not going to be a passing fad. The pendulum was not going to swing back. Although managed care perhaps was going to look different, and although certain reforms were going to be instituted, it was becoming the principal health care delivery mechanism, and fee-for-service arrangements were becoming less prevalent. There may always be a certain niche for indemnity plans, but capitated arrangements and various risk sharing plans are becoming predominant. These plans will take on different parameters as different experiments are tried. Already many primary care physicians have been capitated and have contracts with consultant physicians. In other circumstances, consultants have been capitated with fee-for-service arrangements for primary care physicians. In some areas, so-called gatekeepers are being used while in other areas, plan members can get direct access to certain specialists. Global capitation has also been attempted where whole integrated delivery systems, which can provide all elements of services to patients, receive a per-member-per-month fee to provide all services. All of these various arrangements attempt to align incentives so that costs can be contained; in other words, having the providers, the primary care physician, the consulting physicians, and the hospital all looking for ways to reduce costs together. The cost reduction is then shared in some predetermined fashion. Quality is not supposed to be an issue, since that must be accomplished to maintain marketshare. However, questions about quality have been raised.

There has been an amazing spectrum of development, from small plans simply aimed at providing health insurance coverage for individuals who couldn't afford it, to huge plans which have now become the predominant health care delivery and finance system, with most of the growth in the last five years.[32,33] No wonder there are growing pains, as indicated by all the new and proposed legislation, increased liability activity, and the many critics who have voiced opinions. No wonder physicians are struggling with ways to develop answers to many questions raised by this rapid development.

CLASSIFICATION OF DEVELOPMENT STAGES

It may be helpful to identify some general stages, tracing the evolution of managed care. Many investigators have described the various stages of development. Since the field is new, each researcher has needed to create a new model, with criteria for each stage. We will present five of these models in summary fashion and then, for simplicity, combine the major features of each to form a composite.

In *Managed Care: Origins, Principles and Evolution,* Gillian Fairfeld, et al., described these stages of managed care, dividing them into the following five categories:

- First Generation: characterized by retrospective utilization review, contracts with preferred providers, second opinion programs, and little consumer information or education.
- Second Generation: characterized by proactive utilization review, increased use of capitation and gatekeepers, and prospective payment of hospitals.
- Third Generation: typified by sophisticated utilization management, management of high cost cases, provider profiling, clinical practice guidelines, complex financial incentives, and full capitation or risk.

- Fourth Generation: an increasing interest in health outcomes, health plan report cards, health system integration, and improved information systems and system monitoring.
- Fifth Generation (the end point toward which managed care is working): would have anticipatory case management, community based needs assessment, targeted disease management, integration of clinical services, outcomes based reimbursement, and informed consumers.[34]

Another easily understood description of the stages of managed care was found in the July 1997 issue of *Modern Healthcare*.[35] In discussing Coopers & Lybrand's recent analysis of 57 health care organizations around the country, trying to place them into a managed care matrix, the article describes the stages as follows:

- Stage 1: the professional practice model dominates, costs are uncontrolled, patients get episodic care, access and choice are key, and charges are irrelevant. Examples are Little Rock, AR; South Bend, IN; and Des Moines, IA.
- Stage 2: managed payment dominates, choice and convenience are limited, purchasers gain market power, total cost of care matters, and premiums are flat. Health care becomes a commodity. Examples are Boston, Philadelphia, and Washington.
- Stage 3: organized care dominates, the market defines price, capital is scarce, payers demand reduced utilization, premiums decline, and providers and payers consolidate. Examples are Cleveland, OH; Phoenix, AZ; and San Francisco, CA.
- Stage 4: true medical management dominates; organizations are accountable for medical management, quality, service, and access; and purchasers possess full market power. Examples are Minneapolis, MN and San Diego, CA.[36]

Transition

It is easy to see that managed care has a long history, one that is marked by acceleration over the last several years. Its effects are profound on many aspects of society. It affects employers, employee relations, hospitals, insurers, and of course medical practices, physicians, and patients. Large employers and employer coalitions are struggling with the issue of how to provide costly medical services to their employees in a more controlled, economical way, yet maintain a level of satisfaction with employees. As employers become more involved, and perhaps look to direct contracting, questions arise concerning their potential liability. Insurers are trying to develop new plans so they do not miss out on marketing opportunities. As managed care grows and competition intensifies, many plans will not survive.

Hospitals have been consolidating for some years. As managed care has developed, hospital occupancy has fallen. These trends will surely continue. Hospital health care systems are now being created and many believe that these large, integrated systems soon will become major factors in health care.[37,38] These new systems impact physicians and how they will be practicing in the future. Peter Boland, President of Boland Health Care, Berkeley, CA, says there are many factors which help explain the change that is taking place in the health industry. They include: 1) market forces; 2) structural redesign and reengineering phases; 3) organizational culture; 4) customer focus; 5) population based risk management; 6) statewide reengineering; 7) health satisfaction, and 8) chronic care management. These factors do not only affect physicians, but the entire health industry including institutional providers, organizations, employers, and health care consumers—the patients. He notes that the development cycle varies in different markets (see Table 2–1).

There are multiple definitions of these various stages of managed care. Marion Ford, Department Manager, Medical Economics and Healthcare Delivery, explains it yet another way:

- Stage One: care is driven by few affiliations between independent physician hospitals and employers. Utilization of health care resources is high and market penetration of managed care is 10% or less.
- Stage Two: loose provider networks and weak hospital affiliations are formed. Excess capacity develops and lead HMOs and POs and medical groups emerge. Managed care market penetration ranges from 11–30%.
- Stage Three: hospital systems form and recruit or compete for primary care practices, beds close, and lead HMOs, PPOs, and medical groups amass and begin to consolidate. Managed care market penetration ranges from 31–50%.
- Stage Four: capitation prevails, risk shifts to primary care groups, and purchasers contract with integrated groups and hospital/physician systems to provide comprehensive services.

Our final description is offered by Scott A. Mason, DPA, FACHE, Managing Partner of National Health Advisors, LTD, in Tables 2–2 and 2–3 respectively. Mason describes Stage One as occurring presently in areas such as Little Rock, AR; Birmingham, AL; and Newark, NJ where there is little managed care, community hospitals not yet consolidated, few physician groups that have started to merge and network and, generally speaking, there is an overuse of hospital care fueling an oversupply of beds. Certainly in those areas there are some early signs of Stage Two, which he describes as managed care being essentially discounted fee-for-service and physician groups beginning to organize into larger groups. There may be a lot of PPO activity initially.

Table 2–1 Managed Care Industry Development Cycle

Driving forces	*Stage one*	*Stage two*	*Stage three*
Cost control	Contain specific costs case by case Achieve economies of scale: • membership • geographic concentration • service volume Transition fee-for-service to budget-based reimbursement	Consolidate vendors and distribution channels: • hospitals • medical groups • ancillary services • health plans Contain continuum of cost throughout care delivery	Manage at-risk groups Integrate patient care delivery and health plan administration functions
Network management	Build primary care networks	Integrate continuum of services and providers through multidisciplinary care teams: • primary care • specialty care • behavioral health care • allied health care	Establish interdependent alliances across and within industry sectors
Accountability	Develop aggregate cost reports	Document service and clinical quality	Consolidate information services and reporting functions: • administrative • clinical • financial
Customer focus	Offer comprehensive employee benefits packages and covered services	Increase customer value: • medical management • treatment outcomes • member focus	Document treatment outcomes Improve health status: • members • population groups • community

Source: Reprinted from P. Boland, The Role in Reengineering in Health Care Delivery, *Managed Care Quarterly,* Vol. 4, p. 4, © 1996, Aspen Publishers, Inc.

Later in Stage Two, Mason describes what is depicted in Tables 2–2 and 2–3 as regulatory backlash, where legislators may be concerned about bans on exclusion of a pre-existing condition, physician gag orders, 24-hour maternity stays, new provider provisions, or utilization matters. He describes early Stage Two as being in areas such as Atlanta, GA; Orlando, FL; Cleveland, OH; and Philadelphia. Stage Three is a period of heavy managed care penetration, including governmental programs, and managed care dominates. There is heavy capitation, acceleration of hospital mergers, and specialty groups are beginning to form. At this point, overcapacity begins to shrink and providers are developing a real continuum of care. These markets are seen in Denver, CO; Sacramento, CA; Houston, TX; and Chicago. Stage Four is quite mature where managed care payment predominates and there is little fee-for-service. Networks have developed full continuums of care, and providers and insurers are organizing to serve "covered lives." Penetration is more than 50% of HMOs. Minneapolis, MN is a good example as well as San Diego and Los Angeles. Stage Five he describes interestingly as "end game." Here networks with marketshare form true partnerships and integrated systems are managing patient populations.

Stages of Development, Composite

All five of these noted observers have developed their own classification of the stages of expanding managed care. While there are some significant differences among the various descriptive schemes, there is enough commonality to allow us to draw a composite picture to assist physicians in assessing the situation in their own communities. This may be very helpful in understanding what is happening to the health care system in the community, and how this affects individual practices. The biggest advantage, however, may be in looking at what can be anticipated in the near future based on the experiences of other communities, in time to make preparations. It is interesting to note that no one even mentions the possibility of going down the scale, from a higher to a lower stage. Apparently this has not happened as yet.

On the basis of these analyses, Stage One, or First Generation, in the development of managed care in a community could be expected to have many of these characteristics:

- the professional practice model dominates
- a transition from fee-for-service to forms of reimbursement including capitation
- market penetration of managed care is 10% or less
- community hospitals not yet consolidated
- overuse of hospital care fueling an oversupply of beds

Table 2–2 Five Stages of Market Evolution

Stage 1	*Stage 2*		*Stage 3*	*Stage 4*	*Stage 5*
Unstructured	*Loose Framework*	*Regulatory Backlash*	*Consolidation*	*Managed Competition*	*Endgame*
• Little managed care • Little hospital consolidation • Few insurers active as providers • Few physician groups • Overuse of hospital care fuels oversupply of beds	• Most managed care is discounted fee-for-service; by late Stage 2 some capitation • Hospital consolidation begins • Insurers begin to acquire or partner with providers • Physicians organize in groups; primary care doctors move toward large groups • Oversupply of beds supports deep price discounts	• As the influence of and enrollment in Managed Care Organizations (MCOs) increases, there will be a regulatory backlash in the following areas: — Guaranteed issue and ban on exclusion for pre-existing conditions — Physician gag orders — 24-hour maternity stay — Insurance portability — Recertification requirements and disclosure of provider incentives — Any-willing-provider provisions — Outcomes measurement	• Heavy managed care penetration, including government programs • Managed care dominates payment scene • Some capitation, especially of primary care physicians • Hospital mergers accelerate • Primary care physicians accelerate movement to groups; specialty doctors begin to form groups • Plans begin dropping physicians, hospitals; shift in physician supply begins • Managed care consolidation; providers, insurers begin to align • Overcapacity begins to shrink • Providers develop continuums of care	• Employer coalitions buy health care • Managed care payment dominates • Little fee-for-service • A few large health care “players” dominate • Providers, insurers strongly align • Doctors not in groups pushed out • More pressure to eliminate beds • Shift in physician supply • Use of specialists and their fees driven down dramatically • Networks develop full continuums of care, especially subacute • Providers, insurers organize to service “covered lives” • More than 50% HMO penetration	• Networks with market share form true partnerships with insurers • Providers focus on their unique strengths • Integrated systems manage patient populations

Source: Reprinted with permission from University Hospital Consortium and APM, *Hospitals and Health Networks,* March 5, 1995 (as modified by National Health Advisors), © National Health Advisors, Ltd.

Table 2–3 Five Stages of Market Evolution

Stage 1	*Stage 2*		*Stage 3*	*Stage 4*	*Stage 5*
Unstructured	*Loose Framework*	*Regulatory Backlash*	*Consolidation*	*Managed Competition*	*Endgame*
• Nassau, Long Island • Omaha, NE • Syracuse, NY • Little Rock, AR • Birmingham, AL • Research Triangle, NC • Newark, NJ • Shreveport, LA	• Louisville, KY • Miami, FL • Dallas/Fort Worth, TX • Cincinnati, OH • Tampa/St. Petersburg, FL • Atlanta, GA • Orlando, FL • Cleveland, OH • St. Louis, MO • New York City • New Orleans, LA • Indianapolis, IN • Nashville, TN • Philadelphia	• Since 1990, 47 states including: — Alabama — Arkansas — California — Illinois — Kansas — Kentucky — Maryland — Massachusetts — Minnesota — Nebraska — New Jersey — New York — Wisconsin	• Orange, CA • Milwaukee, WI • Portland, OR • San Francisco/ Oakland, CA • Detroit, MI • Sacramento, CA • Denver, CO • Boston • Salt Lake City, UT • Phoenix, AZ • Washington, DC • Houston, TX • Chicago	• San Diego, CA • Minneapolis/St. Paul, MN • Los Angeles • Worcester, MA	• No markets - yet

Source: Reprinted with permission from University Hospital Consortium and APM, *Hospitals and Health Networks,* March 5, 1995 (as modified by National Health Advisors), © National Health Advisors, Ltd.

- utilization of health care resources is high
- retrospective utilization review
- costs are uncontrolled
- little consumer information or education
- patients get episodic care.

Stage Two has the following general characteristics:

- managed care is essentially discounted fee-for-service
- physician groups begin to organize into larger groups
- increased use of capitation and gatekeepers, and prospective payment of hospitals
- development of a continuum of service in a multidisciplinary way
- excess capacity develops and lead HMOs and POs and medical groups to merge
- managed care market penetration ranges from 11–30%
- greater focus on member satisfaction
- choice and convenience are limited
- total cost of care matters
- proactive utilization review
- premiums are flat
- health care becomes a commodity.

Stage Three is typified by:

- managed care dominates, including governmental programs
- managed care market penetration ranges from 31–50%
- acceleration of hospital mergers, and specialty groups beginning to form
- beds close and lead HMOs, PPOs, and medical groups to amass and begin to consolidate
- hospital systems form and recruit or compete for primary care practices
- sophisticated utilization management, payers demand reduced utilization
- management of high cost cases
- premiums decline
- clinical practice guidelines
- complex financial incentives
- beginnings of a globally capitated system, with complete consolidation and movement towards improving health status.

Stage Four is typified by:

- managed care payment predominates

- purchasers contract with integrated groups and hospital/physician systems to provide comprehensive services
- penetration is more than 50% of HMOs
- networks have developed full continuums of care
- health system integration
- health plan report cards
- improved information systems and system monitoring.

Stage Five (the end point to which managed care is working) is typified by:

- networks with marketshare form true partnerships and integrated systems are managing patient populations
- community-based needs assessment
- anticipatory case management
- integration of clinical services
- outcomes-based reimbursement
- informed consumers.

One can see that in each stage there are changes that occur in a physician's practice. Stage One shows a transition from fee-for-service to forms of reimbursement including capitation, the development of primary care networks, and the tracking of costs. Stage Two involves greater consolidation, the development of a continuum of service in a multidisciplinary way, and greater focus on member satisfaction. Stage Three is indicative of a globally capitated system, complete consolidation, and movement toward improving health status. Identifying where different areas of the country fall into this graph is difficult since these changes are evolutionary in nature and no area will fit squarely into one particular stage. But at each stage providers are striving to meet the customers' needs, improve health status, and lower costs. These are lofty goals and yet expectations are high that whatever has to be done to accomplish those aims will occur.

WHAT WILL WE SEE IN THE YEAR 2000?

Many observers feel that managed care organizations and health care providers generally will become more accountable in the future. Consumers and regulators will have more information than ever about health plans; they will be able to compare and see if, in fact, they deliver what they promise. New and sophisticated ways to collect information will help make this a reality. It is hoped and expected that quality, defined as both better outcomes and more satisfaction, will increase as managed care continues to mature. If patients are not satisfied with their managed care organization, then that organization will not survive. Improving health status, including immunization rates, preventive health measures, focusing on healthy lifestyles and screening, will be standard. Management will become active rather than passive. Disease management will be a standard part of managed care delivery systems by the year 2000, including early identification and interdiction of the disease process, especially as it applies to chronic conditions. Interdisciplinary teams, including nurses, and all types of advanced practice providers, will be working as members of health care teams both in primary and secondary care settings. User friendly information systems, with 1-800 numbers will link patients quickly to their managed care organization, which will be prepared to resolve consumer questions promptly. Technology will continue to push the service revolution.

Patient hospital days will continue to drop. Sachs Group, Inc., an Evanston, IL-based health care consulting firm, has projected that managed care will drive down the number of hospital patient days by an additional 34% by the year 2000.[39] The same organization says the consolidation of traditional hospital providers will continue, and opportunities for patient facilities and primary care networks will increase. There will be more opportunities for the implementation of clinical pathways by case managers. New types of gatekeepers and alternative delivery facilities will be an important part of integrated delivery systems. Systems affiliations or partnerships with home health agencies and long-term care providers will assure that services are in place for a complete continuum of care.[40]

There are additional pressures to reduce costs by creating innovations in the field. For example, Sharp Healthcare in San Diego, CA, has shortened the average length of stay for total hip replacement by doing rehabilitation and discharge planning pre-operatively on an outpatient basis. There are prevention programs (by organizations such as Friendly Hills Medical Center in southern California) where nurses regularly contact and monitor patients with chronic conditions at home to reduce the likelihood of acute episodes needing hospitalizations. They even conduct safety inspections in homes. The medical foundation's Palo Alto voice mail/telephone management system receives patients' questions and helps resolve patient problems, reducing the necessity for office visits. These are all examples of organizations endeavoring to prepare themselves for what will be needed to be competitive in the year 2000.

There will continue to be market consolidation among HMOs. As of January, 1997, the number of HMOs increased to 651 plans, HMO enrollment rose to 71 million individuals.[41] As Medicaid and Medicare begin to offer managed care, the numbers will quickly escalate. Presently, many states provide for Medicaid managed care, a trend which will continue. This brings its own set of new problems, challenges, and concerns about managed care and its potential abuses. With Medicare evolving into managed care, many of the trends associated with disease management and management of chronic medical conditions will simply become even more important. Satisfaction has and always will be at a premium with the Medicare population.[42]

Patient satisfaction surveys will become more and more important. Presently they are essential for the Medicare and Medicaid populations,[43] with the private sector soon to follow suit. There are numerous examples of health care organizations using patient satisfaction surveys both in marketing and in an effort to obtain continuous quality improvement. Using your own survey has several advantages, as will be discussed later in Chapter 9. It allows you to find out how your patients, the health plan's members, are viewing your practice, and gives you an opportunity to work on problem areas instead of waiting for the managed care organization to rate you.

BACK TO DR. SMITH

What does this brief walk through a managed care history and into the future mean for Dr. Smith? It means that he is on a roller coaster ride. It means that his entire industry is changing fundamentally and that he is going to change with it. He may be in a community that is still in Stage One and entering into Stage Two, but two years later he may find himself in Stage Four. To make matters more confusing for him, by the time he gets to Stage Four, the description of Stage Four may change!

It is not as important to analyze exactly what stage you are in as it is to understand that this industry is in a state of flux, with change occurring constantly. It is important for Dr. Smith to realize that change is upon him, that as changes occur he must be informed, be prepared, change with them, and most importantly, be ready to co-exist.

After speaking with hundreds of individuals involved in managing care, physicians, hospital administrators, consultants, lawyers and patients, this was the most important and clearest message we heard; it makes no sense to wage war against managed care; it would simply be waging a war against change. Physicians may not like some of the changes, and may be in favor of significant reform, but this can be done while still working with, not against, managed care.

The remainder of this book is committed to the concept that physicians, and all health care providers, can profit by learning more about the changes that managed care may bring to their practices, and how to be prepared for them, and thrive with them. Many of the early leaders in managed care insist that it was always meant to be patient friendly and patient focused. Of course it was intended to reduce costs but, ultimately, that was to be for the benefit of the consumer, who could no longer afford comprehensive care. While the roller coaster has at times seemed to go off the track, ultimately the successful managed care organization can deliver cost effective health services in a way in which outcomes are improved and patient satisfaction is maintained. The changes will be profound and, hopefully, the following chapters will provide insight for dealing with the various stages in ways that will greatly diminish your malpractice risk. A universal goal of health care providers, but usually unspoken, is to be able to enjoy the practice of medicine or dentistry. Knowing that you have minimized your liability risk is a giant step toward that goal.

REFERENCES

1. G. Fairfield, et al., "Managed Care: Origins, Principles, and Evolution," *British Medical Journal* 314 (1997): 7097.
2. S.N. Burrows, "Healthcast Care: A Direct Contracting Company," *Managed Care Quarterly 5*, no.2 (Summer, 1997): 49.
3. D. Woods, telephone conversation with author of The Economist Intelligence Unit report entitled *The Future of the Managed Care Industry and Its International Implications*, 30 October 1997.
4. S. Gottlieb and T.A. Einhorn, "Current Concepts Review Managed Care: Form, Function, and Evolution," *Journal of Bone and Joint Surgery* 79.1 (1997): 125.
5. "Employers Expect to Rely More on HMOs But Offer More Choices, Mercer Survey Finds," *BNA Managed Care Reporter*, 3.28 (1997): 654.
6. See generally, P.R. Kongstvedt, *The Managed Health Care Handbook*, (Gaithersburg: Aspen Publishers, Inc., 1996).
7. Gottlieb and Einhorn, *Journal of Bone and Joint Surgery*, 126.
8. Gottlieb and Einhorn, *Journal of Bone and Joint Surgery*, 125.
9. E. Ginzberg, "The Healthcare Market. Theory and Reality," *Journal of the American Medical Association* 276 (1996): 777–778.
10. S. Dicarlo and J. Gable, "Conventional Health Insurance: A Decade Later," *Healthcare Finance Review*, 10 vol. 3 (1989): 77–89.
11. C.J. Simon and P.H. Born, "Physician Earnings in a Changing Managed Care Environment," *Health Affairs* 15 vol. 3 (1996): 124–133.
12. L. Prager, "Quality Projects Can Hold Key to Competitive Success," *American Medical News*.
13. J.E. Rare, et al., "Differences in Four Year Health Outcomes for Elderly and Poor Chronically Ill Patients treated in HMO and Fee-for-Service Systems: Results for the Medical Outcome Study," *Journal of the American Medical Association* 276 (1996): 1039–1047.
14. See generally "Managed Care Form Function and Evolution," *Journal of Bone and Joint Surgery*, vol. 79-A, 1, (January 1997).
15. J.E. Rare, et al., *J. Am. Med. Assn.*, 1039–1047.
16. F. Larson, "What Your Doctor Can't Tell You," *Time* (January 22, 1996): 44–51.
17. E.E. Spragins, "Beware Your HMO," *Newsweek* (October 23, 1995): 54–63.
18. R. Kuttner, "The Lethal Side Effects of Managed Care," *Business Week* (August 7, 1995): 16.

19. "Managing Managed Care" *AMA News* (September 9, 1996): 7–8.
20. Sarah Q. Duffy and Dean E. Farley, "Patterns of Decline Among Inpatient Procedures," *Public Health Reports* 110 (1995): 680.
21. Richard C.W. Hall, MD, "Legal Precedents Affecting Managed Care: The Physician's Responsibilities to Patients," *Psychosomatics* 35.2 (1994): 105.
22. K. Swartz and T.A. Brennan, MD, "Integrated Health Care, Capitated Payment, and Quality: The Role of Regulation," *Annals of Internal Medicine* 124.4 (1996): 445.
23. L. Scott, "HMOs Tighten Own Reins," *Modern Healthcare*, 14 July 1997, 54.
24. *BNA's Managed Care Reporter,* 19 November 1997, 1092.
25. E. Weissenstein, *Modern Healthcare,* 10 November 1997, 82.
26. "Mr. Clinton's Trojan Hearse: In it for His Health?" *National Review*, 1 November 1993, 32.
27. "Will Clinton Take a Scalpel to Legal Fees?" *Business Week*, 5 April 1993, 66.
28. "Business Can't Hide its Doubts: Many Fear Clinton's Health Plan is Based on False Assumptions," *Business Week*, 20 September 1993, 30.
29. "Out in the Cold?: Clinton Hates to Mention it but Some Rationalizing of Care is Likely with Reform," *Time*, 4 October 1993, 35.
30. "Faulty Diagnosis: Why Clinton's Health-Care Plan Won't Cure What Ails Us," *Harpers* 287 (Oct. 1993): 57.
31. President Clinton's Health Security Act, H.R.3600, presented to Congress October 27, 1993.
32. "For Profit IPAs, Big HMO Chains Enjoyed Strong Enrollment Growth in 1996," *BNA's Managed Care Reporter*, 11 June 1997, 554.
33. J. Gabel, "Ten Ways HMOs Have Changed During the 1990s," *Healthcare Leadership Review* (June/July 1997): 2.
34. Fairfield, "Managed Care: Origins, Principles, and Evolution."
35. "Look Out for Stage Three," *Modern Healthcare*, 21 July 1997, 35, 37.
36. "Look Out for Stage Three," *Modern Healthcare*: 35.
37. K. Swartz and T.A. Brennan, "Integrated Health Care, Capitated Payment, and Quality: The Role of Regulation," *Annals of Internal Medicine* 124.4 (1996): 442.
38. K.S. Ehrat, C.E. Hollerman, MD, B. Sutton, "Reformatting Healthcare Delivery," *JONA* 26.12 (1996): 5.
39. M.A. Jenkins, *The Managed Care Yearbook, 3rd ed* (The Managed Care Information Center, 1996): 5.
40. *BNA's Managed Care Reporter,* 15 October 1997, 974.
41. "For Profit IPAs, Big HMO Chains Enjoyed Strong Enrollment Growth in 1996," *BNA's Managed Care Reporter*, 11 June 1997, 554.
42. J.E. Sisk, et al., "Evaluation of Medicaid Managed Care: Satisfaction, Access, and Use," *JAMA* 276.1 (1996): 50.
43. J.E. Sisk, et al., *JAMA* 50.

CHAPTER 3

Evolution of Managed Care in a Physician's Office

"A large number of people have, in the face of bewildering events and issues, adopted a struthionine practice; that is, burying their heads in the sand (the adjective struthionine which I have used has a certain polite and esoteric aura, deriving from the Latin struthio = an ostrich)."

Earle P. Scarlett (1896 –?)
Archives of Internal Medicine 118:606, 1966

Source: Copyright © 1997, SC Saxton.

MANAGED CARE BRINGS CHANGE

At a recent national meeting, one of the attendees described his colleagues as "carrying buckets of sand just in case someone began to talk to them about the changes coming." The physician who is most likely to be hurt by managed care is the one who is unable to adapt to the widespread, revolutionary, profound changes it brings and so buries his or her head deeply in the sand. The process is continuing and the changes keep evolving. There are many reasons why a physician should understand the changes it brings:

- Managed care affects the way physicians deliver services and how they receive reimbursement. Without an understanding of how this occurs, a practice can quickly go into deficit.
- As provider panels become more competitive, it may become much easier to find oneself decredentialed, deselected, or disinvited from a plan.
- In many specialties there will be an overabundance of physicians. Even in primary care there will be new types of providers willing to accept the role of coordinating care for patients.
- Managed care changes the liability picture significantly, and magnifies the risk, which can only be addressed when these changes are acknowledged and understood.
- In order to enjoy practice both physicians and dentists need to understand how to make the new arrangements work for them and for their patients.

For these reasons, at the most fundamental level, it is imperative for physicians to understand this new health care environment and how it is affecting them and their communities now, and will in the near future.

Managed care is at different evolutionary stages in different parts of the country. It is a process which, although seemingly having some logical progression, also changes as it matures. However, it has been noted that in areas of the country where managed care has penetrated more slowly, these stages, once initiated, come on quicker or, because of market forces, some stages may be skipped altogether. It is therefore fair to say that managed care is a moving target. No one can predict with precision how managed care will affect a community. However, physicians and dentists who understand how, historically, managed care affected other communities, can understand the potential effect in their own practices. With this understanding, physicians can begin to plan a course of action that will put them in the best position to take advantage of, or at least co-exist with, managed care, to be on the lookout for its pitfalls, and take advantage of its opportunities. Physicians will also be able to realize the risks it brings and endeavor to reduce the liability exposure which stems from those risks.

EVOLVING MANAGED CARE

The above has implications for you. Which organizations should you join? Should you participate in managed care plans? Should you merge your practice with other physicians in a similar specialty? Will this create greater efficiencies or is it simply being done to decrease competition? Should you develop a multi-specialty group? Should you merge with practices in other communities in an attempt to be prepared to offer your health services to a larger geographic area? Health care was always thought to be local but how large is your local area? Is that changing? Should you employ advance practice providers? Should you be working on developing your own clinical protocols or guidelines? Will there be an attempt to purchase your practice? If so, to whom should you sell? Will there be large public companies interested? Should you sell to the local community hospital?

All of these questions are driven by the fact that managed care, when it comes into your community, changes the delivery of health services dramatically. This may not happen initially, where there are negotiations for simple discounted fee-for-service contracts for PPOs, and not even when there is a capitated arrangement for a certain segment of the patient population. However, as managed care develops in your community, and there is a need to reduce costs even further to stay competitive, it becomes clear that to be successful, providers must deliver their health services differently, using less resources while maintaining outcomes and patient satisfaction. Dollars will continue to be squeezed out of the system so that premiums can continue to be reduced to meet the competition.

Managed care, in mature markets, competes not only on the basis of cost but also on the basis of perceived quality. Millions of dollars are spent by managed care organizations to convince purchasers of care that their program should be chosen because of "service excellence," and "providing the best of care." All of these glitzy marketing soundbites are talking about quality, not the cost of care. They are talking about the quality that you, the provider will be delivering.

What society and purchasers of care want is great care, innovative care, prompt care, care that creates favorable outcomes for the patient, and most of all, compassionate care. They also want the whole process done in such a fashion that patients are more involved, more at ease, and more satisfied. Many physicians' initial reaction may well be that this wish is, in fact, unrealistic. However, many have accepted that challenge and are trying to achieve those goals.[1–3] Little effort has been made to explain that societal expectations are out of line with reality. Managed care organizations are trying to create health systems that will deliver the type of care boasted of in the commercials. They are trying to provide high quality care that satisfies patients, yet reduces costs at the same time. They have discovered that to do this, there must be some fundamental changes in how that care is delivered. This is both exciting and threatening, but also has profound liability implications, to be discussed later.

To accomplish the above, it appears that providers will need to deliver their services differently. How will this be accomplished? This is a complex question and the answer is rooted in economics, system redesign, ethics, and politics. The changes, already taking place across the country, can be grouped under three headings, the where, the who, and the what.

Changes in the Where

The location where care is being provided has changed dramatically and will continue to change. This pace of change has quickened and is being driven both by economic pressures and by technology. There has been a move from the acute setting to a subacute setting, an outpatient setting, patient's homes, and even cyberspace.[4–8] Telemedicine is actually becoming an extremely large, profitable, and important part of care.[9] Consider in your community, how the where has changed just over the last several years. The where helps to define the stage of development of managed care in a community and knowing the stage helps a physician to anticipate what changes may be coming.

New technology will continue to change the where. For example, rural offices or hospitals have the ability to obtain a consultation from a pediatric neuroradiologist at a major academic center when presented with a difficult radiological image.[10] Costs are reduced because travel is eliminated and the family's anxiety of waiting is minimized. There are, of course, regulatory, liability, and risk management issues associated with this, but it will forever change the where.

New types of clinics are being developed to treat people with certain diseases such as diabetes and cancer. Special needs can be met in a setting for a specific purpose; for example, a coumadin clinic where prothrombin times can be checked and regulated, which is easy, convenient, and where appropriate patient education can take place as well. Some emergency departments are evolving into triage centers in which care can then be provided at one of many levels, each of which is equipped in a different fashion.[11] Only a small percentage of emergency department patients actually need the expensively equipped facilities that, traditionally, have been designed to take care of patients with major trauma.[12–14]

Some care is now provided from mobile units, allowing thousands of patients to be treated in their own homes. Home health is one of the fastest growing industries.[15] Technology can make available the ability to monitor patients while at home in a setting many hundreds of miles away from the medical facility. The combination of home health, mobile units, and technological changes provides outstanding possibilities to the creative provider seeking to deliver excellent care and patient satisfaction at lower cost. Providing care in a facility to suit the patient could have many favorable effects. It is obviously easier for a patient to be connected to a monitor and speak to a specialist several hundred miles away than to spend a day traveling there for a brief appointment. Patients may be cared for in their own homes who would otherwise need much more expensive institutional care.

A patient who goes to the emergency department because the family doctor's office is closed may be transferred quickly to a primary care center, located near by. This may enable the patient to avoid a long wait and the use of expensive resources, and to have care provided by a more appropriate practitioner. The patient who can have his/her prothrombin times checked in a clinic in the community without waiting in the doctor's office, waiting at a laboratory, and going for another doctor's visit to get the result and waiting again, will be far more satisfied. These new locations do have new potentials for abuses and liability risks, but the where is changing and will continue to change. Studies have indicated that nearly 69% of care will be outpatient by the year 2000.[16] The health facility of the future will be markedly different and there is likely to be some confusion during this period of transition.

Changes in the Who

The who is also going through a very significant change. This is occurring on multiple levels, but all affect physicians, either directly or indirectly. As the competitive environment tightens in the community, there is a tendency for physicians to want to expand their scope of practice to make up for reductions in reimbursement or marketshare. Part of the reason for this decline is that the number of procedures that patients need, or are authorized to have, is shrinking. This will have political consequences and can lead to classic turf battles at the medical staff level. Physicians are advised to review their hospital by-laws closely and enlist the help of their medical specialty societies. They should also consult attorneys experienced in such issues, to define possible areas of dispute in order to avoid conflicts of interest. Many of these expanded scopes of practice are appropriate and provide the public with more choices and are pro-competition. However, others driven by pure economics can be worrisome as some services might be provided by physicians or dentists who are not ideally qualified to do so. Quality, certainly when dealing with specific procedures, often has a relationship to volume. Those who do a procedure most often may be the most qualified. Frequently credentialing decisions are made with that in mind. Striking the right balance is difficult. The stakes are high.

Hospitals—and in the future, managed care organizations—are governed by certain corporate negligence doctrines which mandate that they scrutinize closely the credentials of all providers on a regular basis. They can be held responsible from a corporate liability standpoint if they fail to do so.[17–19] In other words, hospitals have an independent duty to act reasonably and responsibly in their credentialing decisions as well as in their monitoring and recredentialing. Failure to do so opens the institution or organization to liability in the case of a patient who is allegedly harmed by a provider. In the future these corporate negligence doctrines could be applied to medical groups as well. These groups will be responsible for both credentialing and monitoring of those employed professionals who do hands-on care of parents. Failure to do so would put the organization at risk.[20]

There are also state licensing issues; if physicians appear to be practicing outside of their area of specialty an investigation could ensue. This can be a burdensome process which is often not covered by professional liability insurance and therefore could be costly. The accusation might come from a competitor, who could make a formal complaint, or even an anonymous tip because someone feels a provider is encroaching on his or her area of practice.

Primary care physicians are being asked to expand their practice, especially if they have a so-called gatekeeper responsibility. Primary care physicians may find themselves doing procedures that they once quickly referred out such as endoscopy, lump and bump surgery, repair of simple lacerations, or care of simple fractures and dislocations. This not only adds substantially to the work schedule, but has potential liability risk.

Changes in the who in nursing are also occurring at a rapid pace.[21–28] In some institutions, less experienced and perhaps less well-trained, nurses are replacing more experienced or highly trained counterparts. Many commentators have said for years that registered nurses perform tasks in hospitals that could be done more appropriately by someone with less training and experience, freeing up the seasoned registered nurses for tasks that only they are truly equipped and experienced to handle.[29–34] There is obviously a cost factor as well; newer nurses and non-registered nursing personnel cost less. Nursing associations have complained that institutions are reducing staff and reducing the level of experienced staff in an effort simply to save costs but at the expense of quality.[35] There is undoubtedly some truth to both arguments and there is a potential that the patient, and at times the physician, will get caught in the middle. After all, the hospital nurse is the physician's eyes and ears and a vital component of the health care team.

In the future, nurses with varying levels of responsibility will be employed, performing tasks in accordance with their experience, in the attempt to strike this balance. In all likelihood nurses will be stretched as to what they are asked to do, in view of both experience and reimbursement. Resources are shrinking and there is pressure to limit the number of hospital nurses. The needs for nursing services are also changing in regard to the where discussed previously. Home health care, the coumadin clinic, and the triage at the emergency department, are all examples of new and different roles for nurses.

Most importantly in evaluating the change in the who is not the fact that the changes are occurring within physician ranks or within the nursing ranks, but how significantly the responsibilities of each group are beginning to blend. Concurrently there is an expansion of the role of advanced practice providers. Advance practice providers are licensed professionals who provide patient care at varying levels, including nurse midwives, certified nurse practitioners, physician assistants, and certified registered nurse anesthetists, to name a few. There are several hundred programs across the country that are training these professionals who are able to provide an excellent level of care within their scope of practice.[36] The number of these programs have doubled in the last several years.[37–39]

The political dilemma, however, begins when these providers, sometimes referred to as physician extenders, or mid-level practitioners, supplant instead of extend, the services of the physician. Efforts are underway to increase their licensing and the hands-on care that they provide.[40–42] In many respects employing these professionals is an ideal way to provide health services using fewer resources, yet maintaining good outcomes and satisfaction. Many of these advanced practice providers, acting within their scope of training, background, and experience, excel as patient educators, an increasingly important task in the new health care environment. Many of them are able to spend more time with patients and patients often feel less intimidated or threatened by these practitioners. In some practices, patients may request that a certified nurse or physician assistant be their coordinator of care instead of their family doctor.[43,44]

In the future will it be an advanced practice provider who acts as the so-called gatekeeper and who accepts the capitated fee? Will this group then refer to a specialist with the primary care physician's work predominantly in the clinic or hospital setting? Will screening procedures such as a colonoscopy or flexible sigmoidoscopy be performed for the most part by specially trained and certified nurses? Many of these scenarios are already being tried in some practices. The changes in the who are continuing at a rapid pace at all levels, as the health profession explores what physicians will do within their specialty, what nurses will do, and the continued development of new types of providers. Costs are driving much of this, but quality must be maintained. These changes provide some of our greatest challenges.

Changes in the What

The what in medicine is also changing. What level of care will patients receive? Are they going to be offered unlimited services? Should patients be provided services even when the physician determines that the services would be futile?[45] To what extent will services be provided according to practice parameters, care pathways, practice protocols, practice guidelines, and the like? Will the care of patients for certain chronic diseases be redesigned according to the results of clinical research and sophisticated data collection on outcomes? Disease management has turned into a significant industry.

It is clear that managed care is pressing for the development of clinical protocols or pathways which can redefine or re-engineer the way that services are delivered to patients. There is much debate about practice parameters. Some physicians look at it as if "cookbook medicine" were being proposed and that too much emphasis is put on costs and, that ultimately, this may prove to be more costly. Well-developed protocols, however, which have been thoroughly investigated and shown to improve outcomes, may be good news for patients. These are constructed in such a fashion that costs are reduced, but quality, or perceived quality, is believed to be maintained.

Pathways or protocols may involve fundamental redesigning of how a certain disease can be treated, and how variances in treatment courses can be reduced if, in fact, a certain course of treatment has been proven to improve outcomes. One area being studied is earlier intervention of various kinds of malignancies, and then strict adherence to certain protocols. Another area is screening for diabetes, and attempts to achieve greater levels of education of patients so as to reduce the number of trips to an emergency department. One reason that there is so much effort to determine a way to treat patients with chronic diseases more effectively is that they represent close to 80% of health care spending. All of these efforts drastically change the way in which patients are handled. Few will complain if these developments improve outcomes and still maintain quality, in terms of patient satisfaction with the process. Patients often seem to be more concerned about the manner in which they are treated than with eventual outcomes.

What concerns physicians are attempts at micromanagement of patients in their offices. Being told what type of symptoms a patient must have before being approved to go to the emergency department, limiting the type of diagnostic tests ordered for a certain medical condition, having contracts only with certain institutions sometimes requiring patients to travel greater distances, disallowing certain allegedly experimental treatments, limiting the amount of time in the hospital, requiring outpatient surgery, limiting the choices of medications, and limiting the panel of specialists available for referral, are all changes in the what that cause concern.

Utilization review plays a big part in managed care and is going to change the type of care that can be provided. This of course leads to a dilemma for a physician and an inherent conflict, a delicate balance. George Anders in his recent book *Health Against Wealth,* described utilization decisions in the past as follows: "Such everyday predicaments illustrate one of managed care's greatest challenges. Too much compassion and a health plan never saves any money. Too little compassion and the best aspects of American medical care are destroyed in favor of a grim medical assembly line that bounces patients along without any sensitivity to their unique concerns."[46]

A major goal of managed care is cost reduction, which is dependent on utilization review, precertification, retroactive reviews, concurrent reviews, or, in other words, changes in the what. Changing the what in many ways incorporates changing the who and the where as well. Some of these changes are inherent in the advancing nature of medicine. There are now many health care professionals actively engaged in revising the system which is known to be too expensive, permits too many abuses, and does not have enough demonstrable value. The changes are occurring rapidly and there is the danger that new and worse avenues for abuse may be created.

Changes Affecting Your Practice

All of these changes to the where, who, and what create real pragmatic changes in your practice. They may come suddenly and often are simply a by-product of the fact that you are being reimbursed through a managed care arrangement for a larger segment of your practice. However, recognizing that these changes are occurring and, more importantly, being proactive about the fact that they will occur, can help you prepare successfully and be involved in innovative ways to serve your patients better. Many physicians in mature managed care settings are creating radically different models of care which incorporate these changes.[47]

However, one also has to be mindful that with these changes comes potential liability exposure. All of these changes create dangerous gray areas where one can hear the ticking bomb of litigation. Most physicians can deal successfully with the changes that managed care brings when dealing with the easy patient. However, the gray areas, which have always been difficult and exposed doctors to potential liability, have gotten larger, darker, and more numerous. We'll discuss more about litigation later.

EARLY MARKET PENETRATION OF MANAGED CARE

Early penetration of managed care in your practice may simply mean the signing of preferred provider organization (PPO) agreements and negotiating a discounted fee-for-service, allowing you to be included on a certain payer's panel. You may want to do so to retain the marketshare of your patient population. Credentialing will be required and a certain amount of utilization review will occur. These arrangements are usually not problematic, but may become so if discounts are cut and negotiated down each year. For example, one practice manager explained it as follows.

"The first year that we negotiated a fee in the managed care organization, they were brand new. They were just coming into the community, and they were attempting to attract different providers to their panel. They had a lot of ideas about marketing and expected to obtain many of the large contracts from our area employers. The fellow I talked to was very pleasant and knowledgeable and discussed all of this over a wonderful lunch at our local country club. The fee which I tentatively agreed to was actually right in line with what some of our other payers were already reimbursing us and I felt the physicians would be quite pleased with it.

The PPO did a good job marketing and in fact did capture several of the large contracts from local employers. They did a good job of setting up an excellent physician panel, had contracts with the major hospitals and things really seemed to go well. This particular PPO seemed very physician friendly and I thought we would have an excellent longstanding relationship. I was actually surprised at some of the press other managed care organizations were getting nationwide.

The next year came and they negotiated a deeper discount in our fees. The same fellow discussed all of this with me and had explained the progress that their organization was making. I was actually congratulatory about the panel they had developed and it was apparent that they were doing well in the marketplace. This brought up an important point though, since, as my contact explained to me, to continue to grow they needed to hold down their premiums and it meant they simply needed to reduce our fee a little bit more. He also mentioned that they were going to have to begin to watch utilization more closely. The fee was still well within a reasonable range and we also struck an agreement again over lunch, albeit not at the country club. I was able to negotiate a two-year agreement, however.

The PPO continued to grow. By now it was one of our larger payers. Two years went by quickly and shortly before our contract concluded I received a call from the same fellow. He was very busy now. He did not have time for lunch but told me that he would send the new contract. I was shocked when I saw that there were deep cuts in our fees. I quickly called up my contact only to be put on hold and then told he would return the call later. He did so and we had a less than successful conversation. It was amazing to me that they would expect a 20% reduction in our fee, and I explained that this was getting close to our cost and that I did not think it would be acceptable to our physicians. My contact

> explained that the market had tightened even more and not only would he not be able to negotiate any further on the fee, he could not enter into anything more than a one-year contract. He anticipated further cuts. The negotiation power had certainly changed since he now had control of about 21% of our patients. I went back to the physicians who were furious. We reluctantly signed; what else could we do? However, our attention now had to turn in part to how to reduce our costs because it was pretty clear that the reimbursement picture was not going to change!"

This is where the inevitable change in the who, where, and what may start to occur. Physicians will have to start looking at their practices and determining ways to shave costs and/or increase revenues. Some early strategies include increasing volumes to make up for shrinking reimbursements. This has multiple effects on the practice. Are patient visits going to shorten? Are physicians going to attempt to see more patients per hour? Do they extend their hours? Do they cancel their day off? This also leads to problems associated with the staff trying to process additional patients, which adds to an already high stress level. Perhaps the practice should hire an advanced practice provider to see some of these patients. A physician assistant or certified nurse can be an excellent resource for attending to some of the increased volume. Of course this will mean reviewing carefully all the applicable regulations in your jurisdiction and making sure you have credentialing, monitoring, and back-up systems in place. You need to make sure your patients understand the positives of hiring an advance practice provider. You need to make sure you understand their scope and have a plan in place to employ them productively and appropriately. Clearly, however, the old stressors are going to intensify. This means more patients to process, with higher expectations, and resources beginning to get squeezed, for both the physician and staff. Remember Gladys' reaction? Your staff will have to work harder and there may not be more compensation available.

As the practice grows, will your physical setting be large enough? Is your reception area able to accommodate the number of patients who must wait? Are the waiting times increasing, which is still the number one complaint of most patients? When too many of these things occur, it leads to more patient dissatisfaction. This is significant because you will be rated specifically on patient satisfaction. Unfortunately, this can lead to a vicious cycle whereby the practice attempts to increase its volume, patients begin to complain that they cannot get an appointment soon enough, they have to wait too long in the reception area, the staff is unpleasant, they do not always get to see a doctor, and the doctor seems rushed. Patients begin to complain to their managed care organization and now the provider gets called to discuss these complaints: the physician needs to provide a more user-friendly atmosphere. Failure to do so ultimately could lead to contract termination. Under some circumstances patients complain to the local or state medical society or worse yet, to the state licensing agency. Perhaps still worse, you may have engendered enough anger to precipitate a lawsuit, which is one of the increased risks of managed care. That is why physicians need to respond to the changes carefully, thinking through the implications.

Each one of these evolutionary changes cause subtle, and sometimes not so subtle, changes in the physician's practice. Besides an increase in patient volume, and additional stress on the staff, there is also a greater level of reliance on staff members to perform more and different tasks. These might be as simple as receiving more phone calls and asking the receptionist to discuss certain types of clinical information. If this occurs, appropriate education and protocols must be put in place to prevent more problems and to minimize liability risk.

The situation becomes more serious when utilization decisions or triage decisions must be made. For example, a patient may call who is feeling quite ill and wants to go to the emergency department. The call is made to the office of the primary care physician, who is acting as the so-called gatekeeper. The receptionist should immediately transfer the call to someone with enough clinical experience to make a decision as to whether the trip to the emergency department should be authorized, a visit to the office should be arranged immediately, or set up at the end of the day. As managed care penetration increases, staff members must both take on more responsibility and different responsibilities. With reduced resources, this combination can be dangerous if not handled very carefully. If the PPO is successful, a physician can expect decreases in reimbursement and increases in utilization controls as the PPO gains marketshare in the practice. As reimbursements begin to shrink and utilization parameters begin to tighten, and the proportion of your practice involved in such contracting increases, the subtle changes may begin to be more pronounced. It is hard to strike a balance. Providers need to be constantly aware of maintaining quality of care, since the perceived quality will be essential to their overall reputation and the ability to negotiate managed care contracts effectively in the future. This careful balancing act starts even in the early stages of managed care.

FURTHER MARKET PENETRATION

There are also other subtle changes. Much has been written about ethical concerns relative to managed care.[48–54] When the physician has a financial incentive to avoid ordering certain diagnostic tests or making referrals to a specialist, does it impact the decision? At a minimum, it certainly changes the reaction of the patient in a case where there has been a misdiagnosis and that particular test or referral could have yielded some important information. It is very difficult for patients not to jump to the conclusion that the failure to order the test or referral was based on saving money and not sound clinical judgment. We believe that in most cases this doesn't happen, but that does not alter patient perceptions.

Patients are bombarded with marketing materials that affect their expectations and these expectations are already at an all-time high. Marketing materials that are given to employees, heard over the radio, or seen on TV and on billboards, boast care of the highest quality, with convenience, promptness, and excellent service. Millions of dollars have been spent on marketing these ideas to the public. When something goes wrong, or when a family thinks that it has, they are faced with a very difficult and practical dilemma. Has there been negligence? Was there economic motivation? There is an entire industry ready and eager to help, with no initial expense—the plaintiff's attorneys.

Relationships with referral physicians may also be changed. The physician you need to refer to may not be one whom you know. The specialist your patient knows may not be on the panel. This is a significant problem since it goes to the root of the patient-physician relationship. This infringement on the patient-physician relationship is what disturbed many of the risk-management specialists with whom we spoke. The patient who had her total knee replacement successfully done by Dr. X in 1996 is not going to be happy if she is now told she needs to go to Dr. Y. If there is a problem with Dr. Y, the patient may not only blame Dr. Y, but perhaps the referring physician as well. The patient who has been under the care of Dr. Z, a cardiologist, for many years, will be very unhappy when a referral cannot be made. Any patient who does not do well may wonder why it was necessary to be referred elsewhere, to an unknown doctor. What are this other doctor's credentials? Why not Dr. Z, who knew me well, understood my heart, and has all my old records? Was it to save money? If so, for whom?

The other side of the coin is problematic, too. Just as patients are familiar with their physician, so the physicians are familiar with their patients. Dr. Z knows this cardiac patient, and is familiar with the long history of medication interactions, the patient's lifestyle, and how cooperative this patient is, all of which can lead to better clinical results and a more satisfied patient. Changing the referral patterns because of physicians who may not be in the network has liability implications for both the referring doctors and the doctor to whom those referrals are being made. Referring doctors need to have confidence in the consultant panel that has been selected and be prepared to answer questions by their patients as to why the referral is being made to a particular doctor and the level of confidence in that physician. As the doctor being referred to, you need to realize there may be lingering questions and you need to work on creating the right relationship with the patient. You may want to offer to call the original physician. All of this makes communication (which will be discussed in Chapter 6) and creating the right environment (which will be discussed in Chapter 9) increasingly important.

Risks to liability exposure begin to change and enlarge as well. Patients expect more, and if those expectations are not met, the plaintiffs' attorney industry is willing and ready to help them follow up on their rights. The addition of advance practice providers, and the changes in the responsibilities of the office staff can expose the practice to new types of liability. The changes in referral patterns presents additional malpractice risks. The sheer increase in stress to both the doctors and staff can cause liability concerns. However, this is just the beginning.

CAPITATION AND RISK SHARING

As managed care continues to evolve, your reimbursement may not be by PPOs only, but by capitation from an HMO or another risk sharing arrangement. These organizations may have reimbursement arrangements that may give you the opportunity to share year-end profits. The negotiation process for the capitation rate is essential, and you are strongly urged to get help from consultants or obtain thorough training on how to determine a fair rate of capitation. These agreements must be carefully scrutinized to determine what benefits are covered, whether or not any "carve-outs" are included, what the appeal process is, who reviews appeals, and who else will be on the panel.[55,56] An analysis of a managed care contract is not the purpose of this book, but it is an important and sometimes complicated process and a vital part of malpractice prevention. The capitation rate may be very favorable for your practice in the beginning, but later there may be significant reductions, after a major part of your practice is involved in a particular HMO.

Capitation, though, brings other changes and risks to your practice. Not only may the volume increase, but the type of patients you see may change. In primary care, new patients may be coming to see you for complex health problems, requiring more comprehensive medical treatment. This type of medical treatment, as well as health promotion, needs to be provided, according to the contract. For consultants who are capitated, a thorough analysis of the capitation rate must be accomplished, including careful consideration as to what is and what is not covered by the capitation rate. If you are looking at a discounted fee-for-service program, you have to consider what it will do to your overhead. Will you be forced to reduce staff? Will you have to cut corners? What is going to happen to staff salaries? If salaries decrease, will this affect morale and patient care? Some of the solutions include creating more efficient systems or perhaps using advance practice providers; in other words, looking at ways you can change the ***w***ho, ***w***here, and ***w***hat (or the "three W's").

Your patients' expectations will probably climb. When they are recruited for these plans, they are told of the high level of comprehensive and quality care that you will provide; yet you will have to increase your volume and perhaps change the way that you interact with these patients to make your practice profitable. These patients have been told the physicians with whom the managed care organization has contracts are the "finest in the community." They have been told that they will "not have to wait for their visits." They have been told that they will be "very involved and informed about their care" and "involved in all decisions about their care." They have been told that "preventive services and health screening will be provided as well as nutritional education." They have also been told that this health maintenance organization will help them achieve a healthy status and even enjoy life more. They have been told that their primary care physicians will act to coordinate all aspects of their care and that their health is of paramount concern to them.

In that setting, consider the potential surprise when a patient arrives at the office to find a reception area full of patients, since the physician is an hour behind schedule, because earlier there was an urgent and complex problem that needed a significant amount of additional attention. When the patient gets to the physician and has a long list of questions, the physician tries in vain to get through the appointment quickly to try to catch up since there are still hospital rounds. All of this is likely to generate another common complaint, which is that during the visit, the doctor always appears to be rushed or hurried.

A number of other changes also occur. There is a tremendous increase in telephonic medicine. When patient volume increases, the number of telephone calls received by the practice also increases dramatically, especially from patients who are new to the practice. Patients call with concerns about their health, previously unanswered health care questions, or concerns about their treatment or medications, or simply for a new opinion. Many calls are a reflection of the fact that these patients do not understand this new system. Many of these calls take more time than is customary in an established practice. Many of them are clinical in nature and need to be answered according to a specific clinical protocol, or by someone on the clinical staff specifically trained to do so. It may be impossible for the receptionist to handle all of these calls while, at the same time, giving the appropriate amount of attention to the patients coming in to the office. Long-term relationships with patients may be jeopardized.

Patients, unfortunately, but understandably, change plans with some frequency.[57,58] Therefore there will be many patients new to the practice. This has other implications. Have they filled out a history form? Do you have a process in place for them to do so? Have you received prior medical records? Do you have a process for doing so prior to the first visit, if that is necessary? Do you need x-rays prior to the visit? Have pre-procedures instructions been given out if they are coming for a procedure? All of the difficult scheduling and care coordination questions get more difficult as volume increases and as capitation becomes prevalent.

With capitation, there is the possibility of denial of access, one of the gray areas that becomes problematic. Most patients do not want to be scheduled for an unnecessary diagnostic procedure or sent on an unnecessary referral, but when there is a financial incentive, penalizing a physician for excess use, there is a potential for suspicion and for abuse. This is a ticking bomb that has exploded in a litigation context.[59,60] The civil justice system is far behind the changes in health care, and is economically blind. Jurors, who after all are patients themselves, do not accept economic decision making as part of sound clinical judgment. Such abuses are probably rare, but patients perceive that they are occurring, which can be almost as damaging as when they do occur. This will be discussed further in Chapter 10.

If the consultant specialists are capitated also, the unfortunate situation may arise in which neither the referring physician nor the consultant prefers to care for the patient and they refer the patient back and forth. This is also a rare example, but is indicative of the kind of behavior that financial incentives can provoke in this new health care environment. This particular phenomenon has happened often enough to have a name—the bouncing ball syndrome.[61–64] A professional liability representative in Wisconsin explained to us that some patients are slipping through the cracks when referrals are made to specialists. Both the primary care physician and specialist may view their care differently. The specialist may be seeing the patients later in a disease process or referring the patient back to the primary care physician sooner. Neither are very comfortable with their new role and the patient is often caught in the middle. Capitating specialists brings with it some of the same problems and risks as with capitating primary care physicians. The consulting specialists must strive to develop ways in which they can deliver their services in a more efficient fashion to make the capitation rate profitable for them. Many are redesigning the way in which they are providing their services, by altering one or more of the "three W's." Many have done so quite effectively. However, they may still have to face the dilemma of the ever decreasing capitation rate.

Issues relative to disclosure to patients of capitation, or other financial arrangements, will need to be considered. When decisions are made that certain diagnostic tests are not necessary, and a complication occurs, patients or their attorneys may question whether financial motivations were in play. The issues are not that different from those faced by Dr. Smith and many of the same challenges occur.

MATURE MANAGED CARE

As managed care in your community has matured, your practice may have merged with other groups of a similar specialty or formed into a multispecialty group. You may have contracted with other providers and are participating in global capitation. Perhaps a health system contracting with your group or employing its own physicians receives a capitated fee, per member, per month, to take care of members' entire health needs. These include everything from primary care, consultant specialists, diagnostic testing, and hospitalization, to rehabilitation. Your relationships are complex. Everyone is working to try to provide a package of health services in a very patient focused, efficient fashion. You are all working together, yet there is only so much of the capitation pie to divide. Your relationships with patients have been somewhat fragmented. Your pool of patients has now been merged with many other patients and you are often seeing patients for the first time. You rely heavily on advanced practice providers and have spent a great deal of time in developing policies and protocols for them. Your practice is a machine and it takes a lot to run it. You find yourself busier than ever and yet your compensation has leveled out or has been reduced.

Your practice has now merged with your competitors, but quickly new larger competitors developed. You are still responsible to the patient, but that responsibility may be through a health care team. This team may include an advance practice provider, a triage nurse who handles all incoming clinical telephone calls, your colleagues, even specialists and subspecialists who see your patients and whose opinion you must rely upon. Your patients' expectations are at an all time high now and managed care competition has become fierce. Just when you think everything is starting to "settle down," you hear that further costs need to be squeezed out of the system and, by the way, a larger health system is talking about buying your entire organization. Do you have any say about it? No, a committee has been appointed and its deliberations are well under way. It was determined that your organization is simply not big enough to be able to compete in this new environment.

These changes are, of course, profound; only a few years ago you were a private practice entrepreneur. You may now be an employee. You have an employment agreement and your compensation is linked, among other factors, to productivity. Incentives are thought to be aligned and appropriate, but the potential for abuses, or gaming the system, is clearly apparent. Patients are more distrustful than ever. There is a new emphasis on patient satisfaction, and you receive your survey results on a monthly basis. Your income is based in part on results of those patient satisfaction surveys. You are told that you as a physician need to set an example for the staff. Yet you find your schedule more hectic than ever. Liability risks keep on increasing.

Managed care marketing is at its zenith. Patients are entitled to the best care possible, and you have to find ways to continue to conserve resources. It is clear that advance practice providers have become an important part of your system and you are now responsible for the initial screening and credentialing, and monitoring their performance with patients. This is an important part of the job since their mistakes may be your mistakes. You now have new staff members whose sole job is to handle the telephonic communications to and from your office. You are practicing according to multiple practice guidelines and are working on several guidelines of your own. You are setting up clinics with evening hours and have advance practice providers who are totally involved in home health care. The home health providers, however, need a different kind of screening and additional training, and even more careful monitoring. You have centralized scheduling and electronic medical records. Electronic medical recording has introduced new confidentiality concerns and you need to have mandatory training sessions, monitoring, and policies stressing the importance of confidentiality. You also need to review federal and state legislation to inform yourself on the new confidentiality requirements.

The practice of medicine now appears to be more like a business of providing health services to customers. In some of your administrative meetings, you recognize that you are the commodity that is being discussed.

PLANNING FOR THE FUTURE IN MANAGED CARE

However, there are still new opportunities and challenges. Your group may be working on redesigning care in which outcomes are proven to be better and you are able to show that the health status of your particular population is improving. Your work with the advance practice providers and other staff members who now have new responsibilities, may energize the practice and allow you to compete successfully, knowing that you are actually improving, not sacrificing, quality. You are using outcome-based protocols that provide quality care at a reduced cost.

You have probably learned new skills in developing close patient-doctor relationships in much shorter time frames. This can be fostered by relying on other members of the team to do all the necessary mechanics and using your brief time with each patient to focus intently on that person's needs. This can be augmented with timely telephone calls, notes, and using other forms of communication. The patient-doctor relationship is still, potentially, the most potent therapeutic agent a physician has available. Patients are very unlikely to follow advice, take medications, and make changes in their lifestyles, unless they believe that the therapist is competent and that he or she cares about them.

You may have positioned yourself to take advantage of all the new opportunities this environment has provided, opportunities for you to leave most administrative duties to someone else, to work closely with colleagues, to obtain continuous feedback from patient surveys and peer reviews, to have a degree of income stability, and to have the back-up of a larger organization to provide more malpractice litigation protection. There are also opportunities for your patients: an abundance of patient education materials and mechanisms, known costs of their health care, continuously available coverage, and a receptive audience for any complaints.

Of course you also will have developed systems to protect yourself from the liability risks which grow with the changes. Your liability concerns include all the areas discussed previously in this chapter and are magnified by the fact that the care provided may now be less personal and more business oriented. Recognizing the risks and addressing them have now become essential. Your managed care organization cannot afford for you to be taking the time to defend yourself at a malpractice trial, and they certainly do not want the bad publicity, especially as competition has increased.

Fortunately, increased patient satisfaction and addressing both the traditional and the new liability risks introduced by managed care, also increases the quality of health care. In this respect, at least, one of the goals of the patient, the managed care organization, and the physician are synonymous.

So what must you be prepared for? Be prepared for change. Early market penetration of managed care may come in the form of a discounted fee-for-service preferred provider plan. It can be a small percentage of your practice. Even with early penetration, utilization is going to be watched. Practices need to begin to analyze their own costs and overhead, to see how they are processing patients and how they are satisfying patients. This is an important element of preparing for further penetration of managed care.

As you begin to share risk or enter into capitated arrangements, costs are going to be driven down. Your capitation rate, although perhaps initially attractive, may be reduced as the environment becomes more competitive. You will be faced with reevaluating the "three W's."

CONCLUSION

As all of these changes occur, there are a few constants. One constant is that there still needs to be an emphasis on satisfying your patients. This is a nebulous term and will be considered in greater detail in Chapter 9, but it means assuring that the patient feels cared for, literally. This is not only important for you as a provider, whose hallmark, like Dr. Smith's, has always been "taking good care of my patients," but will be of critical importance as your managed care market matures. In the most mature managed care markets, in fact, patient satisfaction is factored into physician compensation.[65]

Another constant is that liability risks change and increase in a managed care environment. In Chapter 5, we will discuss "Who Would Sue You?" Part of the answer to that question is when there is a breakdown in communication. Unfortunately, greater levels of managed care can, at least initially, cause interruptions in patient relationships. You may have less time to spend with patients. Other types of providers may share these interactions with you. If you are a primary care physician, you may have to send patients to consultants whom they have not met before. If you are a consultant specialist you may be seeing new patients who have an established relationship with other specialists. As managed care matures, patients' expectations increase as, unfortunately, do their suspicions. This creates an environment where liability concerns lurk, and systems to reduce these liabilities need to be created as these changes unfold in your practice.

Most importantly, the evolution will not be the same for everyone. It will occur quicker in some parts of the country. Everyone is somewhere on the spectrum and everyone has additional work to do to adapt to these changes. Some people describe the coming of managed care as a war, but it is not. There is not really an enemy. Others have described it as the coming of a plague, but there is not really any disease. It can best be described as a challenge. The challenge is to co-exist and to profit, for you and your patients, from all of the good principles that the early thinkers about managed care wanted to create, while attempting to reduce the potential for abuses, especially in malpractice litigation. It all starts with a greater level of knowledge and understanding, knowledge of what changes this new environment is bringing, and an understanding of how they can affect you and your patients, and what you can do to meet them.

REFERENCES

1. "Quality of Care is Top-Rated Concern in Choosing Health Plan," *CCH Monitor* 4.22 (1996): 7–8.
2. G. Anders, *Health Against Wealth* (Boston: Houghton-Mifflin, 1996): 42.
3. "Kennedy, Dingell Introduce Health Insurance Bill of Rights," *CCH Monitor* 5.5 (1997): 8.
4. D.L. Shelton, "Bridging the Gap," *American Medical News* (4 September 1995): 10.
5. M. Chase, "Physicians Are From Mars, Patients Are From Venus," *Health Journal* (12 February 1996): B1.
6. L. Page, "Managed Care Firms Balk at Patient Rights Agreement," *American Medical News* (December 1995): 3.
7. K. Pallarito, "Thumbs Down," *Modern Healthcare* (26 May 1997): 20.
8. "Senators Unveil Medicare Patient Choice and Access Bill," *CCH Monitor* 5.10 (1997): 10.
9. G. Wilensky, "Technology," *Hospitals and Health Networks* (20 July 1997): 69.
10. S.Q. Duffy and D.E. Farley, "Patterns of Decline Among Inpatient Procedures," *Public Health Reports* 110 (1995): 674.
11. A.E. Balas, MD, et al., "The Clinical Value of Computerized Information Services," *Archives of Family Medicine* 5 (1996): 271.
12. C. Siskos, "Is There a Doctor On the Line?" *Finance Magazine* (July 1997): 12.
13. "Health Agencies Update," *JAMA* 277.11 (1997): 873.
14. R.P. Carlson, "Can Telemedicine Deliver What It Promises?" *Family Practice Management* (March 1996): 36.
15. Physician Insurers Association of America, *Telemedicine* (1996).
16. K. Lumsdon, "A Kinder, Gentler ER," *Hospitals and Health Networks* (5 February 1996): 12.
17. "Many Emergencies Really Aren't," *Hospitals and Health Networks* (5 March 1996): 12.
18. Anders, *Health Against Wealth*, 133.

19. L.C. Baker and L. Schuurman Baker, "Excess Cost of Emergency Department Visits For Nonurgent Care," *Health Affairs* (Winter 1994): 162.
20. C. Kent, "House Calls Return - High-tech Style," *American Medical News* (7 October 1996): 32.
21. "Does the Continuum Ever End? A Patient's Perspective," *Hospitals and Health Networks* (20 November 1994): 38.
22. "Hospital Moves Nursing Outside Its Walls," *Healthcare Leadership Review*: 38.
23. "Hospital Solves Resource Problems By Retaining Nursing Staff," *Managed Care Report* (April 1995): 10.
24. J. Donlevy, "Responsive Restructuring: Part I: Acute Care Nurses Provide Home Visits," *The New Definition* 8.3 (1993): 1.
25. "Home Health Agency Tracks Congestive Heart Failure Patients," *Hospital Outcomes Management* (September 1994): 37.
26. "Have Nurses, Will Visit," *Profiles* (March/April 1994): 8.
27. K. Lumsdon, "Beyond Four Walls," *Hospitals and Health Networks* (20 May 1994): 68.
28. "Psychiatric Home Care for Older Adults," *The Philhaven Perspective* 20.1 (1995): 1.
29. T.A. Dorris and T.H. Stone, "Implications of Negligent Selection and Retention of Physicians in the Age of ERISA," *American Journal of Law and Medicine* 21.4 (1995): 383.
30. S. Boschert, "Malpractice Insurers Worried by Managed Care," *Family Practice News* (1 July 1996): 64.
31. "NCQA Issues Physician Organization Certification Standards," *CCH Monitor* 5.10 (1997): 5.
32. K. Benesch, "Emerging Theories of Liability for Negligent Credentialing in HMOs, Integrated Delivery and Managed Care Systems," *The Health Lawyer* 9:1 (1996): 14.
33. J.D. Blum, "The Evolution of Physician Credentialing into Managed Care Selective Contracting," *American Journal of Law and Medicine* 22.2,3 (1996): 173.
34. "NCQA Announces First Group of Certification for CVOs," *CCH Monitor* 4.22 (1996): 5.
35. J. Shindul-Rothschild, et al., "Where Have All the Nurses Gone?" *American Journal of Nursing* 96.11 (1996): 25.
36. J.D. Moore, Jr., "Mass. Nurses Push Staffing Bills," *Modern Healthcare* (26 May 1997): 6.
37. Shindul-Rothschild et al., *American Journal of Nursing*, 25.
38. J. Donlevy, "Home is Where the Case Managers Are," *Inside Case Management* 1.3 (1994): 2.
39. "Hospital Nurse Cross-over System Eases Agency Staffing Problems," *Hospital Home Health* (June 1993): 80.
40. L. Muir, "Disease Management," *Hospitals and Health Networks* (5 June 1997): 24.
41. D.L. Olmstead and M.L. Williams, "Billing for CRNP Services," *Pennsylvania Medicine* (December 1996): 26.
42. L. Stutz, "The Evolution of Managed Care: New Jobs for Nurses in the 21st Century," *The American Nurse* (November/December 1996).
43. J. Shindul-Rothschild, et al., *American Journal of Nursing*, 25.
44. "PR Practitioners," *Modern Healthcare* (24 February 1997): 56.
45. E.M. Levine, "A New Predicament for Physicians: The Concept of Medical Futility, the Physician's Obligation to Render Inappropriate Treatment and the Interplay of the Medical Standard of Care," *Journal of Law and Health* 9.69 (1994–95).
46. S.N. Rosenberg, MD, et al., "Effects of Utilization Review in a Fee-for-Service Health Insurance Plan," *New England Journal of Medicine* (16 November 1995): 1326.
47. Anders, *Health Against Wealth*, 42.
48. G.J. Apple, "Who Bears the Risk When Physicians Are Also Insurers?" *Minnesota Medicine* 78 (1995): 23.
49. "Extreme Risk—The New Corporate Proposition for Physicians," *New England Journal of Medicine* 333.25 (1995).

50. J. Johnson, "Trial Focus: Public Unease with Physician Incentives," *American Medical News* (12 August 1996).
51. T.S. Bodenheimer and K. Grumbach, MD, "Capitation for Decapitation, Keeping Your Head in Changing Times," *Journal of the American Medical Association* 276.13 (1996): 1025.
52. J. Frieden, "Capitation on Trial In California Case," *Family Practice News* (1 February 1996): 70.
53. D.M. Gianelli, "Giving Ethics Guidance Through Medicine's Moral Thicket," *American Medical News* (7 April 1997): 9.
54. F. Kostreski, "Referral Guidelines Put Heat on Generalists," *Family Practice News* (15 February 1996): 57.
55. D.M. Mulholland, III, "Managing Care and the Risk for Managing Quality," *Managing Care* 7.1 (1992): 12.
56. S. Orlowski, "Pennsylvania Physicians Can Now Share the Risk," *Pennsylvania Medicine* (May 1996): 12.
57. S. Boschert, "Physicians Fight Managed Care Deselection," *Family Practice News* (1 March 1996): 81.
58. G. Aston, "New Medicare Appeal Rules," *Journal of the American Medical Association* 40.20 (1997): 1.
59. K. Davis, et al., "Choice Matters: Enrollees' Views of Their Health Plans," *Health Affairs* (Summer 1995): 99.
60. B. Jancin, "Primary Care Gatekeepers Risk New Liability," *Family Practice News* (15 October 1995): 46.
61. L. Panah, "Common Law Tort Liability of Health Maintenance Organizations," *Journal of Health and Hospital Law* 29.3 (1996): 146.
62. "Oklahoma Court Rules on HMO Liability for Financial Incentives to Physicians," *HDL* 25.1 (1996): 54.
63. "Malpractice Plaintiffs Hit Big," *Hospitals and Health Networks* (5 March 1996): 14.
64. J.F. Tutolo, "Pappas v. United States Healthcare Systems of Pennsylvania, Inc." 546 Pa. 682; 686A.2d 13.2; 1996 Pa. LEXIS 2554.
65. See *BNA Managed Care Reporter,* (October 1, 1997): 914.

CHAPTER 4

True Costs of a Malpractice Suit

"It isn't about winning...it's about not losing."
A physician after a verdict in his favor following a malpractice trial. January, 1997

For a physician in a malpractice suit, winning, however, is still nothing. The costs—win or lose—are enormous. The following are excerpts from a true story published in *Minnesota Medicine* in 1993 (author's name withheld by request), under the title, "Malpractice Nightmare; Good Medicine Didn't Protect Me." The physician had just received a letter serving notice of a wrongful death lawsuit.[1]

> "Naturally, I began to go over the case again and again. But no matter how many times I reviewed my actions, I reached the same conclusion: I would not have done anything differently... The lawsuit has disrupted my practice and my personal life. When I first found out about the suit, I became obsessed with avoiding another lawsuit. I started spending every spare moment reading journals and books. The more I knew, the less chance that this could happen again. I began to withdraw from my family and friends... I realized then that the experience of the lawsuit and my way of handling it had left me mentally impaired to the point where I was unable to continue my practice. I sought psychiatric care.
>
> After my "season in hell," I have been able to resume my practice on a limited basis. Of course, things will never be the same. I now look at every patient as a potential lawsuit. I see far fewer patients because the fewer I see, the less chance I have of being sued."*

Source: Reprinted with permission from Malpractice Nightmare: Good Medicine Didn't Protect Me, *Minnesota Medicine,* November 1993, © 1993, Minnesota Medical Association.

LIMITS OF MALPRACTICE INSURANCE PROTECTION

What happened? Why was this physician so totally devastated? Perhaps, like so many, this physician felt impregnable behind the bulwark of a top level malpractice insurance policy, with the total coverage listed in the hundreds of thousands of dollars, "As long as I practice good, careful medicine, what could go so wrong as to disrupt my whole life?"

Unfortunately, there are two fallacies here. Practicing good, careful medicine will indeed help to prevent medical negligence. It will not, however, save doctors from being human, and, therefore, some will sometimes err. How errors are handled has much to do with whether or not there is a lawsuit. The law, recognizing human nature, will forgive errors in judgment, but not negligence. Patients, however, may not be able to make the distinction, or, if they feel offended, misunderstood, neglected, or ignored, may not choose to do so. They may see their only recourse as a lawsuit.

It is not enough to practice good, careful medicine, practitioners must also be able to prove to others that they did so. The records must demonstrate what they were doing, or not doing, and why, clearly enough to discourage a plaintiff's attorney. Fortunately, good medical records are also an essential ingredient of good patient care.

The second fallacy is the assumption that the malpractice insurance policy will cover all of your potential financial liability. Most policies will cover the cost of your defense, if it is decided that is the best course to follow, or the costs of a settlement. However, there are two disturbing limitations: you could be sued successfully for more than the value of your policy (in the discovery process, the plaintiff is permitted to learn the exact terms of your policy); and the unlikely, but possible, assessment of additional "punitive damages," not covered by most policies.

In a recent case, a group of four family physicians was named in a wrongful death suit against a very large hospital system. The family physicians were only peripherally involved in the care of the patient, having referred the patient to the hospital, with which they were associated, for definitive care. The patient was a 36-year-old man, an executive with a potentially large financial future. Through a series of catastrophic misadventures, the patient died. His widow brought suit against the hospital system, every doctor who had been involved in her husband's care in the hospital, and the family physicians who referred him there. The family doctors were accused of failing to refer him soon enough (but had, in fact, acted quite appropriately).

The case against the family physicians was extremely weak, but the plaintiff's attorney refused to drop them from the suit. However, the case against the hospital system was quite strong, since it appeared that a series of negligent errors had been made.

The family doctors, sure they were totally in the clear, and with the full support of two prestigious expert witnesses, wanted to be vindicated in court. Their combined insurance coverage was $1.6 million. The plaintiff's attorney indicated they would not consider any settlement less than $23 million. The family doctors' attorney pointed out that it was possible that a jury might find in favor of the plaintiff and, if so, could award the full $23 million. The jury might find the family doctors not liable and excuse them. It was possible, however, the jury could decide the doctors did have a 10 or 15% part in the tragic events. In that case, even though unlikely, the doctors' share would be from $.7 to $1.85 million above their insurance coverage—potentially money from their own personal assets.

The normal risks that physicians consider are the time spent out of their practice, the adverse publicity regardless of the verdict, and the stress it would place on themselves, their families, and staff. These doctors were willing to accept these risks but not the potential exposure of their financial resources. That risk they felt was too great. Reluctantly they agreed to a settlement.

Another uncovered hazard is that a jury might decide to award "punitive damages." This as the name implies, is an effort to chastise a physician for perceived extraordinary negligence. Fortunately, this occurs very infrequently and only after a claim for punitive damages is included in the original complaint. If that claim is included, it will be challenged by procedural motions by the defense. If the claim for punitive damages survives these motions, it will be submitted to the jury as an item of damage. This is done with the instruction to the jury that the purpose of punitive damages is to punish the doctor in order to deter such conduct in the future. Awards for punitive damages are not covered by most insurance policies.

OVERT AND COVERT COSTS

The true costs of a malpractice suit are both overt, the actual dollar costs, and covert. Usually the overt costs are covered by insurance. The covert costs, however, are far more damaging and are not covered by the usual malpractice insurance policies.

Covert Costs: Community Reputation

Doctors, especially in small communities, are often prominent people, so when their names are linked with anything of a controversial nature, that automatically becomes news. The public is not aware of a suit until it is scheduled in court. Then, depending on the circumstances, and other news available at the time, it may become a featured article. If the case is settled out of court, most likely there will be no further mention of it in the media, and the accusations linger in people's minds as an unanswered question. If the suit goes to trial, and the jury finds in favor of the plaintiff, it is news. If there is a defense verdict there is rarely a story. If it is a case in which punitive damages are awarded, it may become national news as another contemporary "health care horror" story.

This sequence, even though fairly predictable, is extremely disturbing to physician-defendants, who are outraged at the blatant unfairness. When the physician belongs to a large group, a network, or system, the adverse action is likely to be even more widely publicized and the effects magnified because of the highly competitive market. When a network or system is advertising "comprehensive quality care" in the community, it cannot afford to have a lead article read "doctor's negligence causes death!"

More Covert Costs: The National Practitioners Data Bank

The second, and far more potent covert effect of a malpractice suit, is the looming specter of being listed in the National Practitioners Data Bank (NPDB or Data Bank). The Minnesota physician with the "Malpractice nightmare" experience grieved that his/her record "would be marred forever, even after I die." To this physician, this was an almost intolerable thought.

The NPDB was created by the Health Care Quality Improvement Act of 1986, and began actual operations in September 1990. The purpose of the NPDB was to keep track of physicians, dentists, and certain other practitioners, who had some stigma of possible misbehavior or incompetence. By maintaining such records on a national basis, and making them available to health care entities, it would no longer be possible for these practitioners simply to move to another institution or state, with total impunity.[2]

The stigma used as indicators of possible professional inadequacy includes two kinds of data: reports on "adverse actions" and reports on malpractice payments. No proof is required, other than the action of the various responsible agencies. Adverse action reports are required in four situations:

- when a state medical board or dental board takes licensure disciplinary action for "reasons related to the practitioner's professional competence or conduct." Revisions to actions must also be reported
- when a health care entity, such as an HMO or a hospital, takes actions against a physician or dentist that affect his or her clinical privileges for more than 30 days
- when a professional society takes action against a physician or dentist that adversely affects his or her membership status
- when the Drug Enforcement Agency revokes a practitioner's DEA number.

Malpractice payments must be reported when a payment is made, in any amount, on behalf of a physician or dentist, or other licensed practitioner, to satisfy a malpractice claim.

The Data Bank publishes an annual report each year summarizing its activities for the past year and comparing this with information from previous years. These reports provide a plethora of data, demonstrate some interesting trends, and contain a few startling surprises.

The public currently does not have access to the information stored in the Data Bank. It is available to hospitals, health care entities, state licensure boards, and professional societies. Hospitals are required by law to query the Data Bank when considering a staff appointment for any physician, dentist, or other licensed health practitioner. They are also required by law to query the Data Bank every two years for information on every practitioner on the medical staff. They may also query the Data Bank at any other time.

Managed care organizations may query the Data Bank when they are considering a practitioner for employment or for clinical privileges, and when they are conducting peer review. Medical and dental boards may query the Data Bank at any time, and professional societies may query when they are considering applicants for membership or when they are conducting peer review.

Individual physicians and dentists may obtain information about themselves at any time, but not about any other practitioner. A plaintiff's attorney may also query the Data Bank, but only under very narrowly defined circumstances.

Figure 4–1 indicates the number and type of reports received by the Data Bank, for the past five years. Reports on malpractice payments consistently outnumber all other reportable actions combined.

The number of malpractice payment reports in 1995 was the lowest for five years, but in 1996 the number increased by 12%, to the highest level in five years (see Table 4-1). That same table shows a steady decline in the number of malpractice payments by dentists. In 1992 they comprised 16.6% of all malpractice payments made, but in 1996, that figure decreased to 12.8%. Clearly, dentistry has learned something about malpractice prevention that medicine needs to study.

Donald Mayes, DDS, an authority on managed care in dentistry and author of *Managed Dental Care: A Guide to HMOs*, was somewhat surprised that malpractice litigation was so much less among dentists than physicians, and that the number of suits was actually declining each year.[3] He speculated that there could be several reasons for this phenomenon. One significant factor might be that dentists and oral surgeons are performing fewer of the "exotic" procedures of a few years ago, in part because of malpractice misadventures. These would include newer procedures for temporomandibular joint syndrome and dental implants. Most of these procedures are still being performed, but usually only after specialized training in the techniques. Some dental licensing boards now require proof of such training before granting authority for specific procedures.

Mayes noted that the number of dentists involved in managed care arrangements was increasing; in 1994, 33% of dentists were involved in some form of

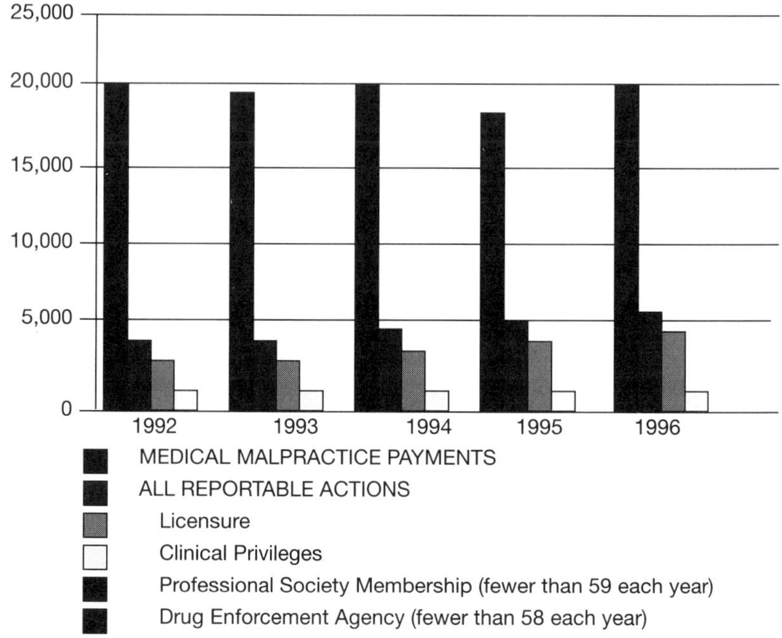

Figure 4–1 Number and Type of Reports Received by the NPDB 1992–1996. Source: Reprinted from *National Practitioner Data Bank, 1996 Annual Report,* U.S. Department of Health and Human Services, Health Resources and Services Administration, Bureau of Health Professions, Division of Quality Assurance.

managed care, with 19% in HMOs. He also noted that dentists have been making notable advances in recent years in presenting dentistry in a less formidable way, much more user friendly. Their practice brochures have increasingly touted, "Family Dentistry," "Gentle Dentistry," and even, "Painless Dentistry." Some of this patient-centered attention may be a direct result of their increasing participation in managed care, and may be a reflection of the managed care organization's goal of pleasing patients. This may be another significant factor in lower malpractice claim rates.

Eighty percent of dentists are generalists, Mayes notes, with an opportunity to develop close patient-doctor relationships, and that also is probably a contributing factor in the continuing overall lower incidence of malpractice litigation in dentistry.

The Data Bank categorizes malpractice payments on the basis of the stated reasons for the suit, i.e., the overt causes. Table 4–2 lists the payments by cause, along with the mean and median amounts of payment for each cause. These are

Table 4–1 Number, Percent Distribution, and Percent Change of Malpractice Payment Reports by Practitioner Type, 1992–1996 and Cumulative

Year	*Practitioner Type*	
	Physicians	*Dentists*
1992		
Malpractice Payment Reports	14,826	3,332
Percent of 1992 Malpractice Reports	73.7%	16.6%
Percent Change (1992–1991)	9.0%	19.1%
1993		
Malpractice Payment Reports	14,602	3,034
Percent of 1993 Malpractice Reports	74.7%	15.5%
Percent Change (1993–1992)	–1.5%	–8.9%
1994		
Malpractice Payment Reports	15,318	2,963
Percent of 1994 Malpractice Reports	76.7%	14.8%
Percent Change (1994–1993)	4.9%	–2.3%
1995		
Malpractice Payment Reports	14,121	2,558
Percent of 1995 Malpractice Reports	77.8%	14.1%
Percent Change (1995–1994)	–7.8%	–13.7%
1996		
Malpractice Payment Reports	15,810	2,541
Percent of 1996 Malpractice Reports	79.3%	12.8%
Percent Change (1996–1995)	12.0%	–0.7%
Cumulative (9/1/90–12/31/96)		
Malpractice Payment Reports	89,801	17,588
Percent of all malpractice reports	76.0%	14.9%

Source: Reprinted from *National Practitioner Data Bank, 1996 Annual Report,* U.S. Department of Health and Human Services, Health Resources and Services Administration, Bureau of Health Professions, Division of Quality Assurance.

Note: This table includes only disclosable reports in the Data Bank as of December 31, 1996. The numbers of reports for 1992 through 1995 may differ from those shown in the 1995 Annual Report because of modifications and voided reports. Modified reports are counted in the year of the modification, not the year of the original report.

Table 4–2 Mean and Median Malpractice Payment Amounts (Actual and Inflation Adjusted) by Malpractice Reason, 1996 and Cumulative

	1996 Only			Cumulative, 9/1/90–12/31/96		
Malpractice Reason	*Number of Payments*	*Mean Payment*	*Median Payment*	*Number of Payments*	*Mean Payment*	*Median Payment*
Diagnosis Related	5,578	$221,596	$125,000	31,931	$190,055	$98,000
Anesthesia Related	553	$223,925	$100,000	3,765	$199,939	$60,000
Surgery Related	5,019	$164,977	$77,500	28,102	$137,043	$60,000
Medication Related	1,045	$161,424	$50,000	7,472	$123,204	$29,999
IV & Blood Products Related	85	$213,100	$83,600	571	$152,981	$40,000
Obstetrics Related	1,411	$363,888	$200,000	8,428	$335,107	$165,000
Treatment Related	5,579	$121,252	$35,000	33,050	$95,796	$25,000
Monitoring Related	251	$197,664	$100,000	1,594	$179,045	$65,000
Equipment or Product Related	88	$55,105	$18,000	553	$59,875	$15,000
Miscellaneous	318	$94,527	$28,500	2,494	$91,159	$25,000
All Reports	19,927	$183,126	$75,000	117,960	$154,431	$52,250

Source: Reprinted from *National Practitioner Data Bank, 1996 Annual Report,* U.S. Department of Health and Human Services, Health Resources and Services Administration, Bureau of Health Professions, Division of Quality Assurance.

Note: This table includes only disclosable reports in the Data Bank as of December 31, 1996. Malpractice payment reports which are missing payment amounts or act or omission codes (n = 251) are excluded.

probably not surprising, with "Obstetrics Related" reasons by far the highest, since those figures would largely be dependent on the care and life expectancy of newborns. The startling finding in this table, however, is the very large increase in payment amounts in almost every category. The only exception is the slight decrease in the "Equipment or Product Related" listing. Even when the figures are adjusted for inflation, the amounts of payments increased alarmingly.

Data are also compiled by the Data Bank on the interval between incident and payment for each year, by reason for the malpractice suit. In 1996 the mean delay was longest for "Obstetrics Related" (6.15 years), and shortest for "Anesthesia Related" (3.56 years). In both of these and nearly all other categories, the delay in 1996 was several months shorter than the mean for the past six years.

A final, and very disturbing, finding is the number of physicians having multiple malpractice payment reports (see Table 4–3). It is probably not surprising that about 20% of physicians who have had one malpractice payment, have had a second. It has been demonstrated that, for totally unexplained reasons, those who have been sued a first time have a greater than average chance for a second suit within one year. The appalling fact is that some physicians have had many suits resulting in payments.

One measure of the NPDB's usefulness is thought to be the number of nonmandated requests received for records. In the past two years this number has increased dramatically, so that now there are as many voluntary requests as those from hospitals, required by law. Figure 4–2 shows the number of queries received, and the changing source of those queries over time. The number of queries jumped by 23.6% from 1995 to 1996. Most of this increase was from health care entities, with only a 4% increase in self queries.

The NPDB has become a major factor in American medicine. Clearly, the data available to every potential practitioner employer will have a significant influence on every employment decision.

Even though the NPDB has been in operation for seven years, many physicians still know very little about what it does and does not do. A survey that measured physicians' knowledge of how the Data Bank operates was published in *Pennsylvania Medicine* in 1994.[4] Among other findings, it revealed that about half of those surveyed did not know that their colleagues, or the general public, did not have access to information about them. More than half thought that physicians would be reported if they had higher than average complication rates.

Access to Information

As established, the data collected may only be released to certain qualified entities. There is mounting pressure, however, to give the public access to this information. The arguments for this change are summarized in the *Health Letter,*

Table 4–3 Prevalence of Reportable Action Reports Among Practitioners Having Malpractice Payment Reports

Number of Malpractice Payment Reports	*Number of Practitioners with Specified Number of Malpractice Payment Reports*	*Number Also Having Reportable Action Reports*	*Percent with Both Malpractice and Reportable Action Reports*
1	61,357	1,926	3.14%
2	10,483	577	5.50%
3	2,556	211	8.26%
4	749	87	11.62%
5	320	44	13.75%
6	116	18	15.52%
7	65	21	32.31%
8	31	8	25.81%
9	21	10	47.62%
10	8	3	37.50%
More than 10	71	25	35.21%
Total	75,777	2,930	3.87%

Source: Reprinted from *National Practitioner Data Bank, 1996 Annual Report,* U.S. Department of Health and Human Services, Health Resources and Services Administration, Bureau of Health Professions, Division of Quality Assurance.

Note: This table includes only disclosable reports in the Data Bank as of December 31, 1995. As of that date, 86,226 practitioners had disclosable reports in the Data Bank. Of these practitioners, 84.5% had one or more malpractice payment reports and had no adverse action reports.

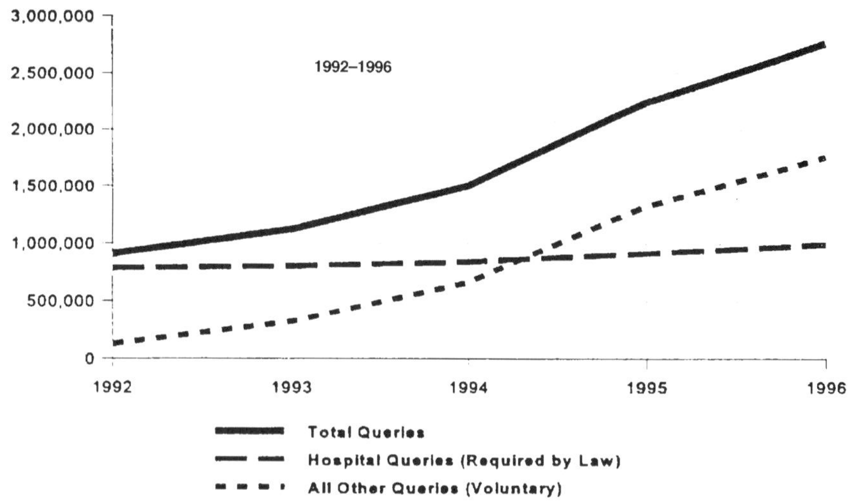

Figure 4–2 Growth in queries, by querier type. *Source:* Reprinted from *National Practitioner Data Bank, 1996 Annual Report,* U.S. Department of Health and Human Services, Health Resources and Services Administration, Bureau of Health Professions, Division of Quality Assurance.

---

a publication of the Public Citizen Health Research Group, an organization co-founded by Ralph Nader and Sidney Wolfe in 1993.[5] They contend that:

- patients need this information in order to choose physicians
- physicians need this information to make informed referrals
- while some of these data are available from other sources, the Data Bank is the only resource that presents the whole picture
- public scrutiny will help to assure the accountability of the data collection system.

Lori A. Bartholomew, a Loss Prevention Consultant to the Physician Insurers Association of America (PIAA), has identified a series of problems with public access to the Data Bank information. She contends that:[6]

- patient relationships could be damaged by misunderstood or incorrect information
- monetary settlements do not necessarily mean negligence, but may be economic expedients

- often several physicians are named in the same suit, but the reports do not identify individual responsibility
- the malpractice data reported are not current, since the average malpractice payment is made almost five years after the incident
- public access would place physicians under additional pressure not to settle out of court, since that would provide a further reason to try to keep from being listed in the Data Bank
- physicians might feel constrained to seek additional, and often costly, ways to practice more defensively.

Regardless of what happens with the federal regulation of the NPDB, individual states may take action to make their own collected information available to the public. In August 1996, Massachusetts became the first state to make it possible for consumers to obtain this kind of information from a single source within the state.[7] This trend seems likely to continue.

The May 17, 1997 issue of *USA Today* contained an article entitled, "Patients Now Checking Up On Doctors." The article noted that the Massachusetts consumer access program was initiated in November 1996, and was already receiving about 200 calls a day. Callers are entitled to request as many as 10 three-page reports on any of the 27,000 licensed physicians in that state. At that time 50,000 reports had been sent.

The reports, or profiles, include the doctor's education and training, specialty, board certification, publications, and any malpractice claims paid or any disciplinary actions against that physician, for the past 10 years. The profiles do not list the dollar amount of any malpractice settlement, but do categorize them as average, above average, or below average.

Consumer groups in Massachusetts would like to add the dollar amount of malpractice claims settlements and also patients' complaints. Doctor groups are opposing these ideas.

USA Today also reported that nine other states are considering similar legislation: Florida, California, Illinois, Maryland, Texas, Rhode Island, Maine, Connecticut, and Vermont. Others are expected to follow.

The NPDB has clearly fulfilled its original expectations of making it difficult for miscreant physicians to move about, escaping their past records, but how serious a covert threat does the present Data Bank system pose to the rest of physicians? James S. Todd, MD, Executive Vice President of the AMA, has pointed out that "there is a difference between data and knowledge."[8] Physicians apparently recognize that raw data, without explanation or context, can be vastly misinterpreted, and remain just raw data. Todd also noted that the Physician Insurers Association of America has reported that even by 1993, 97% of the companies they represent reported that their physicians were more reluctant to settle claims out of court.

The Worst Covert Costs

Personal Threat

By far the most serious covert threat of a malpractice suit against you is the emotional, and possible consequent physical, damage you, your family, and your staff may suffer. The following quotes illustrate the personal trauma that can be experienced due to a malpractice suit:

> "It was mind-shattering, ego-shattering, did everything everybody says a malpractice case does to a physician. . .It shatters you. . .I don't get headaches and I had a headache and was up all night. And you kept questioning your own expertise and what you did" (*Internal Medicine*).[9]

> "In the malpractice situation, you no longer see yourself as an important professional, working for the community. You see yourself as a villain. . . [Y]ou'd be surprised how many times the lawyer indirectly calls you a liar, a murderer, a criminal, and things of that nature. I think that's really devastating to the ego" (*Obstetrics*).[10]

"You are being sued in a court of law" may be the stunning opening phrase of a long and arduous period in your life. It has been likened to having several of your most unwelcome relatives announce that they are moving in with you for the next five years.

Time

The time required to prepare your own defense is in itself an enormous burden. Many hours of prime time must be devoted to answering interrogatories, posing your own interrogatories, attending depositions, preparing for your deposition and trial, and the actual deposition and trial. The trial may only last several days, but could last several weeks. All this, of course, is uncompensated time away from your practice and separation from your family. Some professional liability insurers will pay doctors a per diem for days actually spent in court; however, it certainly doesn't equal the actual time spent out of the office. The time involved is not only the literal time away from practice to participate in the process, but also the time spent contemplating the process, planning your defense mentally, and worrying about the outcome.

A physician recently described the time he spent defending his malpractice case. He explained, emotionally:

> "The time I spent answering the complaint, answering the interrogatories, preparing for my deposition, going through my deposition, and

then preparing for and participating in my trial was actually insignificant compared to the time I spent worrying, contemplating, analyzing my situation. I tried, but I couldn't get it off of my mind. As each event unfolded, I spent hours rethinking our strategy, the implications, reading between the lines of the answers given by my attorney. I must have spent twice the time of the actual process. What I would give to have all that time back now!"

This is a shocking statement when considering the actual time spent, but it is worth noting. This doctor went through all this in even more detail. He described receiving the complaint, poring over the medical record, soul-searching on whether something had been done wrong or not. He recounted many sleepless nights, poring again over the same information during each stage of the process. Although he may have spent as little as six hours with his lawyer preparing for his deposition, he was plagued by thoughts of it for days beforehand. He said that thoughts of the lawsuit crept into his mind when he was seeing other patients, particularly when similar circumstances would arise. He fought hard not to let it affect his decision-making or to become overly defensive in the way he practiced. He was deeply involved in managed care and he found that it affected his utilization, so much that he was contacted by the local managed care medical director. It affected his interactions with his family and made for an extremely stressful time, even at home. He went on to explain that it was not over after the trial, although that ended with a verdict in his favor. He found himself still spending time analyzing each aspect of the trial, again reliving in his mind the criticisms by the plaintiff's expert, which had been made in open court, pondering the negative news articles that described each element of the allegations. He wondered every time he saw patients in the following weeks whether or not they had read the news articles and what their thoughts were, although everyone was peculiarly silent about it. The time he spent never seemed to end.

The Physician Insurers Association of America, in a 1995 report cited by Lori Bartholomew, has stated that the average payment of a malpractice settlement was not made until 58 months after the alleged incident.[11] If the suit goes to court, and there is a verdict in favor of the plaintiff, the average length of time from incident to payment is 76 months. While all of that delay is undoubtedly difficult for the plaintiff, it is an omnipresent and ominous shadow for the defendant physician and family. It is a long and tortuous time.

Credentialing

Another cost of having a lawsuit in the new health care environment is the fact that credentialing has become essential to securing the most desirable practice opportunities. Credentialing is not only required by hospitals, but for managed care organizations as well. In the past, busy physicians may have held the view that having a few lawsuits was indicative of having a big practice. No longer. Because of emerging theories of corporate negligence, hospitals can be held liable for failing to check a physician's credentials appropriately at the time of initial appointment, and for failure to monitor required recredentialing. A physician with multiple claims can expect to have his or her records examined very closely.

Probably even more significant in today's environment is the fact that managed care organizations are also responsible for investigating credentials and monitoring qualifications. This examination is even more tedious than that by hospitals. For any malpractice claim, pending or settled, more details about the circumstances will be required, and a close analysis performed. Managed care organizations are continuously making decisions about which physicians to choose for their closed panels. When there is a surplus of physicians in a particular specialty, if two are similarly qualified, the physician with pending malpractice claims is much less likely to receive the appointment. Although malpractice claims per se often mean nothing about the quality of care provided, questions are raised, "Was the doctor a good communicator?" "Wasn't there adequate documentation for the procedure?" "Why did the patient sue?" This is akin to the assumption that "where there is smoke there is fire" but, unfortunately, this is often the reality. It has now become more urgent than ever to prevent malpractice claims. There is significance not only to having a claim settled, which must be reported to the NPDB, but even having a claim pending has become significant.

Emotional Response

The deep resentment that most physicians feel for the time lost defending themselves against an accusation which they consider unfounded, is only one of the forms of emotional trauma. Physicians, by nature and by training, tend to be sensitive, compassionate people. They have chosen a profession that depends on communication and cooperation, not confrontation and antagonism. They usually have a strong ego and confidence in their own abilities. Indeed, it would be very difficult to hold another person's life in one's hands without the conviction that they could do whatever was necessary for a patient at least as well as anyone else.

A malpractice suit typically challenges both a physician's compassion and ability. The physician, preparing for a court appearance, or even a deposition by a hostile plaintiff's attorney, needs to be prepared to be accused in public of being uncaring, hard-hearted, slovenly, and inept. Time and time again we have heard that no amount of preparation lessens the blow of hearing how you hurt or potentially killed this patient. These comments in court also create attractive sound-bites for the media.

In times of professional stress, it is always helpful to talk to a colleague; but in a pending lawsuit one of the first admonitions of the defense attorney is "Do not talk to anyone else about this suit." The reasoning for this advice is quite simple. Any conversations you have or have had in the past are considered "discoverable"; that is, the opposing attorney has a right to ask you about every conversation you ever had about the case in question. You must respond, under oath, and the other parties could also be queried. The only exceptions are conversations between you and your attorney, or your spouse, which are considered "privileged." You may, and probably should, talk with others about your feelings of stress, but not the details of the source of your stress.

Sara C. Charles, MD is a board certified psychiatrist and a member of the faculty of the Department of Psychiatry of the University of Illinois, Chicago.[12] In 1982 she defended herself successfully in a malpractice suit that involved four years of preparation and a two-week trial. Following this experience she initiated a series of investigations into the nature of malpractice litigation and its effects on physicians.

In 1984 she reported the results of a study of 154 physicians who had been sued and agreed to participate by completing a questionnaire.[13] During the previous five years, about one-third of them had been sued once, and one-third of them had been sued more than once. They were asked to report symptoms, both physical and psychological, they had experienced after being notified a suit had been filed. They were also asked to grade the severity of the symptoms on a scale of 0 (none) to 4 (severe).

When these symptoms were analyzed by clusters, according to The Diagnostic and Statistical Manual III (DSMIII), almost 40% of respondents—all of whom had been sued at least once—had symptom complexes suggesting a major depressive disorder. These symptoms included depressed mood, insomnia, fatigue, feelings of being defeated, and of worthlessness and guilt. They also noted some of the physical symptoms that often accompany depression; gastrointestinal symptoms, anorexia, and headache. More than a fourth noted that these symptoms had lasted more than two weeks.

Approximately 20% had symptoms suggesting an adjustment disorder. Some of these symptoms are, of course, also characteristic of dysphoric mood, particularly fatigue, gastrointestinal complaints, insomnia, and headache. In addition, however, many doctors in this group experienced a pervasive feeling of anger and inner tension, frustration, irritability, difficulty concentrating, and indecision.

Eleven physicians (8%) reported the onset of a physical illness, including three who suffered myocardial infarctions. Ten respondents reported an exacerbation of a previous illness, including hypertension, angina, duodenal ulcer, and colitis. Only six of the 154 denied having any physical or emotional symptoms related to the lawsuit.

Three physicians noted that they had experienced suicidal ideas and four acknowledged that they had abused alcohol or drugs. While these numbers are quite small, the potential danger is great, illustrating again the profound personal impact of a malpractice suit against a physician.

The results of this study were quite startling and the investigators extended their research using a larger number of physicians and a control group. In this study of nearly 1,000 physicians in the Chicago area, more than half acknowledged they had been sued.[14] A questionnaire about symptom complexes they might have experienced, was administered to both the sued and the unsued physicians: 346 of the questionnaires were completed. None of the physicians knew the purpose of the study. The object was to record any symptoms in both groups and assess the possible impact of being sued.

An analysis of the results, as in the previous study, showed that there was a significantly higher number of physicians who reported having symptoms indicative of dysphoric mood in the sued, rather than the unsued group. The same was true for symptoms indicative of an adjustment disorder (see Table 4–4).

More than half (55 to 85%) of the sued physicians had experienced anger, inner tension, depressed mood, frustration, irritability, and insomnia. In contrast, only about half (42 to 56%) of the non-sued noted these symptoms in themselves. There was also a significantly larger percentage of the sued physicians who felt a loss of interest, social withdrawal, a general slowing of motor activity, and a feeling of being misunderstood. Almost three times as many of them reported alcohol abuse, and 6.7% admitted having suicidal ideas, compared with 2.6% of the non-sued physicians.

When asked about their feelings about malpractice litigation, the sued group was much more inclined to say that a plaintiff's case was unjustified. They also were inclined not to view litigation as an affront to their professional competence, but felt that settling a case out of court was tantamount to admitting guilt. Forty-four percent of them said that their families had suffered because of litigation.

In this study there was no difference between the sued and unsued in the number of physical illnesses, but almost twice as many of the sued physicians noted an exacerbation of previous illness. Three sued physicians reported myocardial infarctions. Sixty-two (18%) of the non-sued reported having no symptoms at all, but only eight (2%) of the sued group had no symptoms. The authors noted that some physicians had refused to complete the questionnaire because they found it too upsetting emotionally.

Perhaps the most remarkable finding of all was that even though the litigation process had resulted in all of the emotional trauma and physical effects just described, fewer than 2% of the sued physicians had adverse trial verdicts. This again, drives home the point that it is reducing claims in the first place that has to be our goal.

The sued physicians also reported subsequent changes in their practices; they stopped seeing certain types of patients, they considered retiring early, and they

Table 4–4 Symptomatic Reactions of Sued and Nonsued Physicians

Reaction	*Physicians Who Experienced Reaction*			
	Sued (N = 194)		*Nonsued (N = 152)*	
	N	%	*N*	%
Symptoms				
Anger	166	85.6	70	46.1
Inner tension	161	83.0	86	56.6
Depressed mood	154	79.4	77	50.7
Frustration	149	76.8	73	48.0
Irritability	125	64.4	73	48.0
Insomnia	108	55.7	65	42.8
Fatigue	85	43.8	61	40.1
Loss of interest	73	37.6	42	27.6
Difficulty concentrating	70	36.1	54	35.5
Decreased sex drive	57	29.4	40	26.3
Indecision	54	27.8	40	26.3
Decreased appetite	52	26.8	37	24.3
Social withdrawal	48	24.7	29	19.1
Headache	39	20.1	27	17.8
Gastrointestinal symptoms	36	18.6	32	21.1
General slowing of motor activity	29	14.9	14	9.2
Excessive motor activity	26	13.4	18	11.8
Excessive alcohol use	21	10.8	6	3.9
Exacerbation of physical illness	19	9.8	13	8.6
Increased appetite	19	9.8	10	6.6
Suicidal ideation	13	6.7	4	2.6
Onset of physical illness	10	5.2	9	5.9
Hypersomnia	8	4.1	10	6.6
Elevated mood	4	2.1	2	1.3
Drug misuse	1	0.5	3	2.0
Feelings				
Being misunderstood	80	41.2	51	33.6
Being defeated	66	34.0	39	25.7
Decreased self-confidence	61	31.4	47	30.9
Loss of nerve in clinical situations	55	28.4	34	22.4
Low self-esteem	53	27.3	37	24.3
Guilt	31	16.0	32	21.1
Worthlessness	30	15.5	29	19.1
Shame	28	14.4	25	16.4
Agreement with statements about litigation				
The plaintiff's case is unjustified	153	78.9	47	30.9
Litigation is no affront to my professional competence	119	61.3	62	40.8
Settling equals an admission of guilt	105	54.1	57	37.5
My family and I have suffered	86	44.3	45	29.6
Resentment of counsel's efforts to settle	70	36.1	47	30.9
I am alone in my effort to vindicate myself	61	31.4	37	24.3
My medical practice has suffered	42	21.6	40	26.3

Source: American Journal of Psychiatry, Vol. 142, No. 4, p. 439, 1985. Copyright 1985, the American Psychiatric Association. Reprinted by permission.

tried to discourage other people from entering the field of medicine. In other words, many began practicing the more negative aspects of so-called "defensive medicine."

Three years later Charles and her collaborators reported on the results of 80 follow-up interviews with some of these same physicians: 52 in the sued group and 29 in the non-sued group.[15] The sued physicians were asked about their reactions to the stress of being sued. Most were cognizant of a period of emotional turmoil and that they had experienced either a form of depression, or a cluster of anger related symptoms. Eight percent acknowledged that they had used alcohol excessively as a means of dealing with their feelings.

Both groups were asked about changes in their practice styles in the intervening years. Members of the sued group said that they tended to order more diagnostic tests, exclude certain kinds of patients from their practices, and refer patients to consultants more frequently. More than 75% of the sued physicians indicated that they had altered the way in which they practiced. They also acknowledged trying to dissuade their own children from becoming physicians.

These studies reinforce the obvious to those who have been directly involved in malpractice litigation:

- the fact of being sued has a profound emotional impact on most physicians
- this impact is often severe enough to disrupt the physician's family life and physical well-being
- a suit is often followed by practice changes which may be positive (such as keeping better records) or negative (such as distancing from patients).

Charles reports: "There is no way to completely avoid the feelings and reactions that a malpractice suit generates. Feelings of anger and disequilibrium, often accompanied by somatic symptoms, are normal, human responses to a stressful life event... Not to respond in some way is far more worrisome."[16]

She goes on to say:

> "Individual doctors report different reactions to being sued. There are, however, identifiable clusters of symptoms and behaviors that are commonly reported by doctors who have been sued. In our studies, approximately 33% described symptoms similar to those experienced in a depressive disorder, such as depressed mood, appetite change, insomnia, loss of energy, loss of interest in usual activities, and, on occasion, suicidal ideation. Slightly more than 25% of physicians experienced symptoms which might be described as an adjustment reaction to a major life stress, with malpractice litigation as the psychosocial stressor, characterized by symptoms of intense anger, irritability, inner

> tension, frustration, fatigue, headache, and/or gastrointestinal complaints. Sixteen percent experienced the onset or exacerbation of a physical illness such as hypertension, duodenal ulcer, colitis, and coronary artery disease. A small number reacted by misusing drugs, especially alcohol."

Charles also notes the changes which may occur in physicians' practices such as becoming more defensive, avoiding high risk situations, and distancing themselves from patients. She notes that there is stress on the marital bond and possible repercussions on the children.

Two months after the Minnesota physician published the "Malpractice Nightmare," the same journal published a letter in commentary.[17] The letter writer indicated that in his opinion the physician's concern was exaggerated, that the risk of a malpractice suit is a "risk of doing business," and that worrying about being listed in the National Practitioners Data Bank was an overreaction. The letter was written by a malpractice plaintiff's attorney.

In 1996 a paper entitled, "Physicians' Discourses on Malpractice and the Meaning of Medical Malpractice," as part of The Harvard Medical Practice Study, was published in the *Journal of Health and Social Behavior.*[18] This part of the study was based on interviews with 47 physicians. The authors noted that these physicians had an expectation that they would control the management of their own affairs. A malpractice suit was considered, by them, as a challenge to this autonomy. The physicians found it incredible that patients, and lawyers, were challenging their expertise and, therefore, their autonomy. This raised in their minds the concept of fallibility, a concept that had apparently seemed foreign to them. They did not feel that lawyers, juries, or even judges were qualified to sit in judgment over them. This was a challenge to their professional egos.

Charles has a further explanation for physicians' discomfort in the legal arena:[19]

> "There is a problem inherent to being sued, however, that derives from the very nature of the legal process and that explains one aspect of the intensity of the reaction. It also explains why the "fact" of litigation cannot be out of consciousness continuously. By being sued for malpractice, a doctor is automatically transferred into the legal arena, an environment in which the average doctor is ill prepared to function. It has a different language, proceeds at a different pace, and has rules with a long tradition. It progresses slowly, is punctuated by periods of intense involvement, while at other times one wonders if the malpractice suit has dissolved away for lack of attention. Then suddenly a motion is scheduled, and the doctor is drawn back into the orbit of legal activity and must spend many hours with the lawyer—hours which had

been previously scheduled for other activities. The entire legal process is permeated with unpredictability. A deposition can be scheduled, canceled, rescheduled, and recancelled—all with seeming equanimity. The doctor, meanwhile, who often has to respond to life and death situations at a moment's notice, becomes increasingly frustrated, discouraged, and angry."

The question of why physicians are so often demolished emotionally by a malpractice suit is of particular interest because it may provide some clues as to how to respond to such a stressor in healthy ways. Doctors' two principal psychological mechanisms for dealing with the stress of a malpractice lawsuit are suppression and denial. They are usually able to put thoughts of the impending legal struggle aside and focus on the clinical problems at hand. These mechanisms do not always work. Physicians may then feel distracted, less able to concentrate, and may have difficulty making decisions.

IF A SUIT HAPPENS

In their continuing studies of physicians' reactions to being sued, Charles and her associates discovered a variety of coping mechanisms that physicians had found helpful, including:[20]

- willingness to seek psychological help when stressed
- active, planned, leisure time activities
- frank discussions of feelings under stress, with peers and staff (but not the facts)
- distancing oneself from worrying about a suit, practicing good medicine, and acknowledging intellectually that one could still be sued
- taking an "active" approach to the suit itself—being actively involved in all aspects of the defense
- joining an appropriate physician support group, if one is available in the state (or form one as developed by the Illinois State Medical Society).[21]

All of these are devices that have been tried and found useful by other physicians facing litigation stress. Most, but not all, malpractice suits can be prevented, but if a suit happens, a physician needs to be aware of the covert costs and consider the proven steps to minimize the personal damage.

CONCLUSION

The whole point is that malpractice claims are worth preventing. It is worth taking the time, making the effort or the investment to do so. In the new health care environment, particularly in the new managed care environment, this has become far more important than ever. These claims take far too much time, too much energy, and are too much of an emotional drain, to be accepted as merely the cost of practicing medicine. The "Malpractice Nightmare" can usually be prevented. There are ways to organize one's practice, relate with patients, record essential data, and work in conjunction with managed care, that will make malpractice lawsuits far less likely. When one considers the fact that up to 80% of all claims are actually preventable, it becomes clear that our attention needs to move from winning claims to preventing them in the first place, which is the real win. Once a matter is in litigation, the best which can be done is "not to lose." There are also positive steps that can be taken if there is a suit, to prevent it from becoming a total nightmare.

Chapter 5 will address who is likely to sue and why.

REFERENCES

1. "Medical Nightmare," *Minnesota Medicine,* 76, no.11, (November 1993): 8, 9, 36.
2. *National Practitioners Data Bank 1996 Annual Report* (U.S. Department of Human Services, Public Health Service). For information on the National Practitioners Data Bank, call the toll free Data Bank Help Line 800-767-6732 or 703-802-9380. Copies of the Annual Report are available, without cost, and contain much additional data by state.
3. D.S. Mayes, "*Managed Dental Care: A Guide to HMOs*" (Brookfield: International Foundation of Employee Benefit Plans, Inc., 1993).
4. "NPDB: What Physicians Don't Know Can Hurt Them," *Pennsylvania Medicine,* (July 1994), 10–14.
5. "National Practitioners Data Bank: Why It Should Be Accessible," *Health Letter,* 9, no. 8 (1993): 6–7.
6. L.A. Bartholomew, "Can Public Access to the National Practitioner Data Bank Improve the Quality of Care?" *Medical Practice Management,* 12, no. 4, (1997): 173–176.
7. "Massachusetts Makes Physician Profiles Available to the Public," *Health Letter,* 12, no.12 (1996): 1, 3.
8. J.S. Todd, "Just Numbers or Knowledge," *Public Health Reporter,* 110 no. 4, (1995): 377–378.
9. T. Majoribanks et al., "Physicians' Discourses on Malpractice and the Meaning of Medical Practice," *Journal of Health and Social Behavior* 37 (June 1996): 167.
10. Majoribanks et al., *J of Health and Social Behavior,* 168.
11. Bartholomew, *Medical Practice Management,* 174.
12. "A Different View of Malpractice," *Chicago Medicine,* 87 no. 5, (1984): 338–342.
13. S.C. Charles et al., "Physicians' Self-Reports of Reactions to Malpractice Litigation," *American Journal of Psychiatry,* 141, no. 4 (1984): 563–565.
14. Charles, *Am J Psychiatry,* 142, 437–440.
15. S.C. Charles, "Sued and Nonsued Physicians," *Psychosomatics,* 28, no. 9 (1987).
16. S.C. Charles, "Malpractice Suits: Their Effects on Doctors, Patients, and Families," *Journal of the Medical Association of Georgia,* 76 (1987): 171–172
17. J.F. Eisberg, "'Malpractice Nightmare' Doesn't Ring True." *Minnesota Medicine,* 77 (1994): 3.
18. Majoribanks, *J of Health and Social Behavior,* 163–178.

19. S.C. Charles, "The Physician and Malpractice Litigation," *Journal of Medical Practice Management*, 1, no. 2 (1985): 123–129.
20. S.C. Charles et al., "Coping with the Stress of Malpractice Litigation," *Illinois Medical Journal,* 171, no. 1 (1987): 23–27.
21. S.C. Charles, "Physician Support Group Formed," *Illinois Medical Journal*, 167:6 (1985).

For more information on support groups contact the Illinois State Medical Society, Division of Medical Education, Twenty North Michigan Avenue, Chicago, IL 60602.

CHAPTER 5

Who Would Sue You?

The Doctor's Dream

And thus I dreamt that round me stood
The victims of disease,
The patients I had failed to cure,
Though some had paid my fees.

One said, "It is a happy place,
My bliss is unalloyed;
Through your mistakes just ten years more
Of Heaven I have enjoyed."...

I got here shaky in my shoes,
And asked if they'd attack us,
And raise a rumpus in these courts,
With questions of malpractice.

William Snowden Battles
(1827 – 1895?)

For more than two decades physicians have been urged to practice certain types of "defensive medicine" and to use "risk management" as a means of avoiding the pain of malpractice litigation. Much has been learned from practicing these strategies, but neither has been fully satisfactory in maximizing malpractice prevention. The advent of managed care, on a large scale, has added more factors to the equation, more reasons why patients might sue, and many more reasons to prevent claims in the first place. Traditional forms of defensive medicine will not work in a managed care environment. In order to be successful in preventing malpractice lawsuits, it is necessary to know everything possible about why people sue.

Physician errors, or "medical misadventures" as insurance people prefer to call them, and patients' perceptions that they have been wronged, continue to be significant reasons for many malpractice lawsuits. Given the same set of circumstances, however, why is it that some people sue and others do not? It is also important to consider why some physicians are more prone to be sued than others. It is not so much the area of specialty or type of physician, as it is the behavior or how physicians handle similar circumstances that induce claims. The frequency of litigation varies with the specialty, of course, but there are also variations in the rate of litigation within the specialty. Some practitioners are more at risk than others or their behavior or interactions put them at greater risk.

The purpose of this chapter is to examine each of the issues raised: litigation as a deterrent to actual malpractice, the results of practicing defensive medicine and of risk management, the new factors attendant to managed care, the vulnerability of physicians, and the stated and unstated reasons why patients sue.

LITIGATION AS A DETERRENT TO MALPRACTICE

Many questions have been raised about the effectiveness of the present malpractice system in reducing actual malpractice and in providing just compensation for the injured. Meadow, et al., in the May 1997 issue of *Pediatrics,* reported the results of a study using an unusual technique.[1] The researchers attempted to identify all the physicians in the United States who were practicing neonatal intensive care. They were able to identify 2,498 such specialists and sent each of them a questionnaire. The researchers received 1,813 responses, representing approximately 75% of all physicians practicing in Neonatal Intensive Care Units (NICUs) in this country. While not all of them answered every question, there were at least 1,500 responses to every question posed. In addition to the basic demographic data, the questionnaire asked these physicians about their personal experience with the malpractice system and their views about it.

The investigators discovered that 43% of the NICU physicians had experienced at least one malpractice claim against them. The probability of being sued increased with each year in practice, in a linear mode. Twenty percent of those who had been in practice less than five years were sued; 54% of those who had practiced more than 10 years were sued; and for those who had practiced more than 15 years, 60% were sued.

While these numbers are disconcerting, the frequency of additional suits is even more discomfiting. For NICU physicians who had been in practice fewer than five years, and had been sued, the frequency of one or more additional suits against them was 20%. For those who had been in practice more than 10 years and had been sued, 60% had been sued more than once.

When these NICU physicians were asked for their opinions as to the appropriateness of lawsuits against NICU physicians, only 20% thought that the alleged malpractice claims represented real malpractice. This percentage was approximately the same for those who had been sued and for those who had not been sued. When the opposite question was asked—how many instances of actual malpractice resulted in lawsuits—the answer was only 20%. (This echoes the findings of many other studies, that there are many more instances of malpractice than there are claims, and that most malpractice claims are not based on actual malpractice.)

The NICU doctors were also asked their opinions as to how to correct the current malpractice system: 96% would favor a peer review system to review alleged instances of malpractice; and 72% would prefer a no-fault system to the present arrangement. They also expressed a lack of confidence in the value of the expert witness: 50% thought that the expert witnesses were not truly experts, and 30% thought that they were often actually unethical.

The authors of this study drew some picturesque, but practical conclusions. They noted three theoretical paradigms for medical negligence claims:

- The evildoer hypothesis: most malpractice actions are committed by a small group of physicians who are evil and unprofessional and, therefore, deserve to be punished.
- The evil deed hypothesis: actual malpractice is a rare event and can happen to anyone, at random.
- Malpractice allegations are not related to poor medical care; they are directly related to the need for monetary compensation for bad outcomes.

Meadow, et al., observe that:

> "The evildoer hypothesis does not appear consistent with the data. The relationship between a likelihood of malpractice suits and duration of practice is essentially linear. Over half of all NICU physicians will be sued if they practice 10 years or more. Whatever malpractice allegations are doing in the NICU, they are not identifying a small coterie of bad apples. If the metaphor were appropriate, most NICU physicians would appear to be rotting slowly, and more than half the barrel would spoil each decade."

They believe that the data suggest several possible reforms for the current malpractice system. They feel that efforts to seek out "evildoers," or to identify them through the Data Bank, will be fruitless. They point out that any NICU physician who practices long enough will probably be sued. The authors of this study also believe that efforts to teach doctors to be more sensitive, or to improve their clinical skills, will also be fruitless in preventing malpractice claims, although they concede that it might improve patient care.

The overall conclusion of Meadow, et al., is that our present malpractice system is ineffective as a malpractice deterrent or for providing patients with just retribution, but that it works more like a lottery, "Patients and their families are likely to win at random, but those who win can win big. The costs of this lottery are enormous—doctors are increasingly demoralized, patients are increasingly suspicious, and the lottery payouts are, inevitably, passed on to consumers or taxpayers."

On balance, as will be explained further in this chapter, teaching good communication skills clearly does reduce claims. It may be hard for some practitioners to acknowledge or understand that their communication skills could be improved. At least not until the first lawsuit. No one really knows exactly how many claims good communication has prevented. Has that conduct gone unrewarded? We think not.

DEFENSIVE MEDICINE

We should state at the outset that we question whether defensive medicine ever really worked well. There are many definitions but the American Medical Association (AMA) uses the term defensive medicine in its publications to mean "the performance of diagnostic tests and treatment procedures which, but for the threat of a malpractice action, would not have been done."[2]

Klingman, from the United States Congress Office of Technology Assessment, et al., published a study of defensive medicine.[3] They noted that the term has often been used pejoratively, for example, in referring to medical actions that are "not medically justified and are performed primarily to prevent or defend against the threat of liability." They also noted that it is a goal of the malpractice system to minimize risks for patients. Klingman argued that to some extent, defensive medicine contributes toward the achievement of that goal. In the process, however, it may increase the costs of health care to a particular patient. Defensive medicine may encourage physicians to perform additional procedures, which both increase the costs and pose added risks to the patient. When this occurs, one of the major goals of the malpractice system, safer health care, is thwarted.

The authors of the study describe four possible scenarios concerning costs and outcomes which can occur in the practice of defensive medicine (see Figure 5–1):

- Box A is an ideal outcome: quality is up and costs are down—the goals of both physician and patient are fulfilled.
- Box C represents the opposite: quality is poor and costs are high. This is, however, one of the possible results of defensive medicine.
- Boxes B and D depict the frequent dilemma, a trade-off between health care quality and costs.
- In A and D the question is in deciding which medical procedure is "medically appropriate."

The authors illustrate the problem:

> "Is an expensive test justified for a patient who has one chance in 15,000 of having the disease in question? What if the chance of a positive test result is one in 100,000? What if the disease in question is not very serious? Judgments about questions such as these determine the dividing line between appropriate and inappropriate medical procedures."[4]

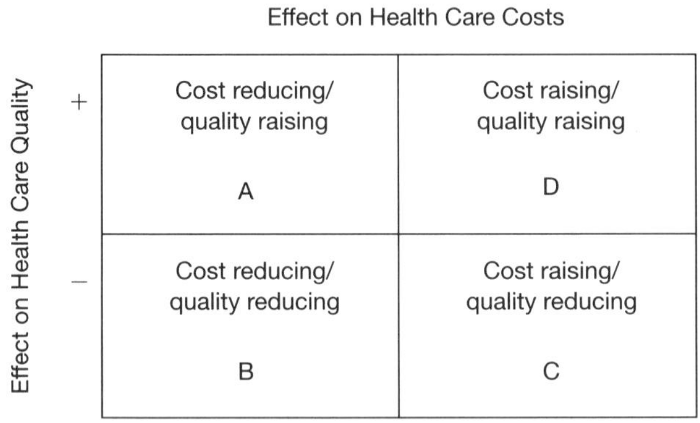

Figure 5–1 A typology of defensive medical practices. *Source:* Reprinted with permission from David Klingman et al., Measuring Defensive Medicine Using Clinical Scenario Surveys, *Journal of Health Politics, Policy and Law,* Vol. 21, No. 2 (Summer 1996), figure 1, p. 89, © 1996, Duke University Press.

The difficulty in assessing the value of defensive medicine is that there is no way to determine the extent to which each of those four possibilities occur in practice. Furthermore, they are a matter of judgment, it is not possible to categorize them uniformly. The authors developed a definition of defensive medicine which is not dependent on a given procedure:

> "Defensive medicine occurs when physicians order tests, procedures, or visits, or avoid high-risk patients or procedures, primarily (but not necessarily solely) to reduce their exposure to malpractice liability. When physicians perform tests or procedures primarily to reduce exposure to liability, they are practicing positive defensive medicine. When they avoid certain patients or procedures, they are practicing negative defensive medicine."[5]

Using this definition, the investigators reviewed a previous study, from the same office, of 47 practice surveys. They found none that answered satisfactorily the questions of the extent to which defensive medicine was practiced, nor how it affected the quality of patient care. They devised a research method to provide additional insights into the problem, based on questionnaire responses to a set of specific clinical scenarios. They noted that, at least in the recent past, physicians were not penalized, and were sometimes rewarded financially, for practicing positive defensive medicine, i.e., ordering more studies. They concluded that the fee-for-service system has encouraged physicians to practice lower risk, and therefore higher cost, medicine.

While the malpractice system is intended to encourage physicians to practice an acceptable level of quality of care, by deterring medical negligence, it is still not clear how well that goal has been achieved. With the multiplication of HMOs and other risk sharing arrangements, there are new incentives to do less, rather than more, which could reduce physician incentives to practice defensively, with the accompanying hazard of doing too little. Not only are the incentives disappearing but there are now disincentives managed through strict utilization control. With managed care, the ability to collect data about utilization and utilization controls, make this kind of defensive medicine nearly impossible.

Imagine the conversation between Dr. Wright, the Medical Plan Director, and Dr. Smith. Dr. Smith has a colleague—one of his former associates and protégés—who has recently been sued. Dr. Smith saw first hand the turmoil that it caused in his colleague's life, and he gained a great understanding of what it meant to have a malpractice claim looming over you for years. He saw his colleague each day when he dragged himself back from the courthouse and remembered reviewing the daily newspaper articles listing all the allegations against his colleague. Fortunately the malpractice case ended in a verdict in the doctor's favor. His colleague was certainly happy, but Dr. Smith vowed that he was not going to let it happen to him. In the clinical gray areas, when he needed to make a decision about whether or not to order an additional procedure, he began making the referral, ordering that extra diagnostic test. He found himself practicing defensive medicine.

This was in sharp contrast to the rules of the system he joined, where he had been asked to look carefully at utilization, be sure that a diagnostic test was indicated and would yield value to the overall clinical understanding of the patient. There were risk pools or pools of money that could be distributed at the end of the year which were dependent, in part, on the number of referrals and diagnostic tests made. Certainly in clear cases he would refer or obtain the test and he would never put the patient's health in jeopardy. He had always been guided by his conscience and good clinical judgment. He was amazed at how many close cases there were where, on balance, it probably was not really necessary, at least at that point in time, to get the referral or test. However, these new feelings, legitimate litigation fears, changed that balance and new habits had developed. It is a subtle insidious process, but it did not go unnoticed.

Dr. Wright showed Dr. Smith several colored graphs which depicted his utilization as compared to others in his group. Dr. Smith was shocked to see the amount of information Dr. Wright had about his practice and the sophisticated presentation he made. The graphs illustrated that his utilization was high in nearly every category. He responded that he really was just using good sound clinical judgment and that there certainly was not any type of change in his approach to his patients. Dr. Wright then brought out another color presentation which showed Dr. Smith's trends. Clearly, over the course of the last 18 months his utilization, that is, his use of expensive resources, had steadily climbed upward. He had no explanation. No, he was not seeing sicker patients. No, he was not seeing a different patient population. No, it wasn't just coincidence. The meeting ended on a down note. Dr. Smith knew that he could not practice this type of defensive medicine and continue to be on the panel.

That scenario is being played out all across the country; the Dr. Smiths are legion. That type of defensive medicine cannot be practiced in a managed care setting. However, on balance, there really is no direct statistical data available that would suggest that type of defensive medicine ever worked. In a managed care environment appropriate tests must be ordered. If not, clearly patients will suffer and litigation exposure will increase. Extra testing and referrals in the gray areas, simply for the purpose of reducing exposure, did not work in the past and in the future will not be tolerated. The good news is that there is a type of "defensive medicine" that can work, but it has more to do with physician behavior, communication, and risk management systems than simply raising shields to protect the physician.

Managed care will continue to draw these issues into sharper, more urgent focus. In many parts of the country, where managed care is still new, this issue is just emerging, but even in areas where managed care has penetrated the market extensively, these issues are taking on even greater significance than before.

Not everyone agrees that defensive medical practice, especially the ordering of unnecessary testing procedures or treatments, occurs because of fear of litigation. In the Netherlands malpractice suits are said to be quite rare, estimated to occur at a rate of one-tenth the frequency in the United States. In a 1994 article in *Family Medicine,* Marjan Veldhuis reported on a series of defensive medical practices in that country.[6] In two studies reviewed it was determined that from 17 to 24% of referrals were made for reasons other than medical necessity. In another study 27% of all tests were said to be ordered defensively, but not necessarily to defend the physician from litigation.

The author concludes that in the Netherlands, and perhaps in this country, defensive medical decisions are often based on non-litigious concerns. The other reason can be considered under the term "relational," and include a perceived lack of confidence by the patient, or a conflict, or a concern for loss of appreciation by the patient.

RISK MANAGEMENT

In the 1970s, in response to the general agreement that the medical profession was undergoing a "malpractice crisis," the concept of risk management for physicians was given a great deal of attention. The idea of curtailing risks was said to have begun in the aircraft industry and later adapted to the needs of the health care profession. The term "risk management" was defined as gathering and using information to lessen the risk of a specific kind of loss. The principal objectives of this strategy to ascertain the frequency of those risks, were listed as:

1. identifying situations that put the insured at higher financial risk,
2. finding ways to circumvent or alleviate such risks, and
3. determining if these recommended remedies were financially sound. Would the cost of such remedies more than balance the probable loss from tolerating those risks?[7]

To address the issues involved in professional liability, the Minnesota Medical Society organized a round table discussion concerning medical risk management.[8] The panel was chaired by a family physician and included a risk manager, a health facility administrator, a malpractice defense attorney, and a neurosurgeon. The family physician moderator opened the discussion by asking what was meant by the term risk management. The attorney risk manager used a three-part definition: a practice style designed to prevent, or curtail, patient injuries, malpractice claims, and malpractice losses. The defense attorney said that he viewed risk management more in terms of maintaining good medical records and following procedures that would improve the effectiveness of a malpractice defense. The neurosurgeon said that he interpreted risk management simply as providing the highest quality medical care, "treating patients and their families in much the same way physicians would wish themselves and their families to be treated." The administrator emphasized the importance of maintaining the necessary policies and procedures which would decrease potential malpractice situations and resultant claims.

The family physician simply noted that these disparate views demonstrated one of the inherent components of the problem of understanding risk management.

In many ways this points out the ongoing confusion with precisely how risk management is defined. Risk management, of course, has been used in many industries. Its primary purpose seems to be to try to determine the underlying causes of harm and then to develop systems that keep those situations from occurring. However, risk management in the health care setting has always been viewed a little bit differently. Risk management is not new to hospitals, many of whom have whole departments who deal with risk management and quality improvement. Their jobs are several fold. Risk managers will perhaps define their primary responsibility as reducing risks to patients, not necessarily to doctors. Of course, perhaps, they are both in essence the same goal. They are not so much in the business of preventing litigation as they are about preventing situations that can lead to litigation in the first place. They have sophisticated incident reporting systems that track situations in the hospital setting that can cause injuries or harm to patients. They use these data collection systems to offer continuous quality improvement. For example, they might attempt to determine why so many falls are occurring in the department of radiology or on a certain floor. Are medication errors occurring too often, and do systems have to be put in place in an attempt to reduce them? Are hospital infection rates climbing above national average or other benchmark indicators? This information, normally protected by various peer review statutes, helps hospitals reduce the incidents of injuries, which of course has the effect of decreasing liability exposure. A peer review statute is one which sets forth that certain discussions, meeting under very particular circumstances between physicians and quality assurance personnel are protected from discovery. In essence their information is kept confidential. The reasoning behind these statutes is that, if this information was not protected, then open and frank discussion about quality of care issues would not take place. Public policy supports such discussions taking place, since it furthers quality of care. However, the risk manager's job does not end there. They also get involved in safety issues, patient complaints, difficult ethical issues, some patient billing issues, some medical staff issues, and public relations issues, all of which can cause liability exposure to the institution if not dealt with appropriately.

Risk management in a general sense deals with continuously studying situations that can cause harm to patients, and concurrently attempting to reduce or manage those situations, thus reducing liability exposure. Of course risk managers have the responsibility of managing the defense of these claims when the litigation process begins, and making sure all the various insurance needs are being met. Although risk managers and risk management departments are commonplace in hospitals, they are not in physician practices. Small practices do not have the resources to contemplate such a task, but even large practices or multispecialty groups do not often assign someone the specific responsibility of risk management. In part this is because they do not have the resources that an institution such as a hospital or health system does. However, the new risks of managed care may change all that. There is a growing need for everyone to be incorporating risk management principles in their everyday practice. Practice management companies which work with physician groups have added risk management as a component of their services; however, with managed care competition pushing efficiency and careful use of resources, this often does not receive a significant allotment of time. Insurance companies, of course, are involved in risk management and encourage physicians to participate in such programs. However, as physicians get busier, attendance at these programs and review of materials provided by carriers does not take a high priority.

A new type of risk management is evolving. It continues to try to strike a balance of reducing liability exposure while at the same time increasing patient satisfaction. It must be done in such a fashion that recognizes that the resource of time is presently at a premium to physicians. It also has to recognize that it is not only the physician who needs information on improved risk management, but everyone on the health care team. The new type of risk management may, in the future, not only reduce the potential of a claim, but also help improve profitability.

WHY PEOPLE SUE

Overt Causes

There are both overt and covert reasons why patients sue physicians, other members of the health care team, and the institutions in which they work. In order to file a lawsuit, a plaintiff must ultimately register a complaint that describes in detail the alleged failures or negligences of the health care provider. This information of record can readily be obtained and forms the database for the overt reasons that people sue.

The Physician Insurers Association of America (PIAA) has been gathering information from more than 60 insurance companies for more than two decades. The PIAA instituted a Data Sharing System in 1985 which has been accumulating information on claims and suits. By 1997, there were data from more than 155,000 claims in the system. A review of this huge collection of data provides much insight into the medical reasons for malpractice lawsuits.[9]

Table 5–1 is an adaptation of a summary of cumulated claims data since 1985. These figures also include data from dentists, paraprofessionals, and residents. However, the PIAA has only recently begun collecting this information and, therefore, the numbers are quite small (total 662) and have no significant impact on the total picture. In this table, the term “no medical misadventure” is used to connote only those cases where there is an absence of any allegations of inappropriate medical conduct on the part of the insured. It is interesting to note that this category was the second highest of total claims, exceeded only by “improper performance,” but while a third of the latter claims were paid, the payout for “no medical misadventure” was less than 1%.

Another notable finding in this summary is in the category “failure to interact or communicate with patient,” which was the principal allegation in more than 3,000 cases, the 10th highest. The claims paid for this complaint were only 20%, perhaps reflecting the difficulty plaintiffs might have in proving the charge. In contrast, for the category “surgical foreign body left in patient after procedure,” the payout was almost 50%, and for “wrong patient or body part,” 65%. This could be assumed to be relatively easy for patients to prove. The “failure to inter-

Table 5–1 Medical Misadventures by Total Claims

Misadventure Description	*Total Claims*	*Total Paid Claims*
Improper performance	40,104	12,590
No medical misadventure	33,539	1,580
Errors in diagnosis	31,981	9,762
Failure to supervise or monitor case	9,511	3,255
Medication errors	5,847	2,014
Performed when not indicated or contraindicated	5,645	1,900
Not performed	4,576	1,791
Failure to recognize a complication of treatment	4,542	1,519
Delay in performance	4,122	1,525
Failure to instruct or communicate with patient	3,153	669
Failure/delay in referral or consultation	2,251	820
Surgical foreign body left in patient after proc	2,220	1,032
Improper supervision of residents/other staff	1,298	271
Failure/delay in admission to hospital	1,014	402
Wrong patient or body part	993	651
Patient positioning problem	933	251
Intubation problems	676	310
Failure to properly respond	547	165
Problems with patient monitoring in surgery	543	247
Tooth injury cases	494	311
Errors in agent use or selection	463	170
Not or improperly performing resuscitation	278	81
Problems with patient monitoring in recovery	194	75
Improper supervision of others	172	72
Surgical/Procedural clearance contraindicated	159	47
Lack or improper perform of preoperative eval	159	49
Problems with admin of blood or fluids	158	58
Failure to delay case when indicated	107	38
Report Totals	155,679	41,655

Source: Reprinted with permission from PIAA Data Sharing Project, 1, 5/1/97, Medical Misadventures by Total Claim, © Physician Insurers Association of America.

est or communicate with patients" category does not apparently include the cases that fall perhaps in other categories but to which poor communication skills probably contributed.

The PIAA Data Sharing System also provides information concerning claims for each specialty, and there are some noteworthy differences among the specialties. In primary care, general, or family practice and internal medicine, the major cause for claims—about one-third of the total—was "errors in diagnosis." In general or family practice this resulted in about a third of the claims paid, although in internal medicine, less than a third were paid. In both fields, the category "failure to instruct or communicate with patient" was 11th on the list, representing less than 4% of total claims.

In most of the non-surgical specialties, including emergency medicine and pediatrics, "errors in diagnosis" were most prominent. In the surgical specialties the category of "improper performance" most often had the greatest frequency of claims.

The total number of claims filed for the specialties most frequently cited, out of a total of approximately 155,000 are: 22,584 in obstetrics/gynecological surgery, 17,976 in internal medicine, 17,711 in general or family practice, 16,704 in general surgery, 15,928 in orthopedic surgery, 8,312 in radiology (non-surgical), and 6,014 in anesthesiology, altogether totaling 105,229.

This represents more than two-thirds of the total claims filed. These figures do not, of course, provide data on the rate of claims per physician per specialty, since the number of physicians practicing in each field has not been considered.

One of the major causes of malpractice suits is malpractice, i.e., some form of medical negligence. How well do the stated causes for claims match with the actual medical errors? What is the correlation between number of medical misadventures and claims filed? In other words, why after a possible malpractice event, is a claim sometimes filed while at other times it is not? These are important questions.

The Harvard Medical Practice Study

Hiatt, et al., in the August 7, 1989 issue of *The New England Journal of Medicine,* published a special report concerning medical care induced injuries and malpractice.[10] Although now somewhat dated, the information is still instructive. The researchers had been conducting a special investigation for the state of New York, under the title of The Harvard Medical Practice Study. They noted that the only substantial data on the extent of injuries to patients as a result of medical care, and the frequency that these were due to medical negligence, was provided by a 1974 study in California. There were no recent studies, on a large scale, to answer the questions being raised in connection with proposed tort reform.

The four components of the Harvard Medical Practice Study are:

- determination of the number of patient injuries sustained during hospitalization caused by medical interventions (or failure to perform indicated interventions) and the percent of these injuries, or "adverse events" due to the negligence of providers
- the cost of these injuries and the extent to which these costs are covered by the present tort and malpractice system
- determination of the proportion of these incidents, whether due to negligence or not, which lead to lawsuits
- measurement of the impact of the threat of litigation on the practice of medicine.

For this study, a random sample of medical records was chosen from 51 hospitals in the state of New York. A total of 30,195 records were examined, representing 1 in 85 acute care discharges in the state for that year. Injuries, or adverse events, were defined as those injuries that were unintended, caused at least in part by medical care, and resulted in a prolonged stay or some degree of disability after discharge. To determine possible negligence, each chart indicating an adverse event was reviewed by two specifically trained physician reviewers. They were instructed to consider the entire context of the event, consult additional specialists as needed, and write independent opinions. In order to determine the incidence in which adverse events led to malpractice suits, the investigators were given access to the insurance claims and litigation records in the state.

The results of the first phase of the study were reported in *The New England Journal of Medicine* in 1991.[11] The authors discovered that adverse events had occurred in 3.7% of the 30,000 plus hospitalizations, or in 1,133 cases. Of these, about one-fourth were judged to be due to medical negligence. While most of the resultant disabilities lasted less than six months, 2.6% caused total permanent disabilities, and 13.6% led to death.

When these figures were extrapolated to the total hospital discharges in the state of New York for one year, it was estimated that 2,550 patients would have suffered total permanent disability, and 13,451 would have died. Even more appalling is the estimate that 877 of these cases of total permanent disability and 6,895 of these deaths were due to medical negligence. It should be pointed out that the term medical negligence is ambiguous at best, and making this determination on the basis of a chart is somewhat arbitrary. Nevertheless, these findings are still startling.

An article in the *Public Citizen* extrapolated these findings even further, citing this same Harvard study. It concluded that this study means that 80,000 people die, and from 150,000 to 300,000 are injured each year in this country due to medical negligence in a hospital. This would make medical malpractice the third leading cause of death in the United States!

In their second report, in the same issue of The New England Journal of Medicine, the investigators described their findings in analyzing the 133 cases of disabling injuries caused by medical treatment.[12] They reviewed each adverse event to determine its relation to: type of error, possible negligence, and degree of disability. They found errors in management in more than half of the cases, nearly half of which were due to negligence.

In this study the most common cause of management error (35%) was in the performance of a procedure. The next most common (22%) was in failure to take preventive measures. Diagnostic errors accounted for 14%. The rate at which these errors were adjudged to be negligent, however, was remarkably different. Only 28% of performance errors were described as negligent, but 60% of preventive errors and 75% of diagnostic mistakes were considered to be due to medical negligence (see Table 5–2).

It is interesting, but not surprising, to note that these categories of most frequent errors due to negligence do correspond roughly with the data from PIAA on claims paid (see Table 5–1).

Part III of the Harvard Medical Practice Study matched hospital medical records with malpractice claims.[13] The authors found that there were 47 malpractice claims in the 30,000 plus patient records. The investigators also determined that in this set of records there had been 1,133 adverse events, of which 288 had

Table 5–2 Types of Errors Leading to Adverse Events, as Classified by the Reviewers in a Weighted Sample

		Errors Observed	
		In Entire Sample	*Ultimately Judged Negligent*
Type of Error	*No. of Reviews*	*percent*	
Performance	537	35.2	28.2
Prevention	232	21.9	59.6
Diagnosis	168	13.8	74.7
Drug treatment	87	8.9	52.8
System and other	32	2.4	66.0
Unclassified	220	17.9	43.4
All	1276	100.0	47.3

Source: Reprinted with permission from B. Leape, et al., The Nature of Adverse Events in Hospitalized Patients—Results of the Harvard Medical Practice, Study II, *The New England Journal of Medicine*, Vol. 324, pp. 377–383, Copyright 1991 Massachusetts Medical Society. All rights reserved.

been judged due to negligence. Only eight of those had been among the 47 claims filed; the other 39 had filed claims for reasons other than medical negligence. When medical negligence had caused injury to a patient, there was less than a 2% statistical possibility that it would result in a lawsuit.

Some general conclusions from the three reports on this massive study are apparent:

- the number of patient injuries and deaths in this country attributable to medical management is enormous
- the frequency of medical negligence as a cause of these errors is significant
- the likelihood of a lawsuit resulting from a particular act of medical negligence is, however, quite small, less than 2%.

The question raised at the beginning of this chapter was, "Why do people sue?" An equally enlightening question is, "Why don't more people sue?" Medical errors, with bad results, have been shown to be a huge problem. Does this represent a great untapped resource for plaintiffs' attorneys?

The authors of the Harvard Study speculate on possible reasons why some people who have been subjected to medical negligence choose not to sue:

- patients may feel that they have received adequate insurance benefit
- they may not want to break a close patient-physician relationship
- they, or their attorneys, may not consider the effort worth the cost
- they may "find attorneys repugnant"
- they may not recognize that their care was negligent.

In the quest for prevention of malpractice suits, each of these reasons needs to be considered. It would appear that the second and fifth reasons, especially in combination, are the best explanations for why patients do not sue. The patient-physician relationship is the factor that a physician can best control. Further, it is this close patient-physician relationship that is most in jeopardy in a managed care environment.

Another consideration is the changes in the health care environment which patients are now experiencing. There have been significant differences since this study was initiated a decade ago. If we assume that malpractice occurred with a greater frequency than we were aware of in the last decade, and that it was during a period of time when managed care market penetration was slight, physicians had the luxury of spending more time with patients, and did not need to be concerned about additional diagnostic tests and referrals or strict utilization controls, what will happen to the liability claims rate now? The overall environment in which physicians are practicing presently is not as favorable as it was in the 1980s.

As a recent American Hospital Association (AHA) supported study shows, nearly a fourth of patients surveyed felt as if they were not obtaining the amount of information they needed to make decisions about treatment.[14] Other surveys show that the population is generally becoming distrustful. As will be seen later in this chapter, this is a major reason for malpractice claims. The combination of changes in attitudes with the potential for increased incidences of maloccurrences could become explosive. In the future we must not only endeavor to reduce maloccurrences, but we must also address the other, more prevalent, reasons why people initiate a claim.

The result of the Harvard Study was reported in 1991, but the disturbing climate does not appear to have improved. The February 1997 issue of *The Lancet* described a more recent study.[15] The investigators followed 1,047 patients who were in an intensive care unit or a surgical care unit in a large American hospital. They found that 17.7% of patients had "serious adverse events," ranging from physical disability to death. By far the most frequent cause of these events was poor performance or poor judgment.

Covert Causes

The overt causes of malpractice suits are the medical negligence allegations stated in the plaintiffs' complaints. There is a glut of them and, unfortunately, many of them are valid. The valid complaints, however, do not match the real medical negligence experience. There are far more errors than there are suits, and the suits most often are not based on the demonstrated medical negligences. An exploration of the covert causes of malpractice lawsuits will shed much light on the real reasons that patients decide to sue.

One way to find out why people sued is to ask them why they made that decision. Several investigators have done that. In addition, we have had the combined experience of interacting with malpractice litigants on thousands of occasions. Almost always a breakdown in communication is lurking in the decision-making process of patients who have initiated a lawsuit. When a maloccurrence happens, the patient or the patient's family needs information more than ever. Their attitudes, and even their entire psyches, change when something unexpectedly goes wrong. Communication at that point is crucial and a lack of information, especially during a crisis, is a frequently cited instigating factor. Research by others has confirmed this observation.

In England, medical negligence litigation has been increasing steadily in the past few years. In 1994 a study was published in *The Lancet* based on information obtained from 227 people who were currently in the process of suing physicians for medical malpractice.[16] A group of 466 people were identified and invited, by mail, to participate. Almost half agreed to do so and completed the questionnaire.

Most of the 227 participants were patients, although 72 were relatives suing on behalf of a child, and 22 were relatives suing because of a deceased patient.

The questionnaire asked people to rate their level of agreement or disagreement with a series of statements. They were also asked to state, in their own words, their reasons for bringing suit. The responses followed four major themes:

- concerns for the standards of care—they did not want the same thing to happen to someone else in the future
- people wanted an explanation of what had happened and felt that their questions had been ignored
- they wanted monetary compensation for their own pain and suffering, or for future care
- they wanted someone to be held accountable for what had happened.

The questionnaire also revealed the intense emotional responses that were generated by the adverse incident: 90% expressed anger; 80%, bitterness; 55% felt betrayed; and 40% felt humiliated. The respondents wanted better, and more timely, explanations of what happened. Only 15% felt they received a satisfactory explanation. About 20% did not receive an explanation for at least a year, and more than a third never received an explanation. When explanations were given, they were often unclear, inaccurate, or not given by a senior physician. Often the patient or relative was not given an opportunity to ask questions.

A final question on the survey form asked, "Once the original incident occurred could anything have been done which would have meant you did not feel the need to take legal action." Nearly half responded and their answers are shown in Table 5–3. These responses reflect the major themes discovered in the

Table 5–3 Actions After the Incident That Might Have Prevented Litigation

Explanation and apology	37
Correction of mistake	25
Pay compensation	17
Correct treatment at the time	15
Admission of negligence	14
Investigation by drug company/hospital	3
Disciplinary action	4
If listened to and not treated as neurotic	5
Honesty	4

Source: Reprinted with permission from C. Vincent, et al., Why do People Sue Doctors? A Study of Patients and Relatives Taking Legal Action, Vol. 343, p. 1612, © by *The Lancet,* 1994.

study and the emotions evoked. By far the most frequent complaint was a lack of explanation or an apology.

This study demonstrates the importance of the covert causes for suing. Almost half of the litigants who were invited to participate made the effort to complete the questionnaire sent them. That fact in itself is an indication that many people had strong feelings about the process. While concerns for the standards of care were expressed by the greatest number, failure of communication was a close second. The emotional responses were intense; anger, bitterness, betrayal, and humiliation were expressed by the majority of the participants. When asked to write accounts of their experiences, most related these strong emotional reactions to a failure of the doctor to communicate with them on a personal basis.

When asked what could have prevented litigation, in addition to the answer of an explanation or an apology, a significant number of people cited that an admission of negligence, not having been treated as though neurotic, or plain honesty would have made a difference. We are certainly not recommending that physicians who have a less than desirable result immediately admit liability or negligence. Too often physicians may jump to the conclusion that negligence has occurred and are too harsh on themselves. The conclusion that one has committed malpractice, except in unusual circumstances, should not be reached without an expert reviewing the circumstances and expressing that opinion. The question of causation needs to be addressed as well. An apology may be indicated but has to be done carefully so as not to be misunderstood by patients. Perhaps apologizing that a complication has occurred or sympathizing with the patient may be appropriate but not in the context that an error has been committed. There is a real difference in feeling sympathy that something has occurred (feeling sorry) and apologizing for a result.

It is evident, at least in this study, that failed communication, a covert reason to sue, was more problematic than the overt causes, the alleged malpractice. The powerful emotional responses appeared to be the major instigating cause for suit.

A similar study was conducted in this country with some overlapping results.[17] Mothers of infants who had suffered permanent injury or death between 1986 and 1989, and had closed malpractice claims, were invited to participate: 127, or 35% of those asked, agreed to do so. They were each interviewed by telephone, using a structured questionnaire, but with open-ended questions. When they were asked what was wrong with the care their child received, the 127 mothers offered more than 300 complaints. The complaints fell into three general categories: physician performance errors, physician unavailability, and failure to consult.

When asked exactly what had prompted them to sue, they offered 179 reasons. Each of these was recorded and then analyzed by the research team, who found that they could be grouped into six categories. The most frequently reported reason (one-third) was that they had been advised by someone else to sue. Most frequently the advice had come from someone in the medical profession. Contrary to popular notion, in only eight instances did the advice come from someone in the legal profession, and in only one of these was the family approached directly by a lawyer. (This should not be surprising since the code of ethics prohibits attorneys from directly seeking out or soliciting lawsuits.) Twenty-four percent said that they needed the money for long-term care of the injured child; 20% said they sued when they realized their child would have no future; and 24% said that they sued because they became aware that the doctor had not been honest with them or deliberately misled them. Twenty percent said they thought the court was the only place they would learn the truth about what happened. Almost the same number said they wanted to punish the doctor and prevent this negligence from happening again. This comment has to be considered in part due to the same communication problems cited above.

The issue of communication was investigated with further questions. Almost half of the families thought that their physician had misled them; a third said their physician would not talk or answer questions; 13% said their doctor would not listen, and 70% said that no one warned them of the possible bad outcomes.

A different approach to the same question was reported by Beckman, et al., in a 1994 issue of the *Archives of Internal Medicine.*[18] They chose at random 45 plaintiffs' depositions from malpractice suits that had already been settled. All of the suits concerned one large metropolitan health center.

Plaintiffs' depositions, typically, are interviews by defense attorneys, conducted in the presence of representatives from both sides, and recorded verbatim by a court stenographer. Statements that a person makes in a deposition cannot be contradicted in court without an acceptable explanation or at the risk of having one's credibility greatly diminished. The total of the 45 depositions reviewed amounted to 3,878 pages. A majority of the plaintiffs were the involved patients themselves, although 20% were spouses. In general, the group was young and well-educated, and all but two were employed.

The nature of the adverse outcomes, as alleged in the depositions, were anatomic deformity (16), death (12), emotional impairment (9), and functional deformity (6). In two there were no adverse outcomes discussed in the deposition.

When the question was asked, "Why are you suing?," 71% identified problematic relationship issues. It was thought that the actual number could be even higher, since the interrogation process in a deposition is dependent on closed-ended questions and plaintiffs were not invited to express themselves freely. These relationship issues fell into four general categories:

- The doctor was not available, or considered himself/herself too important and sent a surrogate (see Table 5–4);

Table 5–4 Categories and Frequency of Relationship Issues Identified in 45 Depositions

Issue	*No. (%)*
Desertion	
Perceived as unavailable	2 (5.3)
Abandoned	7 (18.4)
Physician too important	2 (5.3)
Sending a surrogate	1 (2.6)
Total	12 (31.6)
Dysfunctional delivery of information	
Failure to provide an explanation	4 (10.5)
Failure to keep a patient and/or family up-to-date	2 (5.3)
Blaming a patient and/or family for bad outcome	2 (5.3)
Insensitively informing a patient and/or family	2 (5.3)
Total	10 (26.4)
Devaluing patient and/or family views	
Discounting a patient and/or family opinion	2 (5.3)
Discounting a patient's illness and/or suffering	4 (10.5)
Not listening	3 (7.9)
Discounting a family's attempt to advocate	2 (5.3)
Total	11 (28.9)
Not understanding the patient and/or family perspective	
Failure to solicit patient and/or family opinion	1 (2.6)
Inattention to patient's discomfort	3 (7.9)
Failure to recognize the psychosocial impact	1 (2.6)
Total	5 (13.1)

Source: Reprinted with permission from H. B. Beckman, et al., The Doctor-Patient Relationship and Malpractice, *Archives of Internal Medicine,* Vol. 154, p. 1368, Copyright 1994, American Medical Association.

- Information was delivered in a dysfunctional manner. This involved failing to keep a family current on what was happening. The patient or family felt they had been abandoned. The most frequent complaint was not getting enough information or even providing no explanation at all. Some physicians were perceived to be insensitive, or blamed the family for a bad outcome;
- The patient or the family felt that their own values were debunked. Physicians were described as disregarding or disparaging the patient's, or family's opinions, and minimizing the patient's illness and suffering;
- Doctors did not understand the patient's, or family's perspective. Physicians were perceived as not recognizing the social impact of the illness, or not appreciating the degree of the patient's discomfort.

These assertions may or may not have been factual, but they were the patient's or family's perceptions.

In about two-thirds of the depositions there was an exploration of the question, "Was a maloccurrence suggested by a health professional?" More than half answered affirmatively, most often citing a consultant as being critical of the defendant referring physician. Although not specifically stated, this often occurs when a consultant or subsequent treating physician simply responds to questions by the patient with surprise or body language. Time and time again in depositions a patient will say something like, "Oh, Dr. X never directly told me Dr. Y had done something wrong, but you could tell the way he was asking questions and the look he gave me when I told him what Dr. Y had told me. Then he concluded our conversation by saying… 'well, the most important thing is that we get you better.' Isn't that practically an admission?" This is an area where there has to be greater sensitivity by subsequent treating physicians or consultants. Not a conspiracy of silence but compassion and common sense. The demeanor and body language as well as the statements of the subsequent physicians will be remembered forever. If there is a question of malpractice involved, relating to the quality of care that was given, and you have enough information to be certain, then this should come to light. If asked, physicians should be forthright. Peer review committees, perhaps, should be contacted. However, if you do not have all the information, no criticism should be offered. In this instance there was no mention of an attorney suggesting that medical negligence had taken place.

The authors of this report conclude with:

> "This study suggests some important hypotheses about the effect of the process of care on a patient or family's decision to litigate in the face of an adverse outcome. There appear to be a series of predictable, high-risk behaviors that may be prevented by educational interventions. While these findings should be validated in other settings, our study suggests that professionals should be attentive to their communication style with patients and families as one means to decrease the likelihood of being involved in malpractice suits."[19]

Another approach was employed by Shapiro, et al.[20] They surveyed a group of 642 suing patients, sued physicians, and non-sued physicians, using parallel forms of the same survey instrument. Questionnaires were completed in full by 40 patients, 67 sued physicians, and 93 non-sued physicians. An analysis of the demographics of the patient group indicated that they represented the general adult population.

All three groups were asked about reasons for filing malpractice claims by responding to a series of statements of possible causes of malpractice actions.

Patients and sued physicians' responses were based on their own experience, and those of the non-sued physicians on a theoretical basis. Table 5–5 tabulates these responses. Each respondent was asked to respond on a scale of 1 (not a factor) to 4 (a major factor).

The non-sued physicians identified many factors that they thought would be a major influence, but those involved in suits did not. The most pronounced of these differences were unavoidable consequence of medical treatment, physicians' directions were not followed, physician-patient personal conflicts, and unreasonable patient expectations.

Table 5–5 Perceived Reasons for Malpractice Action*

Cause	*Suing Patients, %*	*Sued Physicians, %*	*Nonsued Physicians, %*
Physician error	96	20	66
Physician negligence	97	10	51
Unanticipated complications	64	52	86
Unavoidable consequence of medical treatment	34	39	66
Physician's directions were not followed	0	23	44
Patient's desire for financial compensation	22	83	85
Patient withholding pertinent health information	3	16	20
Physician's failure to pursue pertinent health history	22	8	29
Physician/patient personal conflicts	11	11	75
People expect too much from medical technology and/or the physician	3	44	95
Need to place responsibility for injury	41	66	85

*Combines responses choosing 3 or 4 on a scale: $P<.001$. Respondents were asked to rate the above as a cause in their malpractice action (suing patients and sued physicians) or theoretically (nonsued) physicians) on a scale ranging from 1 (not a factor) to 4 (a major factor). *Source:* Reprinted with permission from R.S. Shapiro, et al., A Survey of Sued and Nonsued Physicians and Suing Patients, *Archives of Internal Medicine,* Vol. 149, p. 2192, Copyright 1989, American Medical Association.

Fewer than half of the suing patients and sued physicians agreed with these opinions. Only 11% of the members of these two groups identified personal conflicts as a factor, whereas 75% of the non-sued physicians thought that it would be. Both physician groups thought financial compensation was a major reason (83 and 85%) but only 22% of suing patients concurred.

Another set of questions explored their perceptions of physician-patient relationships prior to the malpractice action. The non-sued physicians responded on the basis of their own physician-patient relationships in general. Table 5–6 tabulates these responses and reveals some striking differences in perceptions. Sixty-two percent of the sued physicians thought their pre-claim relationships were

Table 5–6 Perceptions of the Doctor-Patient Relationship*

Respondent Classification		*Continuum* 1	2	3	4
		Closed to Open†			
Suing patient	No. (%)	7 (21)	2 (6)	12 (35)	13 (38)
Sued physician	No. (%)	9 (7)	14 (11)	24 (19)	77 (62)
Nonsued physician	No. (%)	2 (5)	0	5 (13)	33 (83)
		Dishonest to Honest‡			
Suing patient	No. (%)	7 (21)	3 (9)	9 (27)	15 (44)
Sued physician	No. (%)	7 (6)	4 (3)	16 (13)	96 (78)
Nonsued physician	No. (%)	0	0	2 (5)	39 (95)
		Perfunctory to Personal‡			
Suing patient	No. (%)	8 (28)	13 (45)	5 (17)	3 (10)
Sued physician	No. (%)	18 (15)	32 (26)	35 (29)	37 (30)
Nonsued physician	No. (%)	0	3 (8)	23 (58)	14 (35)

*Respondents were asked to indicate where on the above continuums they would place the doctor-patient relationship involved in the malpractice claim (suing patients and sued physicians) or their doctor-patient relationships in general (nonsued physicians).

†$P<.01$.

‡$P<.001$.

Source: Reprinted with permission from R.S. Shapiro, et al., A Survey of Sued and Nonsued Physicians and Suing Patients, *Archives of Internal Medicine,* Vol. 149, p. 2193, Copyright 1989, American Medical Association.

quite open, but only 38% of the suing patients agreed; 78% of the sued physicians thought the relationship was honest, but only 44% of patients believed that it was, and 21% thought that it was actually dishonest!

Only 10% of patients found their physician-patient relationships to be personal, and 28% thought they were just perfunctory. In contrast, 30% of the sued physicians thought they had personal relationships, and only 15% characterized them as perfunctory. Not surprisingly, the non-sued physicians thought their relationships were open (83%) and 95% were sure they were honest. Ninety-three percent rated their relationships on the upper side of the perfunctory to personal scale (see Table 5–6).

A final set of questions asked all groups for suggestions to reduce malpractice litigation. The only idea which all three groups agreed on (nearly two-thirds of each group) was the need for improved doctor-patient communication (see Table 5–7).

The authors of the study concluded:

Table 5–7 Suggestions to Reduce Malpractice Litigation

	Very Effective[*]		
Suggestion	*Suing Patient, %*	*Sued Physician, %*	*Nonsued Physician, %*
Better doctor/patient	65	63	62
communication	28	2	3†
Increased government involvement	61	15	10†
Enhanced peer review			
More disciplinary power to state	79	19	38†
medical examining board	15	58	76†
Limiting noneconomic damages			
Encouraging alternative dispute resolution mechanisms	35	35	30‡
Eliminating the contingency fee arrangement	32	79	70

*Percentage choosing No. 4 on a scale ranging from 1 (minimal effectiveness) to 4 (very effective).

†*P*<.001.

‡When respondents choosing Nos. 3 or 4 are combined, percentages are the following: sued physicians, 74%; suing patients, 74%; and nonsued physicians, 87%.

Source: Reprinted with permission from R.S. Shapiro, et al., A Survey of Sued and Nonsued Physicians and Suing Patients, *Archives of Internal Medicine,* Vol. 149, p. 2194, Copyright 1989, American Medical Association.

> "Effective medical care depends on a trusting, mutually trustworthy fiduciary relationship between physicians and patient. Our survey demonstrates that our current malpractice litigation system creates distrust in, and places stress on, that relationship. This damaged relationship prevents the physician from doing his or her best for patients, and it interferes with the patient's choices in taking necessary steps in the disease prevention or healing process. The litigation experience and the perceived threat of litigation encourage patients and physicians to view one another not as partners in a health care program, but as potential adversaries in multi-million dollar lawsuits. To begin a therapeutic relationship on the basis of suspicion makes conflict—legal or otherwise—virtually inevitable."[21]

These investigations, using a variety of research models, all demonstrate that many, if not most, people who sue physicians for medical negligence do so for personal reasons. The most prominent feelings that prompt such actions are anger, bitterness, humiliation, abandonment, and being ignored or misunderstood. This information is of critical importance and has been underestimated for years. It means that changes in behavior and the development of communication skills can go a long way toward reducing one's liability exposure. There is not a great deal of cost, from an economic standpoint, in doing so. Often physicians believed that risk management meant spending dollars. It meant additional staff, a different type of physical plant, extensive documentation and more time, all of which they did not have, especially in a managed care setting. These things, to a certain extent, are important and will be discussed later.

There is the potential for a significant reduction in claims exposure through a basic low-cost effort. Building communication systems, improving skills, and forming new habits does take hard work and there are some costs associated with the educational endeavor, but they are minuscule in comparison to the expense of having a malpractice claim. Equally important, the same behavioral and communication systems are a must in the new health care environment. Physicians, to be competitive in the future, will need to have these skills. These principles, which go to the heart of malpractice exposure, need to be learned by the entire health care team and incorporated into the practice. Too often, in the past, the training was nothing more than a lecture or a reminder and acknowledgment that "communication skills are important." That is not enough and is obviously not working, since malpractice lawsuits are proliferating and contemporary studies show that patients feel uninvolved and uninformed.[22]

Understanding both the overt and covert reasons for malpractice litigation is a basic first step in the development of an effective prevention strategy. The answers to two additional questions may also help: "Are there physicians who are most likely to become targets?" and "Are there people who are most likely to sue?"

PHYSICIANS AT INCREASED RISK

Some useful information on this issue was revealed by a retrospective analysis of all closed malpractice claims against physicians in the state of Florida between 1975 and 1988.[23] The findings reaffirmed the relative risks of different specialties. Claims against physicians in the medical specialties were quite low. Eighty-five percent had no claims experience during that time and for the claims made, the payments were relatively low. Claims against surgical specialists were much more frequent and the payments higher. The obstetrician/anesthesiologist group had both the most frequent claims and by far the highest payment rate. Almost half of the physicians in this group had claims against them. Surprisingly, in all three groups, 85% of all the claims made were against fewer than 10% of the physicians in that group.

Another analysis of the risk factors showed that, in general:

- older physicians were less likely to have claims against them;
- those who engaged in teaching or research had the same risk as those who did not;
- physicians in the surgical and the obstetrician/anesthesiologist group who worked in direct patient care more than 60 hours per week were more likely to have claims, and more costly claims, than those who worked less than 60 hours—this was not true in the medical group;
- physicians with degrees from less developed countries had the same risk as their counterparts;
- physicians with prestigious credentials had no better claims rates than others.

The authors note that their study did "not demonstrate that claims experience is a valid indication of physician quality, although it does correlate with future claims experience."

A follow-up study was published in 1994.[24] The object of this investigation was to assess the quality of care of obstetricians who had malpractice claims against them.

Four groups of physicians were identified as those with no claims experience, and those with claims experience, graded further by frequency and level of payment. The medical records of 446 deliveries by these obstetricians were analyzed both objectively and subjectively. The investigators were not able to find any correlation between previous claims experience and technical quality of care.

Another effort to identify those physicians at high or low risk was published by Charles, et al., in 1991.[25] They conducted a survey of 248 physicians, about half of whom were thought to be at low risk for malpractice litigation, and half who had demonstrated high risk histories.

They also found high risk associated with the surgical specialties, but unlike the Florida study, they found that increasing age correlated with increasing risk. They also found that increased risk was associated with greater time away from practice, and with an attitude that the litigation climate was "unfair." Practice styles that increased patient comfort and promoted better patient-physician communication were associated with lower risk. This included scheduling more time to talk with patients and answering telephone calls directly. Curiously, the low risk group also acknowledged more personal emotional symptoms.

The only clear conclusion to be drawn from these studies in order to lower one's own malpractice risk, other than changing specialties, is better communication with patients. This requires both time and skill. Of course, increasing time with patients in a managed care environment is often impossible, but adding different types of communication is not. Methods to increase the ability to communicate more effectively can be learned, as will be demonstrated in the following chapter.

KNOWING WHEN YOU ARE AT RISK

The literature has demonstrated to us over and over that a minority of malpractice claims are in response to actual malpractice. Malpractice occurs many times without resulting in a claim. Nevertheless, physicians continue to try to eliminate their errors. Physicians know, both from training and experience, that they, like the rest of the population, are more likely to make mistakes when they are rushed, stressed, or have insufficient help. These are all common problems in practice, especially on certain days, or even at certain times of the year.

Because this is such a common phenomenon, most physicians have learned to proceed more deliberately, more cautiously, when in a tense situation, both as a means to provide better health care, and to reduce liability risks. However, malpractice is not the principal cause of medical negligence claims, miscommunication is. While many physicians may pay meticulous attention to the clinical details of the work they are doing during a rushed or stressful situation, they may pay much less attention, or even ignore, the need for close communication with the patient or family.

From reviewing many physician and plaintiff depositions, the authors have observed that the "trigger event," the moment that seems to ignite a patient's decision to sue, most often occurs during a period of stress. These times have some degree of predictability—at the last appointment on a busy day, or on a Friday afternoon, or on the eve of a holiday. These are often times of intensity, not only for the physician, but for every member of the staff. For conscientious and caring people, working intimately with patients who are hurting, troubled, sometimes irritable, anxious or depressed, can be exhausting. Adding one more patient, or one more hour, unexpectedly, is another stress for most people. And the extra patient must have special needs, or have convinced someone of the importance of immediate attention. Either situation can add to the tension.

Even the time of the year can make a difference. Many people find it hard to concentrate during a frantic holiday season. Everyone who has ever worked in a teaching hospital knows that the absolute worst time to be admitted is on July 1. Nearly all of the house staff are changing rotations, and medical students are making the mighty overnight leap to becoming doctors.

Recognizing when your own practice is at greatest risk can be very helpful. Perhaps scheduling changes can be made, a few appointment slots left open, hours shortened, and more help made available. Above all, it is important that everyone on the health care team be aware of these periods of heightened vulnerability.

It is easy for a disgruntled patient to file a lawsuit. It is probably not only the fact that there are so many lawyers available, advertising their services, that instigate these claims, but the ease with which one can proceed with the process once an initial consultation with a lawyer is made. Plaintiffs' cases are normally handled on a contingent fee basis. Costs are often held until litigation has been concluded and then taken out of the proceeds. Therefore, individuals have no financial risk at the outset. If this was not the case many patients with legitimate claims could not get their day in court. However, it has led to many actions without merit proceeding through the process and ultimately ending in verdicts for physicians; but only after a great deal of cost and anguish.

PATIENTS MORE LIKELY TO SUE

There has been a long standing belief that poor people, or people on Medicaid, are more likely to sue their physicians. This myth has sometimes been used by physicians as a reason to avoid providing care for the indigent. The question was addressed by Molly McNulty, JD, in a letter in answer to an inquiry about this issue, and published in *JAMA*.[26] She identified several reasons why this belief was illogical:

- Plaintiff awards are usually based on anticipated income, so any award to a low income person is likely to be quite small and, therefore, a disincentive to plaintiffs' attorneys, who usually work on a contingency fee basis;
- Many Legal Service lawyers are barred from pursuing malpractice suits unless the plaintiff has previously been refused by two private attorneys;
- In many states Medicaid recipients would not be permitted, by Medicaid rules, to keep a monetary award. They might also lose their Medicaid status.

Not the Poor or the Elderly

McNulty cited unpublished work in progress in Maryland, which demonstrated no increased litigation by Medicaid patients. This research was published by Mussman, et al., two years later.[27] They had examined all malpractice claims filed in Maryland for two years, a total of 1,037 cases, and counted the number of those who were Medicaid recipients. This proportion was compared with the proportion of Medicaid recipients in the state of Maryland. They found that the number of malpractice claims by Medicaid recipients was actually less than that of the general population.

Burstin, et al., as part of the Harvard Medical Practice Study cited earlier, reviewed 31,000 hospital records from the state of New York for the year 1984.[28] They also found that poor people, and the uninsured, were significantly less likely to file malpractice claims. They found that the elderly, those aged 65 and over, were also less likely to sue. Further, they found that the poor who were not injured were also less likely to file inappropriate malpractice claims.

The finding that the elderly were less likely to sue was reported also by Sager, et al., in 1990.[29] They analyzed 431 claims and found that the elderly had filed only 10% of the claims. The elderly population of the state was 12%, but their usage of the health care system was far greater than that of younger people. The authors theorized that the reasons for the low proportion of suits by the elderly might be because of stronger patient-physician relationships, lower expectations of the health care system, and the smaller malpractice awards they could anticipate.

These studies effectively refute the myth that care for the poor, the indigent, the uninsured, or the elderly cause an increased malpractice risk. Indeed, the risks are demonstrably less.

There are two groups of people who are more likely to sue than others. This is an important consideration, not so that these people can be shunned, but so that they can be given the extra attention that they need. It has been traditional to assume that any patient who has a lawyer in the family poses a litigation threat, but this has proven not to be the case. There are no more suits from lawyer families than from others. The two groups more likely to sue are the unhappy and those who do not understand.

The Perpetually Unhappy Patient

The unhappy are usually easy to identify. They often complain about their care, express their anger, and overreact to minor inconveniences. They may also be understandably angered by something the physician, or the staff, has done, or failed to do. They may be unhappy because of circumstances in their lives unrelated to their health care. Their discontent may be shown in more subtle, passive aggressive behavior, by being late, missing appointments, or failing to follow advice. They may have a history of past or current litigation.

Regardless of the cause of the unhappiness, these people need more caring, careful attention from the whole health care team. This may be difficult, as the natural instinct is to get them on their way as expeditiously as possible. It is also difficult for the staff to understand, for the same reasons, especially if the patient becomes reluctant, resistant, or even rude. While it may not be possible to assuage their anger, above all they need to be listened to, and they need to know that they have been heard. When a problem occurs, these patients may for psychological, or perhaps for pure litigation purposes, blame the doctor for all of their problems. For example, there was a case which dealt with a simple tooth extraction that did not go as smoothly as anticipated. It took longer and admittedly caused a great deal of discomfort. Imagine the dentist's surprise when the patient complained, during the course of litigation, of hand pain, neck pain, pain in the arms and legs, vaginal pain, work loss, and disruption of her relationship with her husband (even though they were divorced)! Every problem she ever had became the fault of the dentist.

Patients Who Do Not Understand

The group of people most likely to sue that is clearly the largest, is those who do not understand. There can be many reasons for this, and they are not all the physician's fault (although the physician may be held accountable). These include patients who may not be able to understand because of intelligence, perceptual impairment, language, or culture. Further, perhaps the most dangerous group, those whose lack of understanding is easiest to overlook, are the "too busy." These are often colleagues, acquaintances, friends or family, who just say, "Do what you have to do, Doc," or "I trust you or I wouldn't be here." If something unexpected were to happen, though, the entire relationship may change.

The whole informed consent process is designed to prevent misunderstanding and, if properly conducted, can be most effective. Care must be taken at all times to use language that patients do understand. It is important to be aware that patients sometimes feel ashamed to reveal their lack of understanding, a particular hazard with colleagues. It is also important to remember that people who are anxious, as many people are in a doctor's office or a hospital, have trouble hearing and remembering. Patients with anxiety disorders of any kind are often the ones who call an hour after their appointment to ask what the doctor said.[30] Physicians are expected to recognize anxiety in their patients and take potential forgetfulness into account when they explain something. Written information and documentation are absolutely essential for these patients.

For people with perceptual difficulties, it is necessary that a treating physician find the best available means of communicating, so the patient can make a truly informed consent. The Americans With Disabilities Act is intended to assist people with various disabilities, such as deafness. If the patient is deaf, the physician may not only want to find interpretive help, but may actually be required to do so by law under certain circumstances. The same principles may apply when there is a language barrier.

The art of medicine is an interactive process. Without clear communication, there can be no interactive process and there will be no possibility of optimum health care.

CONCLUSION

Actual medical malpractice could be described as almost rampant. So are medical malpractice claims, but the two are not even closely related. Miscommunication, however, is rampant and is directly and causally related to malpractice claims. All physicians can think back to an error for which they might have been sued, perhaps even appropriately. Oftentimes the patient did not sue because of adequate, supportive communication and a good patient-doctor relationship. The health care provider's actions, attitudes, and behavior have more to do with what causes lawsuits than medical errors. In a managed care environment it becomes even more important, and in some ways harder, to put the systems in place to prevent these claims. However, it is not optional; these risk management skills and systems will become a necessary component of practices in the near future. In some ways there is a great opportunity because any changes that can be made now to reduce liability exposure can prepare you for the competitive environment of the future at the same time.

REFERENCES

1. W. Meadow, A. Bell, and J. Lantos, "Physicians' Experience with Allegations of Medicare Malpractice in the Neonatal Intensive Care Unit," *Pediatrics* (May 1997): 10.
2. *Professional Liability in the '80s, Report I of the American Medical Association Special Task Force on Professional Liability and Insurance* (Chicago: AMA, 1984).
3. D. Klingman et al., "Measuring Defensive Medicine Using Clinical Scenario Surveys" *Journal of Health Politics, Policy and Law* 21(1996): 94–205.
4. Klingman et al., *Journal of Health Politics,* 198.
5. Klingman et al., *Journal of Health Politics,* 198–199.
6. M. Veldhuis "Defensive Behavior of Dutch Family Physicians. Widening the Concept," *Family Medicine* 26 (1994): 27–29.
7. *Risk Management in Practice* (Washington: American Society of Internal Medicine, 1982).
8. P.S. Sanders, "Confronting Professional Liability: A Roundtable Discussion of Medical Risk Management," *Minnesota Medicine* 70 (1987): 142–148.

9. Data Sharing System of the Physician Insurers Association of America, (Rockville: 1997).
10. H.H. Hiatt, et al., "Special Report: A Study of Medical Injury and Medical Malpractice," *The New England Journal of Medicine* 321, no. 7 (1989): 480–485.
11. T.A. Brennan, et al., "Incidence of Adverse Events and Negligence in Hospitalized Patients," *The New England Journal of Medicine* 324, no. 6 (1991): 377–384.
12. L.L. Leape, et al., "The Nature of Adverse Events in Hospitalized Patients," *The New England Journal of Medicine* 324, no. 6 (1991): 377–384.
13. T.R. Localio, et al., "Relation Between Malpractice Claims and Adverse Events Due to Negligence," *The New England Journal of Medicine* 325, no. 4 (1991): 245–251.
14. The Picker Institute, *Eye on Patients*, (American Hospital Association: 1997).
15. L.B. Andrews et al., *Lancet* 349 (1997): 309–313.
16. C. Vincent, et al., "Why Do People Sue Doctors? A Study of Patients and Relatives Taking Legal Action," *Lancet* 343 (1994): 1609–1613.
17. G.B. Hickson, et al., "Factors that Prompted Families to File Medical Malpractice Claims Following Perinatal Injuries," *Journal of the American Medical Association* 267, no. 10 (1992): 1359–1363.
18. H.B. Beckman, et al., "The Doctor-Patient Relationship and Malpractice," *Archives of Internal Medicine* 154 (1994): 1365–1370.
19. Beckman, et al., *Internal Medicine*, 1365–1370.
20. R.S. Shapiro, et al., "A Survey of Sued and Nonsued Physicians and Suing Patients," *Archives of Internal Medicine* 149 (1989): 2190–2196.
21. Shapiro, et al., *Internal Medicine,* 2196.
22. Picker Institute, *Eye on Patients.*
23. F.A. Sloan, et al., "Medical Malpractice Experience of Physicians," *Journal of the American Medical Association* 262, no. 23 (1989): 3291–3297.
24. G.B. Hickson, et al., "Obstetricians' Prior Malpractice Experience and Patients' Satisfaction with Care," *Journal of the American Medical Association* 272, no. 20 (1994): 1583–1587.
25. S.C. Charles, et al., "Predicting Risk for Medical Malpractice Claims Using Quality-of-Care Characteristics," *Western Journal of Medicine* 157 (1992): 433–439.
26. M. McNulty, "Letter," *Journal of the American Medical Association* 262, no. 10 (1989): 1391–1392.
27. M.G. Mussman, et al., "Medical Malpractice Claims Filed by Medicaid and Non-Medicaid Recipients in Maryland," *Journal of the American Medical Association* 265, no. 22 (1991): 2992–2994.
28. H.R. Burstin, et al., "Do the Poor Sue More? A Case-Control Study of Malpractice Claims and Socioeconomic Status," *Journal of the American Medical Association* 270, no. 14 (1993): 1697–1701.
29. M. Sager, et al., "Do the Elderly Sue Physicians?" *Archives of Internal Medicine* 150 (1990): 1091–1093.
30. T.L. Leaman, *Healing The Anxiety Diseases,* (Plenum Press: 1992).

PART II

The Response

CHAPTER 6

The Importance of More—and Better—Communication

"Patients don't care how much you know until they know how much you care."
Sir William Osler (1849 – 1919)

CHOOSING A DOCTOR

Almost everyone is a patient from time to time, and unless in a managed care plan with limited options, they must choose a health care provider. Those who are medical professionals probably make their choices based on personal knowledge or reputation within the profession. For those who are not professionals, however, and must choose a physician in the private health care sector (as compared to a managed care setting), the choice is a bit of a gamble. There is very little "scientific" data on which a family can base such an important decision. The result of that decision could be the difference between a "good" doctor and a "bad" doctor, with literal life and death implications—far more important than choosing a new car, house, or location in which to live. Fortunately, it is usually much easier to change doctors than a car, house, or location. Fortunately, too, the odds are quite favorable.

In 1996 the *Health Letter*, published by the Public Citizen Health Research Group, compiled its fourth list of doctors who had been sanctioned either by the federal government or by a state medical board.[1] The result was a book entitled, *13,012 Questionable Doctors,* available as a three volume set or by individual states. The book lists the specific disciplinary actions reported and the offenses for which physicians were disciplined. The book also includes the name and location of each physician. While these numbers are disturbing, the editors of the *Health Letter* believe that, in view of the known rate of medical errors, the number of disciplinary actions against physicians should be more than twice the reported rate. Considering that there were calculated to be 689,121 non-federal physicians practicing in 1996, the odds remain quite good, but are still a gamble.

The Female Patient magazine, in its March 1997 issue, discussed the problem of choosing a physician and noted that many patients are beginning to use more sophisticated methods.[2] In addition to mentioning the *13,012 Questionable Doctors* book, the article identified a Web site (http://medseek.com) for checking on board certification and hospital affiliations. Readers were also informed about the value of an initial "get acquainted" visit and the sorts of questions to ask when interviewing a doctor. Most doctors now are amenable to this visit, even though no charge is made, and it is during a period when time is at a premium.

Recently, lists of "best doctors in the state" have been available, published in the local press. These are usually compiled by querying physicians about who they would choose for their families in each field of medicine. While this is very nice publicity for the physicians chosen, it probably has limited usefulness for potential patients, because if the doctors are that well known, their practices are likely to be closed, except for personal referrals. Further, they are often in metropolitan areas which would be less helpful for those not living in that city. In a managed care environment, people would wonder if they are on their plan's particular panel.

All of these suggestions may be of help to patients in making their decisions, some in a positive way and some in a negative way. But most patients will still need to rely on what they have read, observed, or heard from others. The advice of others, of course, is also based on subjectivity. Few people are in a position to make informed judgments about the quality of care provided by a physician, but they are able to judge whether they like or dislike, trust or doubt, a physician. In this one respect, every patient is his or her own expert, and this probably remains as the single most persuasive factor in choosing a doctor.[3] As Dr. Osler has been quoted: the first consideration for patients is a caring relationship. Likability and trust are both ingredients and products of a good patient-physician relationship, which can become the basis for a therapeutic relationship. It has been established that this can be a major determinant of health care outcomes. Interestingly, once in a courtroom, the lack of trust in a particular physician as a witness is one of the major reasons why jurors find against that doctor and in favor of a patient or plaintiff.

Unfortunately, in one recent celebrated case it was discovered that a psychiatrist, who had seen hundreds of patients, was allegedly unlicensed, yet had been apparently credentialed by a managed care organization.[4] This is an example of an additional problem for patients in the private sector. There is very little, if any, monitoring of a physician's practice. Physicians are expected to practice within the standards of care for their discipline, to maintain accurate records, and to keep abreast of developments within their field. They are honor bound to do so, and most do, but there is no mechanism in place in most private practices to maintain any kind of surveillance. Most patients are unaware of this, assuming that there is at least a minimum of oversight within the profession. A trusting relationship is essential, but fortunately, when trust wanes, patients are quite free to go elsewhere.

DOCTORS IN A MANAGED CARE SETTING

In a managed care setting, there is an entirely different dynamic. Patients may have a very limited choice of physicians, and they may even tend to dislike or mistrust a physician in part, at least, because they were unable to participate in the selection process. However, they can usually be assured that all of the physicians whom they see will have had their credentials examined by experts. Usually those with responsibility for credentialing will know the relative value of training in different institutions, in different countries, the difference between board eligibility and board certification, the extent and limits of training in each discipline, and the applicability of each physician's previous employment history. They will have the information from the Data Bank available to them and they will scrutinize it carefully. They also often review records, notes, and charts from the physician's practice. Even if all this information were available to the public, most consumers would not be able to evaluate it.

Managed care organizations, and hospitals to a lesser extent, are in part mandated to seek all of this information, and it is in their best interest to analyze it carefully, and make their appointments accordingly. Moreover, they are also obliged to keep this information current. A hospital is required to query the Data Bank at least every two years about each physician who has any privileges in that institution.[5] Hospitals and managed care organizations monitor physician behavior at some level on a continuous basis. In the past, however, it was customary only in the hospital setting. This may begin to change as more hospitals employ physicians. They may be responsible for the physician's actions or the employees in the physician's office from a corporate negligence standpoint.

However, in a managed care environment, every physician's practice is more closely monitored. Data collection in almost all aspects of care is a continuous process and the information obtained is compared with that of other physicians doing comparable work. Any substantial deviation from the norm in diagnoses, procedures, prescriptions, patient complaints or satisfaction, number of patients seen, and dollars generated, or a host of other variables, is subject to investigation. In a private practice, outside of a managed care setting, it is quite possible that no one will ever review the medical records, or even ascertain whether or not there are complete records.

In managed care, records are maintained on each physician's continuing medical education (CME) activities, and on recertification in those specialties that require or offer it. In a private practice this information is unknown, unless the patient asks for it.

The problem for the family seeking a private practitioner is the lack of information on which to make a decision, and the absence of any assurance of continuous monitoring by other professionals, of the physician's practice, and continuing education. The problem for the private practitioner is instilling the kind of trust, and developing the kind of relationship that can be therapeutic.

The problem for the family in a managed care setting, where it ought to be easier, is learning to like and trust, or at least get along with, the physicians to whom they are assigned, and in developing confidence in the managed care organization which they have joined. Most people want to like their doctors and to put their trust in them. When choices are limited, however, there are nagging thoughts which may interfere with the process: "Why couldn't I have Dr. X?" "Was this new doctor cheaper?" "This doctor is not like my old doctor!" "I have heard that doctors in the system get paid more for cutting costs—does that affect my doctor's decisions about my care?" "How do I know?" The questions are endless and unanswerable; they can only be addressed on the basis of trust.

A problem for physicians in the managed care system, even though it ought to be easier, may be in developing close patient-doctor relationships, especially if they are not the patients' prime choice, and are simply perceived as "working for the company." It is important for the physician, and the organization, to portray a sense of being fair, credible, and having the patient's best interest foremost. To the extent that this portrayal is honest, it is also in the patient's best interest, as a basis for a therapeutic relationship. Physicians in a managed care setting must begin a patient education process to change any negative perception, which could both hinder a therapeutic relationship and increase liability exposure. If patients

Source: Copyright © 1997, SC Saxton.

are wondering every time advice is given what the motivation of the doctor may be, they may be harmed from a health standpoint, never really comfortable enough to follow their treatment regime. If there is ever a case of a late or allegedly missed diagnosis, the doctor will have a nearly impossible hurdle to get over convincing the patient that good clinical judgment drove that decision.

Even though the problems for the patient seeking a private practitioner and those of the patient using managed care are quite different, the remedy for these two sets of problems is essentially the same. The key is in communication, patient to physician and physician to patient.

COMMUNICATION CREATES AN IMAGE

Communication takes many forms. It begins with the first mention of a particular physician, or group or system, or the first words identifying them in print. What people hear about a health care provider sets the background for a like or dislike, and a trust or mistrust by a patient. An individual physician has very little control about what people say, except in the development and guarding of his/her reputation. A publicized lawsuit, although at one time not having much of an effect, now can be quite disconcerting to a managed care organization whose success rests on building a reputation of having the "highest quality" providers. Developing a positive image for an organization is becoming extremely important, especially as the managed care market matures.

An organization does have some control over what is said about it, other than by its reputation alone, through advertising. In a fully developed managed care environment, advertising is impressive and very important. It seems that the media message, "We really care about you" would not have any impression on the public. It is a variation of the same message from car dealers, grocery chains, and repair people. Apparently the market research does demonstrate its effectiveness. So the "we care" message continues to be a central theme of advertising and a remembered slogan by patients. When anything goes amiss, long waits, billing errors, impatient words, or any other kind of miscommunication, the patient tends to feel a personal affront. The patient who feels angered or hurt or humiliated is the one most likely to sue. All the advertising in the world will not prevent patients from walking away from a plan if they feel personally mistreated. Managed care and, in fact, everyone in the health industry, is learning that it takes not only image building through advertising, but continuous attention to patient satisfaction in order to receive good ratings. Managed care organizations also know that it is more costly to attract patients than to keep them.

Patients often have a choice about which health care plan they will join. That decision will be based partly on the terms of the agreement, but also on everything they see, hear, or feel about that organization. Having made their choice, they will be alert to anything they see, hear, or feel that either tends to validate or negate that decision. What happens to each patient every step of the way, from appointments to how a complaint is handled after the visit or procedure, is extremely important. As is often pointed out, a positive comment is repeated two or three times, which is good press and important. However, just as important to remember is that a negative comment is repeated ten or twelve times.

OFFICE COMMUNICATION

No one doubts the importance of good office communications. It would be near the top of any practice consultant's list, considering either malpractice prevention or just good patient care and good practice management. The widespread interest and increasing educational endeavors in this area show that there is still a need and a lot of work to be done. Breakdowns in these communications are still occurring, and are still one of the major reasons for malpractice litigation. In the managed care environment, communication is both *more* important and *more* difficult than ever. Simple patient focused principles move from being a nicety to mandatory. Patients now have questions, not only about their health, but about the system they hope will serve them. Staff members become key players on the health provider's team. Available time seems to be shrinking, but the need for communication is expanding.

Susan Keane Baker, a practice consultant and author of *Managing Patient Expectations,* writing in the February 24, 1997 issue of *The American Medical News,* described "10 steps to better service."[6] These are based on her own experience, and that of her organization, in risk management. They are intended to help make a practice hassle-free, improve patient satisfaction, and reduce the risk of malpractice litigation. These include:

1. Staff know who patients are and why they are there
2. Staff members are willing to take responsibility to make things easier for patients
3. Physicians and staff remember to explain what is going to happen and why
4. There is a willingness to improve systems for patients' convenience
5. Patients are told how long the wait will be, and the waiting is made enjoyable
6. Forms are readable
7. Important information is provided in writing
8. Patients don't have to take their clothes off more than once
9. Billing statements can be understood by 10-year-olds
10. Voice mail is user-friendly.

These steps are fairly simple and can be implemented by a dedicated and enthusiastic staff, with competent supervision. Baker says, "In a hassle-free practice, every staff member views the patient as his or her reason for working in health care rather than an intrusion into daily routine."[7]

MISCOMMUNICATION AS LIABILITY

Reducing medical mistakes, euphemistically called medical misadventures, is and probably always will be, a major goal of all physicians and their employers. As has been shown previously, however, they are not the major cause of malpractice lawsuits. It has been demonstrated that approximately 1% of all hospitalized patients suffer injury due to some form of medical negligence, but that malpractice claims are filed in behalf of fewer than 3% of those injured or killed.[8]

It has been demonstrated again and again that failed communication is the major instigating factor in lawsuits. It is a far more frequent cause than medical misadventures. The Physician Insurers' Association of America data, as shown previously, lists "failure to instruct or communicate with patients" as only the tenth most frequent cause of medical misadventure claims (see Table 5–2).[9] It accounted for only 315 claims, or less than 2% of the total, and then only a fifth of these resulted in payment. However, there were also 33,539 claims classified as "no medical misadventure," meaning nothing bad happened medically, but the patient, or family, were suing anyway. Most of these also could be assumed to be a result of failed communication at some level. Less than one half percent of these were paid, from which one could conclude there was little true negligence involved. When there is actually negligence that is causally related to injuries, there usually is a payment by way of settlement or a greater chance for a verdict in the plaintiff's favor.

At first glance, these figures might seem to indicate that communication failure is really an insignificant cause of lawsuits. However, the data collected by insurers are based on the claims filed in court by plaintiffs, which alleges the overt basis for the suit. It does not describe the covert causes, the personal feelings of the offended patient and family, which prompted them to initiate a lawsuit. There is, in the authors' experience, a point in time, literally a moment, during which a suit is contemplated seriously by a patient. That moment in time can clearly be affected positively or negatively by the relationship, and the environment that has been created by the physician. Whether the billboard or commercial with the offer for free legal advice becomes attractive to them, or they take up a co-worker's offer to meet a brother, the lawyer, may well depend on that moment in time.

In the previously reported study based on an analysis of plaintiffs' depositions, 71% of them identified problematic relationships in response to the question, "Why are you suing? (see Table 5–4)."[10] The survey of sued and non-sued physicians and suing patients asked for suggestions to reduce malpractice litigation in the future. The primary response of all three groups was "better doctor-patient communication" (see Table 5–7).[11]

The survey also confirmed the observation that a poor doctor-patient relationship frequently preceded a lawsuit. Similar findings were noted in the other studies described in Chapter 5.[12–14]

The fact that poor communications between doctors and patients is a major risk factor for malpractice seems incontrovertible. In order to do anything constructive about the problem, however, a much more detailed definition is needed. Is there a pattern to miscommunication? How much of patients' perception depends on time spent, physician mannerism and attitude, and how much on the content of the message? Exactly what behaviors do patients experience as negative?

TIME MANAGEMENT

Time is vital to the patient-doctor relationship, important to both patient and doctor, but also to the managed care organization. For the patient, time spent waiting is often resented if it exceeds a certain tolerance, usually considered to be about 20 minutes, especially if it is on a repetitive basis. This time is often measured by patients who tend to know exactly how long they had to wait in the reception area. Time with the physician, however, is not usually measured by a clock but by whether they have had sufficient time to tell their story, whether they feel they have been heard, and whether they at least have had their questions acknowledged. Often it is not just the actual time but the tone of the visit.

Lester and Smith reported on a study designed to evaluate "the hypothesis that the way physicians communicate with patients and the degree patients perceive physician fault for bad medical outcomes are risk factors for the initiation of malpractice lawsuits."[15]

They enlisted 160 adults to participate in the study. This panel was divided, at random, into two groups and each group was shown a videotape of a simulated patient-physician encounter. The clinical situation portrayed was of a patient with a skin lesion which the physician-actor diagnosed and treated. One group saw a physician exemplifying positive communication skills, including "eye contact, a friendly tone of voice, presentation of information and requests for information, smiling, appropriate physical touch (shaking hands), self-disclosure, acknowledgment of verbalizations, reflections of affect, appropriate praise, and a relatively long period of contact (videotape length, 5 minutes 2 seconds)."

The other group saw the same doctor and patient actors, in the same setting, addressing the same problem. However, with this group the doctor-actor displayed negative communication behavior, including no eye contact, harsh and clipped tones of voice, criticism, a minimal presentation of information and minimal request for information, non-smiling expression, no friendly physical contact, no acknowledgment of verbalizations, no reflection of affect, no praise, and a relatively short period of contact (videotape length, 2 minutes 2 seconds).

After seeing the videotape, each participant was given one of four possible outcome reports. One of these reported a good outcome, but the other three all noted a bad outcome. In one of these the physician was clearly not at fault, in another there was uncertainty about his blame, and in the third the doctor had definitely erred. Participants were then given questionnaires asking them to rate the physician they had viewed, in light of the outcome report that they had read. They were asked to rate him on the basis of how professional, caring, friendly, trustworthy, and competent he was, whether they considered him to be negligent, and whether they would file a suit against him.

Not surprisingly, the results did support the hypothesis that the way in which physicians communicate with patients is a risk factor for a malpractice suit. When there was a bad outcome, the physician who related to the patient in a "negative" way, in a very short interaction, was much more likely to be sued than the physician who related to the patient in a "positive" way, with the longer interaction. This was an entirely contrived situation, of course, but it provides an illustration of the implications of the brief and unpleasant encounter.

The investigators expressed some concern that their "negative communicator" might be too negative to be credible. However, they overheard many participants commenting that such behavior was quite real and commonplace. There can be little doubt that the perceived time with the physician is one of the major determining factors in a patient's degree of satisfaction with the care offered.

Most people have had no training in how to be a patient, or how to relate their history in a logical sequence, focusing on the important and ignoring the trivial. These skills are taught in medical schools and are important in establishing a framework for the patient's story. It is a good thing, however, that patients are not taught to make formal coherent presentations. The way in which they tell their story, the effect that the telling has on them, the subtleties of voice changes, and non-verbal signs provide a rich source of information to the physician.

Inviting patients to describe their symptoms in their own way, at their own pace, can produce patient satisfaction, but can it provide the information needed within the time allotted? Some patients seem to be eternal fountains of information! With some patients, endless ventilation is an expression of unbounded anxiety. Can a balance be reached between physician time available, the patient's emotional needs, and the patient's sense of satisfaction? This is not a new problem and has been approached successfully in many different ways.

In 1956 Michael Balint, an Austrian psychiatrist, initiated a series of experimental teaching sessions with groups of 8 to 10 general practitioners at the Tavistock Clinic in London, England.[16] He was concerned about the enormous and, to him, obvious effects of psychological problems on physical illness. He met with the same group of physicians for several hours each week. Thc physicians described their patients' problems to the whole group, and they explored together the possible psychological implications and made suggestions for further inquiry and a therapeutic approach. On subsequent meetings each physician gave a brief report on his or her patient's progress. The therapy that the group developed, under Balint's guidance, proved to be remarkably effective. (The general practitioners were so impressed by the outcomes in their practices that they continued to attend the weekly sessions for several years, some traveling as far as 200 miles.)

The British general practitioners working with Balint and Enid Balint, his wife, also a psychiatrist, were concerned about the time involved in exploring a patient's psychological needs. The usual office visit in England at this time was from 5 to 10 minutes. When they realized that many of their patients' problems had a psychological basis, they began asking open-ended questions and encouraging their patients to tell more about themselves. They quickly discovered the use of the "long interview," a block of time, often after hours, when a patient would be encouraged to tell their whole story. The long-term time saving was illustrated by one example in which a woman had required about three visits per month for a long time, but after a "long interview" had "opened the floodgates," she was so relieved that she needed only an occasional visit. Her original symptoms had nearly disappeared. Summing up his conclusions on interview techniques, using open-ended statements or direct questions, Balint observed, "if you ask questions you get answers—and hardly anything else."

Encouraging patients to share their deepest concerns, fears, hopes, worries, frustrations, dreams, and hurts can provide penetrating insights into understanding the patients. It also provides physicians with opportunities to offer help when it is needed. This may mean a carefully chosen consultation or referral. It might also mean that physicians will choose to do some simple psychotherapy. Even this can be managed in a reasonable time period. Stuart and Lieberman, in *The Fifteen Minute Hour*, describe just how this can be done.[17]

Smith and Hoppe described two interviewing techniques, which they call patient-centered and physician-centered.[18] They believe that everyone has a story, an interaction of his or her biological, psychological, and social aspects. The physician who wishes to understand a patient needs to know that story, in order to gain insight into the diagnostic and therapeutic issues and why the patient is seeking the physician at this time. The mechanism for learning that story is the patient interview. The authors also note that this level of understanding requires that a physician use both patient-centered and physician-centered approaches to interviewing.

In the patient-centered interview, the physician focuses on the concerns, comfort, and desire for information of the patient. In this kind of interview, the patient leads the exchange, generating the ideas, and controlling the direction of the conversation. "The physician follows the patient, much as one follows a dance partner."[19] The result of this approach is a much more humanistic interaction; patients are heard and understood; doctors can express respect, humility, empathy, and sensitivity. Patients experience a sense of responsibility and self-sufficiency as they recognize the sharing of power and their own increasing autonomy. The authors also note that the patient-centered approach increases the bonding between patient and physician, part of the "spiritual or transcendent dimension of medicine."[20] They also cite evidence that this approach to interviewing is an integral part of healing, of the placebo effect, and of both patient and physician satisfaction.

Physician-centered interviewing is understood by the authors to be an equally important component of a good interview. It is especially useful in defining possible organic disease. It usually begins with non-directive, open-ended questions, but as symptoms are identified, it becomes directive, focusing more and more on the specific characteristics. The authors point out that "closed-ended interviewing can introduce considerable bias into the patient's medical story, but this bias can be minimized by proceeding from the general to the specific; consider doing the following:

- using single questions
- not suggesting a response by wording of a question, tone or non-verbal communication
- giving equal weight to alternative answers
- not interpreting data while gathering it
- balanced attention to all aspects of the story
- not confusing the patient with technical language or rapid shifts
- and making the conversation congruent with the patient's education, language, cultural, social and stylistic capabilities."[21]

This style of interviewing is essential in making diagnostic decisions. Smith and Hoppe believe that an interviewing approach that integrates the two styles is ideal and applicable in all practice settings. They have found that the proportion of time required for the patient-centered interview amounts to only from 5 to 20% of the total time available. The variations in time required are dependent on the extent of the patient's personal concerns. Since those concerns are probably the basic reason for the visit, the time allocation is appropriate.

It is always wisest to ask these exploratory questions early in the interview. Otherwise too much time may be spent on some minor complaint and the real reason for the visit appears much later. Every doctor in primary care can relate tales of the patient who, with a hand on the door knob, says, "Oh by the way, Doctor..." followed by "What about this hard lump?" or "Why is my urine always red?" or "I forgot to tell you, my twin brother killed himself last week."

Not all of these "by the ways" are avoidable, but some choice open-ended questions in the beginning can help.

Some patients bring lists of problems, questions, and complaints, with the apparent goal of seeking advice on each one, in numerical order. Such lists can be very helpful to both patient and doctor, and many doctors encourage their use. However, it is a good idea to ask to see the whole list, because the BIG QUESTION, the true reason for the visit, may be at the end and because it helps in the allocation of time.

In their experimental work, (described in more detail later in this chapter), Roter, et al., paid particular attention to the time involved in using interview techniques that addressed patients' emotional distress.[22] They recognized that many physicians feared that "opening Pandora's box of psychological concerns will lead to unmanageable and interminable visits."[23] This has not been their experience. They did note that at three-month and six-month follow-ups after special training, that even though the doctors had changed their interviewing style to decrease patients' emotional distress, there had not been any significant increase in time utilized.

This type of interview can be incorporated into multiple practice styles, whether it be primary care, specialty care, or by an advanced practice provider. The key is understanding patients and giving them an opportunity to tell their story.

Time management is always a prime consideration. In a private practice situation physicians may choose freely to give time away whenever they choose to do so, although in the present environment that luxury is quickly disappearing. When a physician is employed, however, there is an obligation to account for time to the employer, who has the responsibility to assure profitability. Without profitability the practice cannot continue. It is, therefore, in everyone's best interest—patient, doctor, and organization—that time is used most effectively. We now know the kinds of specific communication skills that are most desirable, that these can be taught, and that learning to use them can make a difference in outcomes. We also know that these skills can be exercised with no increase in required time.

This is corroborated by our observation of thousands of depositions in which patients—now plaintiffs—described circumstances in which they perceived they were mistreated: "I always had to wait so long, he obviously did not care about my time;" "the receptionist never gave me the time of day, she did not even look up when I came in;" "he never even returned my phone call;" or "I just felt like another number." Patients in depositions talk more about those comments and about breakdowns in communication, than the alleged malpractice!

COMMUNICATION SKILLS

Lester and Smith believe that doctors may be able to decrease their risk of malpractice lawsuits by learning to improve their communication skills.[24] They also believe that better patient education may also help reduce the risks. They note that when patients are well enough informed to recognize that a particular bad outcome is clearly not the fault of the doctor, they are less inclined to sue. Remember, patients know the least about managed care and what they know is often through misperceptions.

Roter, et al., conclude:

> "The positive results of the present study suggest that attempts to lower litigation risk by using extra medical procedures and tests, consultation, and extensive documentation, often known as 'defensive medicine,' may miss the point. Although such efforts may be preventive in that their 'double-checking' may help to avoid some bad medical results, they will not prevent them all. And when a bad result does occur, even lack of physician fault and the presence of extra procedures seem unlikely to diminish litigious feelings and the resulting chance of a lawsuit. Defensive medicine is not so much a tool to prevent lawsuits as it is to win them if they do occur. It can help provide the necessary courtroom evidence that a physician provided an appropriate standard of care. But if the intention is to prevent a lawsuit in the first place, forging a physician-patient bond that can effectively resist the pressures of our litigation-crazed and socially antagonistic society seems indispensable. An important way of accomplishing this may be through improving physician communication skills and patient education."[25]

Adamson, et al., used a different approach to gain further understanding of the patient-physician relationship.[26] They identified 107 physicians, from the disciplines of surgery, obstetrics-gynecology, anesthesiology, and primary care, who agreed to participate in the research. The group included those who had no claims as well as those who had one or many claims. The physicians' length of time in practice averaged 19 years and their average age was 51. The average number of claims per physician, since the beginning of their practices was 4.4.

Survey instruments were then given to this panel's patients and approximately 2,000 of them were completed satisfactorily. The survey form contained 52 opinion items, under the headings: Understanding and Empathy, Competence, Accessibility of Physician, Helpfulness of Office Assistants, Explanations, and Absence of Communication Problems. The results were then plotted against the physicians' records of number of claims filed against them.

The study noted that it has long been claimed that failure of communication between doctor and patient is a major cause of malpractice claims, whether or not these claims were meritorious. They believe that their study suggests that there is a relationship between patients' opinions of communication and the physician's history of malpractice claims.

The results of this study were mixed, with some variation in responses by sex of the patient and by their level of education. The most consistent and striking difference was in the area entitled "Explanation." In the area of "Competence" the scores awarded by patients were quite high, 90 out of a possible 100. Under the headings of "Understanding and Empathy," and "Communication," the scores were somewhat less in all of the specialties. The scores under "Explanations" however, were much less, 20 points lower than any other scale.

The significance of this finding is that these patients did not feel that their physicians explained all aspects of the procedure that was about to be performed in a manner that they could comprehend. Even though the physicians were perceived as showing empathy and communicating, their actual explanations apparently did not meet the patients' desire to know.

The authors suggest that a lack of information may lead patients to have unrealistic expectations about the outcome of their treatment, and when these are not met, they may be inclined to sue. The authors conclude:

> "Physicians must learn to adapt their communication styles to the individual variations of their patients' intellectual and emotional needs. When a patient prefers less explanation, care must be taken to see that an adequate informed consent is given. In this study, the inverse perceptions reported by male and female patients and more-and less-educated patients about physicians with few and many claims reinforces the importance of this."[27(p.360)]

Another effort to define the specific communication behaviors associated with doctors with and without malpractice claims was reported by Levinson, et al., in February 1997.[28] They noted that there did not appear to be a relationship to being sued and quality of care. They did acknowledge that there was a relationship between malpractice claims and miscommunication.

The investigators identified a group of 124 physicians, about half in primary care and half in general or orthopedic surgery. About half of the primary care group and one-third of the surgical group had malpractice claims experience. In each of the physician's offices, 10 patients were selected. Patients were chosen who were adults, were not having an acute problem or a procedure, and in the primary care practices, had at least two prior visits, and were not scheduled for a complete physical examination at that visit. A regular office visit was then audiotaped for each of the 124 physicians with their 10 patients.

The resulting 1,240 audiotapes were then analyzed by specifically trained coders, using a standardized coding system. Communication behaviors, including every utterance by the physician, were sorted into one of three categories: Content, Process, and Emotional Affect.

Content included questions asked about the patient's medical condition, therapy, and psychosocial and lifestyle issues, or giving information or counseling about these same topics. Process consisted of facilitation and orientation. Facilitation included paraphrasing, interpretation, and asking questions about the patient's opinions and understanding. Orientation was described as giving instructions and directions concerning the medical visit process, and transitional statements. Emotional affect was measured by the physician showing approval, worry or concern, criticizing a third party, showing empathy, and by laughing and the use of humor (see Table 6.1).

The results were then compared statistically by specialty group, primary care or surgical, and, within each group, according to claims or no claims experience.

Primary care visits lasted an average of 16.5 minutes and surgical visits 13.6 minutes. The authors note that previous studies indicated that suing patients often complained that their visits felt hurried and rushed. This study also demonstrated that shorter visits were associated with more frequent malpractice claims against primary care physicians. This was not necessarily true of the surgical group.

In the Content category there were no significant differences between claims and no claims physicians in either specialty group. In the primary care group, however, there were significant differences in both the Process and Emotional Affect categories. Non-sued primary care physicians used more orientation techniques than the sued group, with statements such as, "First I'll examine you and then we will talk the problem over" or "I will leave time for your questions."[29] These statements help patients understand the process.

Primary care physicians with no claims also used facultative comments, such as, "Go on, tell me more about that," or asked patients for their opinions as to what was happening to them or should be done about it. They also laughed and used humor more often, portraying friendliness and warmth. The researchers commented on the importance of this finding, indicating that "how a physician says something may be as important as what is said."[30] They note that this projection of warmth is especially important because it bolsters the long-term relationships that characterize primary care.

None of these differences between no claims and claims physicians was detected in the surgical group. The explanation for this is not known, but may be because patient expectations of surgeons are different. However, what is expected of consultants, or secondary care physicians, both by patients and by managed care, may be changing. Some consultants in a managed care environment are thought of as the primary care or coordinating physician for the patients under their long-term care. For example, a cardiologist may be regarded as the primary care physician for a cardiac patient or a pulmonologist for an asthmatic patient. This may pose additional risk for all concerned since the training and experience of a specialist may not be well-suited for the primary care role. What may work

Table 6–1 Categories of the Roter Interaction Analysis System

Category	*Communication Behavior*	*Example*
Content	Question asking related to medical condition	What can you tell me about the pain?
	Question asking related to therapeutic regimen	How have you responded to the medication?
	Question asking related to psychosocial and lifestyle issues	What's happening with your son?
	Giving information–medical	The medication may make you drowsy.
	Giving information–therapy	You'll need to take the antibiotics every day for 10 days to have it work.
	Giving information–psychosocial and lifestyle	It is important to get out and do something every day. The Senior Center is a great place for company and they'll give you lunch too.
	Counseling–medical/therapy	Call me if you aren't feeling better by next week.
	Counseling–lifestyle/psychosocial	You really need to get out and meet more people.
Process	Facilitation (asking for patient opinion, asking for patient understanding, paraphrasing and interpretation)	What do you think it is? Go on, yes, aha. Do you follow?
	Orientation (instructions and directions regarding the medical visit process, and transitional statements)	Get up on the table, take a deep breath. Well, okay, let's see.
Emotional affect	Shows approval	Good, I'm happy to hear you are feeling better.
	Concern/worry	I'm concerned that this may happen again in the future.
	Criticism of third party	It's pretty stupid of the insurance company to do that.
	Empathy	You look worried.
	Laughs, humor	My son said that college life is one big party. "That's not what I want to hear, Andrew!"

Source: Reprinted from W. Levinson, et al., Physician-Patient Communication, *Journal of the American Medical Association*, Vol. 277, No. 7, p. 555, Copyright 1997, American Medical Association.

out better is to have the specialist coordinate the care for a certain disease, letting the primary care physician handle other health needs. Regardless, for the time period when the study was conducted, and even now for some consultants, the relationships tend to be short-term and patients may see them as technical experts, consulted for particular advice or a procedure.

These three studies have demonstrated some of the specific aspects of communication that are associated with lower malpractice risk, and increasing patient satisfaction. This addresses two of the major goals of managed care. However, none of these studies addresses the problem of time. Many of the positive communication behaviors require extra time, more than might be required for a simple standard history. The Levinson study noted that the average time required for a visit with a no-claims physician was more than 16 minutes, significantly higher than what many primary care physicians schedule for follow-up patients; however, the amount of extra time in the Levinson study was only approximately four minutes. We believe the real difference in time is probably how the time is spent with the patient and not so much the amount.

CHANGING COMMUNICATION SKILLS

Using more time per patient may be contrary to the requirements of managed care to increase productivity in order to be competitive. Can both be accomplished? The answer is clearly yes, by improving the quality of the interaction and avoiding the appearance of being rushed or harried. Most primary care physicians do not spend 16 minutes with each patient, nor is it practical to do so. The amount of time that needs to be spent with a patient will clearly vary depending on the presenting clinical picture, whether it is a follow-up appointment, the questions posed by the patient, and the complexity of the medical history of the patient. The lesson from the studies is that the quality of the time is paramount.

There are several strategies that a physician can employ to communicate a caring and interested attitude. Asking open-ended questions initially and then honing in on the particulars later, maintaining good eye contact, a friendly demeanor, avoiding watching the clock, or becoming absorbed in the chart, all help to reach this goal. It also helps to have systems in place that will provide patients with more initial information. The employment of a clinical coordinator or having an office nurse who can review the history and answer some initial questions, may streamline the process. It also helps to have literature that has previously been sent to the patient concerning a certain procedure and answering perhaps the top ten repeated questions by patients concerning the procedure, phrased in a patient-focused, easy to understand fashion. The physician then has the benefit of incorporating all of these other educational processes that have taken place into a visit. In other words, the physician will get "the credit." The time actually spent with a patient does not have to differ significantly at all for good patient-doctor communication to take place.

The goals listed in these various studies can be met by improving communication skills, improving and expanding communication systems, involving others on your staff in the process, and avoiding negative communication pitfalls. While physicians have all learned the basic behaviors of good interviewing in medical school and beyond, it is worth doing a quick review of these techniques to see if they have developed any bad habits. You have been told to try to keep your eyes on the same level as your patient's, maintain good eye contact, don't allow a desk or other piece of furniture to come between you, use appropriate touching, avoid becoming distracted by the chart or the clock, and listen. Allow the patient to tell the story, both because you need the information, and because you know that the telling has a positive therapeutic effect.

The ways of a physician in secondary or tertiary care may seem mysterious to patients, especially those who have been exposed only to primary care in the past. The specialist, with the advantage of a referral letter, and perhaps films, may need to ask only a few questions and do a very quick and focused examination in order to answer the question for which the patient was referred. "No, there is nothing structurally wrong with your knee," or perhaps, "Yes, you will need surgery to correct that problem." Patients often do not understand that the orthopedic surgeon has seen hundreds, perhaps thousands, of knees with similar problems before, and that there are only a few clinical signs and symptoms that are of concern. However, the patient may not be ready to have such a momentous decision made ("cut open my knee or not") so abruptly. Much patient anguish, and possible liability claims, can be avoided by a more direct explanation by the physician, preferably augmented by pertinent written materials. This goes a long way toward helping patients feel as if they have been given their due.

If physicians do a better job in communicating with patients as to what to expect in a particular visit, so they are not taken by surprise, the whole experience is more likely to be a positive, not a negative one. This is one of the keys to relationship bonding and malpractice prevention.[31] It may also have a powerful therapeutic effect.

Another major goal of managed care is improved health care outcomes. What effects, if any, can be expected from improved doctor-patient relationships in this area?

BETTER HEALTH THROUGH BETTER COMMUNICATION?

Two recent reviews have addressed this question. Moira Stewart published the results of her review in 1995.[32] She analyzed selected studies to measure the effects on patient health outcomes of the quality of physician-patient communication. She selected 21 studies for review, all of which were either randomized controlled trials or analytic studies in which health care was an outcome variable.

Stewart's review illustrated the extent of the physician-patient communication problem: "50% of psychosocial and psychiatric problems are missed," "physicians interrupt patients an average of 18 seconds into the patient's description of the presenting problem;" "54% of patients' problems and 45% of patients' concerns are neither elicited by the physician nor declared by the patient;" "patients and physicians do not agree on the main presenting problem in 50% of visits;" and patients are dissatisfied with the information provided to them by physicians.[33]

In general, the studies described communication problems in two areas, from patient to physician in history taking and from physician to patient describing the management plan. However, she also noted that "most of the studies also point to the importance of emotional support as a dimension of communication. In addition, the distribution of power and control in the physician-patient relationship, particularly with regard to decision-making, is an implicit or explicit concern in all the studies reviewed."[34]

An analysis of the 21 research projects reviewed showed that 16 reported positive findings, and 5 either had insignificant or inconclusive findings in regard to the effectiveness of physician-patient communication in improving patient health outcomes. This is a strong affirmation of the potential value of the therapeutic relationship. The specific outcomes that were affected, in decreasing order of frequency, were "emotional health, symptom resolution, function, physiologic measures (i.e., blood pressure and blood sugar level), and pain control." [35]

Stewart concluded that the studies reviewed identified the elements of communication that could be addressed in continuing medical education programs. There were several themes most prominently suggested by these 21 studies. In taking histories, physicians are urged to ask a wide variety of questions, including those about patients' feelings and concerns, about their own understanding of the problems, how they affect the patients' ability to function, and what they are expecting from treatment. Continuing education programs should also emphasize ways in which clear explanations can be given to patients and how physicians can provide emotional support.

A recurring and overriding theme was the need for active patient participation. As Stewart noted in her conclusions, "agreement between physician and patient was found to be a key variable that influenced outcomes. In my view, such agreement implies that decision-making was a shared 'egalitarian process.'

The second review was published by Rosenberg, et al., in 1997.[36] They analyzed 40 sources, both original work and reviews, including that by Stewart. They were specifically interested in how communication between physicians and patients affected health outcomes. They noted that the research indicated that patients actually felt better when they were actively involved in their health care process. They cited studies in which headaches resolved, and a wide variety of other symptoms cleared more quickly.

In order to try to understand why this occurs, they first identified the purposes of the medical interview:

- to define, understand, and monitor patient problems
- to develop a therapeutic relationship
- to explain management plans.

Rosenberg, et al., found ample evidence in the medical literature to demonstrate that patient health outcomes could be affected by improvement in at least the first two of these. While benefits from the third seem obvious, there is a paucity of research to prove the effects conclusively.

Identifying psychological and social problems seems especially difficult for many physicians, and yet one-third of patients consulting primary care physicians have these problems as a major cause of their discomfort and the reason for the visit. The authors point out that "while history taking is important in the diagnosis of all disorders, it is the sole tool available to diagnose psychosocial problems."[37]

Physicians who are most successful at detecting such problems are those who ask open-ended questions, ask direct psychological questions, make empathic comments, and interrupt their patients less frequently. One suggestion is to ask patients how much of their difficulty they think might be due to psychological stress. When patients do make any kind of a psychological statement, physicians are urged to follow up with appropriate additional questions.

THERAPEUTIC RELATIONSHIP

The physician-author met with Michael Balint in 1968 and was permitted to attend several of the sessions provided that he "stay in the background and say nothing." Dr. Balint explained that he attributed much of the therapeutic success to what he termed, "the drug, doctor." As the general practitioners recognized their patients' psychological needs, honoring the validity of their patients' complaints and addressing them, they developed a potent therapeutic relationship, strong enough and predictable enough to be considered a drug.

As an extension of the therapeutic relationship, Rosenberg, et al., assume that patients' healing, in general, would be enhanced if patients were more compliant with their doctors' instructions. They note that the literature indicates that compliance rates can be improved when physicians make more positive, and fewer negative, comments. There was also improvement when physicians asked a fewer number of total questions, but asked questions that, directly or indirectly, probed the actual compliance of a patient with a previously given instruction. They suggest asking patients whether or not they are taking the pills, for example, what they are taking, and how often.

The term "compliance" has been used here, as used in the article by Rosenberg, et al., and is widely accepted in the medical literature. However, the authors of this book find it to be an objectionable term. It connotes acquiescence, or yielding, in a subservient way, to the will of another, in this case, a physician. This is the antithesis of co-active practice, in which all important decisions are made jointly, by an informed patient and physician. Patients as partners would be a better description.

COMMUNICATION AND PATIENT SATISFACTION

The therapeutic relationship also involves patient satisfaction. Improving patient satisfaction can be expected to improve patients' cooperation (compliance) and, presumably, health outcomes. One of the identified ways of achieving this is by providing more information to patients. It has been shown that patients do want more information than their doctors usually provide and that doctors, when asked, vastly overestimate the time they spend giving information to patients. This information can be provided through practice brochures, pamphlets, videos and audiotapes; but these are intended to supplement what the doctor is saying, never to supplant it.

Rosenberg, et al., point out that the patient-physician relationship is an asymmetric one. The encounter usually occurs in the physician's milieu, office, or hospital, and the physician sets the agenda and the rules. This may be quite intimidating to patients and they may need to be encouraged to ask questions and to play a more active role in their own health care. Another proven communication technique is to focus on the patient's perspective, asking patients for their views and suggestions, and addressing their requests and concerns. Simply inviting patients to ask questions can improve their feeling of satisfaction with the encounter.

Those physicians who make home calls will readily understand the vivid difference that the environment creates. Patients, and their families, when seen in their own home, are obviously more "themselves;" they are at ease, speak more freely, and their interactions are casual and unguarded. When the physician comes to their abode, an intense therapeutic relationship is easily established.

Pleasing patients must always be a major goal of managed care, so long as patients have a choice of plans. Profitability depends on patient volume and marketshare. Ultimately, in a mature managed care setting, the managed care organizations that are going to be successful are the ones that attract and maintain patients. It has been demonstrated that patient-physician miscommunication is the major source of patient dissatisfaction. It has also been shown that patient satisfaction is an essential ingredient in the development of a therapeutic relationship. A strong therapeutic relationship has been demonstrated to improve patient cooperation, with the expectation of better health outcomes, another major goal of managed care.

In January, 1997 the American Hospital Association (AHA) released the results of a study entitled "Eye On Patient; A Report to the American Public."[38] This report was the initial result of an on-going investigation commissioned by the AHA and conducted by the Picker Institute of Boston. The purpose of this effort was to "gather information about patients' perceptions and experiences with care and to help health care providers and organizations find ways to be more responsive to patients' needs."[39] It was based on the stated conviction by the AHA that a key to improving the health care system lies in understanding patients' viewpoints.

This study was intended to provide an overview of patients' concerns and experiences during 1996. The work is continuing and is expected to produce additional reports on in-depth investigations into particular aspects of health care. The methods used to collect data for the first report include both the use of focus groups and surveys of 23,762 hospital patients and 13,363 patients in clinics and doctors' offices.

The authors of this report note that the results of "satisfaction surveys" are notoriously unreliable. In this study, for example, 70% of hospital patients surveyed said their care was "good" to "excellent" (see Figure 6–1). In spite of that glowing report, a large percent of hospital patients reported significant problems (see Figure 6–2). It is interesting to note that in the area of physical comforts, perhaps the area given most attention in hospitals, the problems reported were quite low, only 10%. However, in all of the personal areas, Respect for Patients' Preferences, Coordination of Care, Information and Education, Emotional Support, Involvement of Family and Friends, and Continuity and Transition, problems were reported by 20 to 25% of patients in each area. When asked to discuss their care, however, such as in focus groups or in written commentary, the story was often quite different. This appeared to be true regardless of geographic location, level of education or income, or ethnicity. Many patients reported deep concerns over the changing health care system, especially noting:

- reduced access to care
- higher costs to the patient
- doubts about the quality of care
- doubts about the quality of the caregivers
- interactions were cold and impersonal
- doubts about whether or not their own best interests were being served.

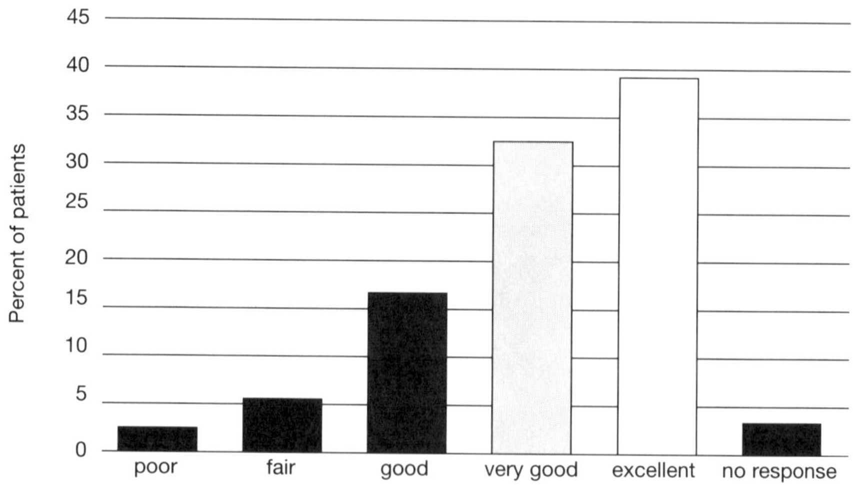

Figure 6–1 Overall ratings of care based on surveys of 23,763 patients. *Source:* Reprinted with permission of the American Hospital Association and The Picker Institute, copyright 1996.

Some of the concerns are reflected in the survey of hospital patients, which identified problem rates at different hospitals (see Figure 6–4). It is interesting to note that Courtesy of Nurses (based on a fair to poor rating on a five-point scale) was the lowest percent of problems reported, with the smallest difference between hospitals (less than 15 percentage points). The second lowest percent of problems was in the area of "trust in the doctor treating you," from 5 to 15% reporting problems, with the mean at 12%. While this is quite low, compared to the frequency of the other problems presented, its importance is more profound than any other. It means that the 12% of patients who do not trust their physicians are not likely to have an effective therapeutic relationship. The implications of this finding affect not only satisfaction, but health care outcomes, as well.

All of the other areas of problems reflect difficulty in physician to patient communication. Hospital patients were asked whether they received answers that they could understand when they questioned their doctors (Figure 6–4). While there was a significant difference from hospital to hospital, the median response was that 25% of patients said that they had problems. When asked if they had trouble finding someone in the hospital to talk to about their concerns, the median response was even higher, 35%.[40] Even more patients complained that they were not told about possible side effects of medication, what danger signals from their ailment to watch for, or when they could resume specific daily activities. Perhaps

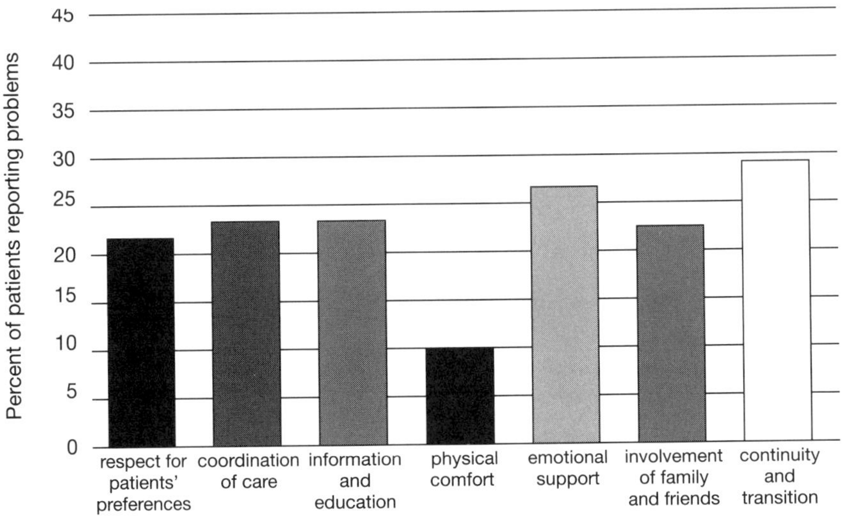

Figure 6–2 How hospitals scored. Based on surveys of 23,763 patients. Numbers reflect mean percentage of patients who reported problems. The higher the number the worse the score. *Source:* Reprinted with permission of the American Hospital Association and The Picker Institute, copyright 1996.

the most significant finding was that 31% noted that they did not feel they had enough say in their own treatment.

In clinics and doctors' offices, the principal complaint was access to the physicians. Of the 13,363 patients surveyed, more than 20% identified this problem (see Figure 6–4). When specifically asked, "Were you able to get an appointment as soon as you wanted?," the responses varied most widely. At some clinics or offices only 5% of patients reported problems, while in others it was as high as 44% (see Figure 6–5). After getting an appointment, from an average of 30% said they had to wait "too long" in the reception area. The length of time was not stated, but patients were clearly dissatisfied.

Almost 20% of patients surveyed in doctors' offices and clinics mentioned a lack of information and patient education as a problem. When asked directly if they got as much information about their condition and treatment as they wanted, about 28% answered in the negative. While only slightly less than 10% identified a lack of emotional support as a problem, this could also have serious consequences. The fact of being ill, and the environment of health care, even a physician's private office, can be anxiety producing. Untreated anxiety symptoms frequently cause exacerbation of other illnesses, and may even precipitate new ailments. Failure to provide emotional support is another form of miscommunication.

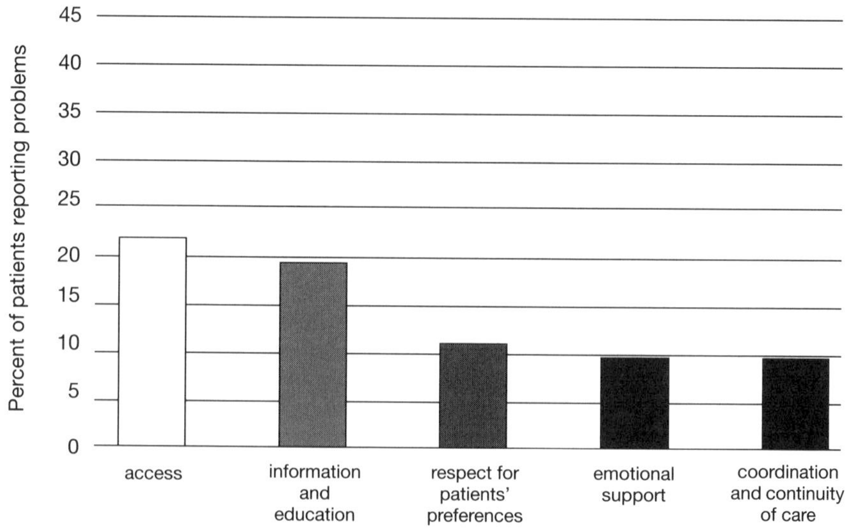

Figure 6–3 How clinics and doctors scored. Based on surveys of 13,363 patients. The numbers reflect mean percentage of patients who reported problems. The higher the number the worse the score. *Source:* Reprinted with permission of the American Hospital Association and The Picker Institute, copyright 1996.

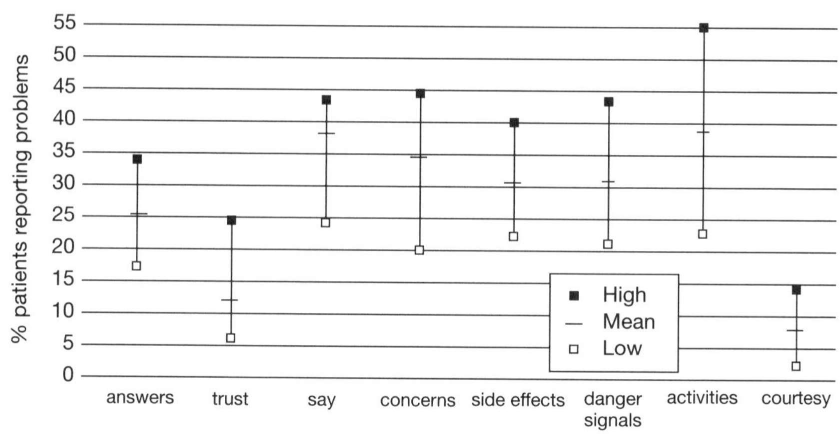

Figure 6–4 Problem rates on hospital patients. *Source:* Reprinted with permission of the American Hospital Association and The Picker Institute, copyright 1996.

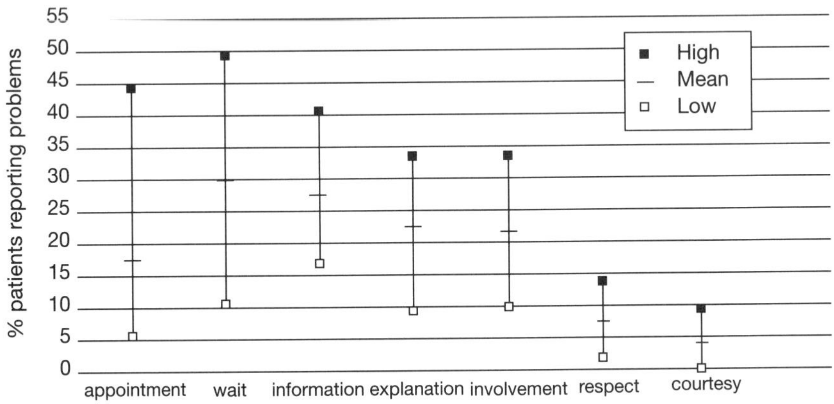

Figure 6–5 Problem rates for clinic and doctors' office patients. *Source:* Reprinted with permission of the American Hospital Association and The Picker Institute, copyright 1996.

Another troubling problem, listed by 10% of patients, was a perceived lack of coordination and continuity of care. While this may have reflected a basic administrative or bureaucratic problem, it too, is a form of failed communication. In the open-ended survey, when patients were simply invited to list problems, 22% mentioned a lack of respect for their own preferences as patients (see Figure 6–3). When asked the direct question, "Were you as involved in the decisions about your care as much as you wanted?," from 10 to 33% said "No" (see Figure 6–5).

These findings are especially important because they are based on a very large number of patients, in many different settings. They are reinforced by the comments of people in focus groups. The patients meeting in focus groups complained very little about the "hotel" amenities of hospitals, such as the quality of food and variety of menu choices. The degree of courtesy shown them in doctors' offices and clinics was also of little concern. However, they expressed deep concern about the health care system itself. Instead of a planned health care system, they feel there is a "confusing, unreliable, and often impersonal disassembly of medical professional and institutions." It seems to them to "block access, reduce quality, and limit spending for care at the expense of patients." They related many stories of trying to get approval from their managed care organizations for what they, or their doctors, thought they needed. They stressed how necessary it was for them to be assertive in order to get answers, and they worried about what will happen when they are no longer able to take charge.

This report from the Picker Institute, with continuing support from the AHA, makes it quite apparent that there is great dissatisfaction with the present health system. Dissatisfaction provides the perfect breeding ground for malpractice litigation. An added value to this particular study is that it provides a base line against which trends can be plotted. When placed in the context of greater market penetration of managed care it is especially troubling. One of the potential effects of the expanding managed care penetration is even keener competition, pushing the doctor and staff even harder. Potentially this could lead to less time with patients, less of their involvement in decisions, and more distrust. The statistics in this type of study could get worse before they get better. The types of feelings described in the study are the same feelings that lead to lawsuits. Could we be on a collision course?

TEACHING COMMUNICATION BEHAVIORS

There is ample, clear evidence in the medical literature that if physicians need to learn to improve their communication skills, they can do so. These abilities are not genetic, not something that "you either have or you don't." Quite aside from the scientific data, the fact that improved communication behaviors can be learned is self evident; what physician cannot look back five years and recognize that his or her interviewing skills have changed, simply on the basis of experience? Formal education programs, however, can identify particular skills or behaviors that need improvement, focus educational efforts on these areas, and measure the results. Communication skills are, in essence, simply good or bad habits of interrelating that have been formed slowly over the years. With work, or lack of attention, either can change.

Steven Cole has recently summarized the functions of effective communication, noting that they fall naturally into three areas: data collection, rapport building, and information giving (also referred to by Rosenberg, et al.).[41] The specific skills needed in each of these areas can be identified, the physician's abilities in each of these areas assessed, and an appropriate teaching intervention developed.

Data Collection

Data collection includes four basic skills: questioning, both open-and closed-ended, facilitating, surveying, and summarizing.

- Data gathering, or history taking, should begin with open-ended questions, inviting patients to tell their story in their own words. This permits them to voice all of their concerns and provides the physician an opportunity to sense the weight of these concerns to the patient. This is followed by a series of closed-ended questions, gathering more details on each of the problems presented.

- *Facilitation* is any behavior that encourages a patient to continue talking after an open-ended question. It can be accomplished by a few encouraging or inquiring words, or non-verbally, by head nods or simply by attentive silence.
- *Surveying* is a technique for avoiding last minute surprise complaints or statements. After the patient has responded to the initial open-ended questions, augmented by the physician's facilitative actions, a simple surveying question may be asked, such as, "What else?" Patients' lists of problems, especially in primary care where every possible health concern is acceptable, are often too long to be addressed in a single visit. However, after the last "What else?" and the list appears complete, patient and physician together can negotiate a priority list, addressing first those problems that seem most urgent, or that can be dispatched quickly. Part of the management plan should be an appointment for follow-up on the remaining issues.
- *Summarization* is the final step in the data gathering process; the physician recounts, briefly, the patient's story. This step helps to obviate any misunderstandings and, equally important, it lets patients know that they have been heard and understood.

Rapport Building

Rapport building is probably the most crucial communication skill. It can begin to be developed during the data gathering phase and be reinforced during the information giving process. There are specific techniques, however, that can help to develop a bond between physician and patient, a potentially powerful therapeutic relationship. The basis for maximizing rapport is understanding a patient's emotional concerns. Sometimes the patient's response to topics being discussed is obvious, evidenced by expression, tears, agitation, hand actions, or other non-verbal clues. These should be acknowledged by the physician, with a comment such as, "You seem to be feeling. . . ." This lets the patient know that the physician understands and accepts his or her feelings, and encourages the patient to discuss them openly. This is actually one of the keys in developing a therapeutic relationship described as an important goal earlier.

Cole suggests five specific responses that physicians might use when a patient's emotions become apparent, although he noted that other techniques might also be helpful:

- reflection—as just described, simply lets patients know their feelings are acknowledged
- legitimation—refers to comments by the physician which tend to validate the experienced emotion, "I can understand why you would feel..."

- support—promises the physician's help in addressing the problem
- partnership—statements to the effect that the physician will work with the patient to manage the situation together
- respect—affirmation and reinforcement to the patient for any positive coping behaviors that they have demonstrated

The principal reason for concern about this area of communication skills is that patient health outcomes are so dependent on the effectiveness of the therapeutic relationship. Miscommunication in this realm, however, is a major cause of malpractice litigation. Good communication is also important to satisfaction, which is key to member retention and attracting patients for managed care organizations.

Information Giving

Information giving is simply all the information that physicians give to patients, primarily by what they say, or by what is said by the physician's staff, but supplemented with materials in all available media.

Roter, et al., have conducted an elaborate investigation into the value of communication skills training on the effectiveness of physicians in recognizing and caring for patients in emotional distress.[42] They reviewed the medical literature noting that 30 to 40% of primary care patients have significant levels of emotional distress; that most of those who do seek care consult primary care physicians rather than mental health professionals; but that a high proportion of these emotional ills are unrecognized and undiagnosed. The authors of this study also note that the literature provides abundant evidence that communication skills can be taught effectively.

In order to test the effectiveness of specific educational interventions, Roter, et al., conducted an experiment involving 69 physicians and 648 of their patients. The physicians who were recruited were all primary care physicians; about half were in internal medicine and half in family medicine, all were full time, average age 40, and they represented a wide variety of practice arrangements. They were divided at random into three study groups. The physicians in two of the groups each received eight hours of CME training, one group emphasizing emotion-handling skills and the other problem-solving skills. The third group received no training, until after the experiment, and served as a control group. Patients were recruited from the physicians' reception rooms, based primarily on their willingness to participate. They were asked to complete a written questionnaire, designed to detect emotional distress. The patient-physician encounter was then audiotaped.

The CME programs were presented in two four-hour sessions, one week apart. A variety of educational techniques were used, including presentations, round table discussions, and role play. The physicians were asked to audiotape themselves practicing their new skills, after the first session. These tapes were then used during the second session for critique and discussion. The difference between the two groups was in the focus of the training. One group followed a Rogerian, emotion-handling, model and the other the work of Lesser, in problem solving (see Table 6–2).

The questionnaires completed by patients were analyzed and sorted for the presence or absence of evidence of significant emotional distress. There were 301 patients who were scored as positive for emotional distress. Each of these patients was interviewed by the research team at intervals of two weeks, three months and six months.

The results of the experiment were that the trained physicians, by both methods, had gained significant skills in recognizing emotional distress and emotional problems, and that they made use of appropriate management strategies in handling these issues. The Problem Defining group scored slightly higher than the Emotion Handling group in both of these areas.

Roter, et al., concluded that there were four especially important findings from this work:

1. "physicians' use of communication skills in their practices changed as a result of an 8-hour CME program
2. physicians trained in specific communication skills recognized more psychosocial problems in their patients than did untrained physicians
3. patients of trained compared with untrained physicians showed greater reduction in emotional distress for as long as six months after their medical visit
4. these results were not associated with longer medical visits or increased utilization of medical services."[43]

These studies are examples of the evidence that specific communication skills, necessary to practice effective medicine, have been identified, that curricula and methods to teach them are being developed, that physicians can learn them, and that it does make a measurable difference in patient care outcomes. Although the above study dealt with primary care physicians, there is little doubt that the same type of conclusions can be associated with all health care providers. The first step may be just recognizing how important good communication is and emphasizing that to your staff. Maintaining continued vigilance in the form of reminders, a yearly educational review on the subject, and special training programs will make a difference. This is a constant concern by managed care organizations since it goes to the heart of patient retention, a critical issue to all health plans.

Table 6–2 Targeted Skills in the CME Program*

Emotion-Handling Skills
Signaling receptivity by
1. Asking patients about their feelings
2. Listening more, talking less
3. Following up on signs of patients' emotional distress
Showing positive regard by
4. Complimenting patient efforts
5. Making statements of legitimation (explicitly stating that patients' feeling/views are normal or understandable)
Expressing mutuality by
6. Expressing empathy (accurately acknowledging an emotion expressed by the patient)
7. Making explicit statements of partnership or support
8. Providing appropriate reassurance
Problem-Defining Skills
Eliciting the full spectrum of patient concerns by
1. Resisting immediate follow-up of the patient's first expressed concern
2. Asking the patient explicitly about other problems or concerns ("anything else"), including problems of daily living and stressors
3. Prioritizing with patients (negotiating use of time)
Delineating the patient's problem by
4. Starting with open-ended questions
5. Using facilitative statements to help patients tell their story in their own words
6. Assessing the effect of the patient's problem on psychosocial functioning
Understanding the patient's perspective by
7. Probing explicitly for patients' understanding and expressing concern about their problem(s)
8. Clarifying patient expectations for the visit

*CME indicates continuing medical education.

Source: Reprinted with permission from D.L. Roter, et al., Improving Physicians' Interviewing Skills and Reducing Patients' Emotional Distress, *Archives of Internal Medicine,* Vol. 155, p. 1882, © 1995, American Medical Association.

COMMUNICATION AS THE ENVIRONMENTAL KEY

The environmental key, therefore, is communication. This primarily means the direct communication between physician or provider and patient and the quality of that interaction. It does not necessarily mean more time has to be taken, but skills must be polished, so that patients know that the time with their doctor is well spent and that the doctor was caring and truly listening. It also means that every member of the health care team needs the same type of skills and understanding as to the importance of these interactions.

As managed care penetrates a community market, the environment does change, often subtly at first. As you become part of a new system, you might have a new or different type of location, different types of personnel on staff, and practice medicine somewhat differently. The environment is changing not only for you but also for your patients. It is an ideal time to take a critical look at every aspect of your interaction with your patient/partners.

REFERENCES

1. "13,012 Questionable Doctors," *Health Letter*, 12, no. 4 (1996) 1–3. This book has been available in two forms: *Questionable Doctors* listing information for one state, at $15; and *13,012 Questionable Doctors* as a complete three volume set, for $250. A new edition should be released about the time this book is published. Contact *Public Citizen Publications,* 1600 20th Street, NW, Washington, DC, 20009. Tel: (800) 588–7734.
2. "Shopping for a Doc," *The Female Patient* February, 1997.
3. "Eye on Patients" [Online]. Available: http://www.amhpi.com/eyeonpatients/seethree.html. See Press/Garm list and chart.
4. Katlin v. Tremoglie et al., No. 2703 June Term 1997 (PA Ct. Comm. Pf., Phila. Cty. Complaint filed June 23, 1997).
5. R.D. Weber, "Managed Care and the Data Bank," *Michigan Medicine* (February 1996): 8.
6. S. Keane Baker, "Ten Steps to Better Service," *The American Medical News*, 24 February 1997: 13–14.
7. S. Baker, *Managing Patient Expectations*, (New Canaan: Jossey-Bass, 1997): 13. (Baker may be contacted at 6 Kelley Green, New Canaan, CT 06840. Tel: (203) 966-4880.)
8. T.A. Brennan, et al., "Incidence of Adverse Events and Negligence in Hospitalized Patients," *The New England Journal of Medicine* 324, no.6 (1991): 377–384.
9. Data Sharing System of the Physician Insurers Association of America, (Rockville: 1997).
10. H.B. Beckman, et al., "The Doctor Patient Relationship and Malpractice," *Archives of Internal Medicine* 154 (1994): 1365–1370.
11. R.S. Shapiro, et al., "A Survey of Sued and Nonsued Physicians and Suing Patients," *Archives of Internal Medicine* 149 (1989): 2190–2196.
12. C. Vincent, et al., "Why Do People Sue Doctors? A Study of Patients and Relatives Taking Legal Action," *Lancet* 343 (1994): 1609–1613.

13. G.B. Hickson et al., "Factors That Prompted Families to File Medical Malpractice Claims Following Perinatal Injuries," *Journal of the American Medical Association* 276, no. 10 (1992):1359–1363.
14. R.S. Shapiro, et al., "A Survey of Sued and Nonsued Physicians," *Archives of Internal Medicine* 149 (1989): 2190–2196.
15. G.W. Lester and S.G. Smith, "Listening and Talking to Patients: A Remedy for Malpractice Suits," *Western Journal of Medicine* 158 (1 March 1993): 268–272.
16. M. Balint, *The Doctor, His Patient and the Illness* (New York: International University Press, 1964).
17. M. Stuart and J.A. Lieberman, *The Fifteen Minute Hour Applied Psychotherapy for the Primary Care Physician*, (Westport: Prager, 1986). This book is a wonderfully simple primer for learning basic counseling skills for primary care physicians. It was written by a practicing psychologist and a seasoned family physician.
18. R.C. Smith and R.B. Hoppe, "The Patients Story: Integrating the Patient and Physician Centered Approaches to Interviewing," *Annals of Internal Medicine 115* (1991): 470–477.
19. Smith and Hoppe, "The Patients Story," 470.
20. Smith and Hoppe, "The Patients Story," 471.
21. Smith and Hoppe, "The Patients Story," 474.
22. D.L. Roter, et al., "Improving Physicians Interviewing Skills and Reducing Patients' Emotional Distress: A Randomized Clinical Trial," *Arch Int Med* (25 September 1995): 1884.
23. Roter, et al., *Arch Int Med*, 1884.
24. Lester and Smith,"Listening and Talking to Patients," 268.
25. Roter, et al., "Improving Physicians' Interviewing Skills," 270.
26. T.E. Adamson, J. Tschann, D. Gullion, and A. Oppenberg, "Physician Communication Skills and Malpractice Claims: A Complex Relationship," *The Western Journal of Medicine* 150.3 (March 1989): 356–360.
27. Adamson, et.al, "Physician Communication Skills and Malpractice Claims: A Complex Relationship," 360.
28. W. Levinson, "Physician-Patient Communication," *Journal of American Medical Association* 277.7 (1997): 553.
29. Levinson, "Physician-Patient Communication," 558.
30. Levinson, "Physician-Patient Communication," 558.
31. Levinson, "Physician-Patient Communication," 558.
32. M. Stewart, "Effective Physician Patient Communication and Health Outcomes: A Review," *Canadian Medical Association Journal* (1 May 1995): 152(9).
33. Stewart, "Effective Physician Patient Communication and Health Outcomes: A Review," 1424.
34. Stewart, "Effective Physician Patient Communication and Health Outcomes: A Review," 1424.
35. Stewart, "Effective Physician Patient Communication and Health Outcomes: A Review," 1424.
36. E. Rosenberg, et al., "Lessons for Clinicians from Physician Patient Communication," *Archives of Family Medicine* 6 (May/June 1997).

37. Rosenberg, et al., "Lessons for Clinicians from Physician Patient Communication," 280.
38. American Hospital Association, "Eye on Patients," (Internet presentation, available at http://www.amphi.com/eyeonpatients/charts.html).
39. American Hospital Association, "Eye on Patients."
40. American Hospital Association, "Eye on Patients."
41. S.A. Cole, "Reducing Malpractice Risk Through More Effective Communication," *The American Journal of Managed Care,* 3.4649.
42. D.L. Roter et al., "Improving Physicians Interviewing Skills and Reducing Patients' Emotional Distress: A Randomized Clinical Trial," *Archives of Internal Medicine* (25 September 1995): 1884.
43. Roter et al., "Improving Physicians Interviewing Skills and Reducing Patients' Emotional Distress: A Randomized Clinical Trial," 1883.

CHAPTER 7

Documentation: Not More, Better

"The horror of that moment," the King went on, "I shall never, never, forget!"
"You will, though," the Queen said, "if you don't make a memorandum of it."
Lewis Carroll, (Charles Lutwidge Dodgson) 1832 – 1898

INTRODUCTION

More is not better. The reasons for documentation have proliferated in managed care, which means that physicians need much better documentation, but not necessarily more. The old harangue of, "Document, document, document," has been replaced by "document right!" Quantity does not make up for quality.

In the managed care environment, all the reasons for having good documentation simply increase. All the problems associated with not having good documentation intensify. It may be a good time to relook at some of the fundamentals of documentation and rethink the way in which we document the essential elements of patient care. Documentation has always played a big role in liability claims, both preventing them and helping to obtain a successful result when they do get to the courtroom. However, documentation also plays a key role with patient care and achieving greater levels of patient involvement.

There is little doubt that, at its most fundamental level, documentation can and does prevent malpractice claims. Almost all risk management consultants and continuing education sessions on risk management devote time to documentation. Such attention is appropriate. A well-documented chart is the physicians' shield protecting them from many allegations, including negligence. Plaintiff attorneys contemplating suit will send the physician an authorization with a cover letter requesting a copy of the patient's complete chart. They will then pore through the chart to see if it is consistent with what their potential client has said, before deciding whether or not to take their case. Many have staff members in their offices trained in clinical matters, or sometimes even physicians, to review the chart and get their impressions of whether there is a viable claim for medical negligence. A cynical, but realistic, view is that if you look close enough at any chart you can find a misstatement, a note that may have been left out, a procedure that could have been described more accurately, a laboratory test that is not initialed. Many of these would not be the basis for malpractice litigation, but there could be some that could be construed to have the causation necessary to a malpractice claim. Perhaps the laboratory report was not initialed and filed before the physician saw the result. Perhaps the patient was not even notified until the next visit, and was only then told of the elevated prothrombin time and that the coumadin needed to be adjusted. If nothing untoward happened to the patient, it could be argued that the failure to contact the patient caused no harm; therefore, the necessary causation element was not present, and as such, there cannot be a claim. If anything unforeseen did happen to your patient, the attorney might view your negligence as the cause. The point, however, is that your chart is the starting point at which a plaintiff's attorney gets involved and could help determine the decision as to whether or not the claim goes forward.

DOCUMENTATION BASICS—DIFFERENT IN MANAGED CARE

Documentation needs to be considered differently in a managed care environment. Responsibilities to patients are different. The physician has new responsibilities to a third party, the managed care organization. Patients are being seen under different circumstances, perhaps by a different level of provider, but still under the aegis of a physician. We believe that the documentation does not need to be more extensive, or longer, in most practices, but it does need to be more specific, more focused, and better organized. Documentation is far more than the medical record: it is every recorded interchange between you and your patient. It begins with the information, or advertisements, about your practice, disseminated by your managed care organization. These provide records, or documentation, to your patients of representations made to them by you or in your behalf. These are important documents to review carefully, since in some court cases these representations are portrayed as promises. When the promise is unmet a breach of contract claim could ensue.

Documentation also includes every recorded communication between your patient and you. It can be designed to achieve greater levels of education and patient involvement, especially important in the managed care environment. Documentation in the way of checklists can create systems for you and other members of the health care team, to simplify the process and allow your patients to move through your system in a more efficient fashion. Documentation by way of protocols can be used to make sure that the receptionist follows a certain telephone pattern. Documentation of past history and future plans can be used as a care map, and then as verification that these plans have been accomplished for the patient.

Preprinted, yet tailored, forms can be used for informed consent, pre-op and post-op instructions, rehabilitation, preventive care services, healthy habits instructions, appropriate use of medications, pre- and post-procedure instructions for diagnostic procedures, explanation of the importance of following through on laboratory and other diagnostic tests, safety issues, and even ongoing instructions on how to work most effectively with your office staff in a managed care environment. Documentation needs to be considered in a broader context in a managed care environment. One of the goals in managed care is to increase patient involvement. To do this, you need to inform patients in a manner that they can understand, and these efforts also need to be documented.

As the health care system has evolved, clarity of documentation has become even more essential. No longer are most physicians practicing alone, or in a small group where shortcut methods of documentation were commonplace, yet understood. As groups have merged together or multispecialty groups have formed and networks developed, many members of the health care team will be relying on your documentation.

DOCUMENTATION BASICS

Even though the needs for documentation are different in managed care, the basic principles still apply, and their importance is actually amplified. There are three basic principles: documentation should be complete, clear and concise, and appropriate.

Completeness

The patient's medical record is the net by which all patient care can be caught and noted and, if necessary, will verify the good care that was provided by the physician. Of course the greater importance of documentation is not preventing malpractice claims, but in providing information that a physician, or any other member of the health care team, can use in ongoing care. It is critical to good patient care. The record must be concise, or it will not be read. It must be complete or it will be of little use for either of its major purposes.

The medical record, at a minimum, includes the basic demographic and insurance data, past history, family history, lifestyle, allergies, present illness, and recorded physical examination. In primary care it should also include a history of preventive procedures.

The real problem for most practitioners is in writing the current notes. Most use the SOAP method, as originated by Weed.[1] This system, used correctly, has the structure needed to avoid important omissions. When keyed to the Problem List, it simplifies the task of following a particular problem. The Problem List is a chronological, numbered listing of all of a patient's continuing health or health-related problems. It serves both as a summary of health concerns and as an index to the medical record. This is especially important in primary care, where patients, typically, have many disparate problems that the same practitioner is following. SOAP stands for the following:

- S (subjective): symptoms can be listed, along with their essential characteristics. There is no need for complete sentences or correct punctuation. Relevant negatives should also be listed;
- O (objective): list the body parts examined and describe only the positive findings;
- A (assessment): your impressions, or tentative diagnoses;
- P (plan): actions you will take, or recommend to the patient. Patient education is usually included here.

Example:

S: List symptoms: headache
• characteristics: occipital
• onset: struck by leg of lamb
• etiology: irate husband
• circumstances: patient found in bed with neighbor's wife
• additional relative information: neighbor's husband 6 foot, 250-pound butcher
• avoid irrelevant information: wife, blue-eyed blond
• include relevant negatives: wife says she is HIV negative.

O: Parts examined: head—occipital ecchymosis
• neurological: negative
• psychological: negative.

A: (This is a crucial area and one for which physicians are often attacked in court. The assessment should be a logical impression, or group of impressions, based on the findings thus far.) In this case:
• contusion
• concussion
• rule out fractured skull, intracranial hemorrhage
• unresolved domestic problem
• avoid pejorative comments: stupidity.

P: (The plan should be a logical set of steps to address the assessment. It should include both immediate and long range plans.)

- head trauma instructions
- CAT scan if symptoms persist or increase
- neurological consult if CAT scan positive
- schedule family conference
- advise legal consult
- consider SDT testing
- call tomorrow
- avoid inappropriate plans: discussion of nutritional value of lamb; advice that lamb may be hazardous to your health.

The SOAP note does take time and thought, but it expresses in writing the essence of the encounter, culminating in the plan. The Plan presents your thoughts, exactly what the patient is seeking, your only real "stock in trade;" that is, what you are being paid for. Your thoughts, ideas, and considerations can be jotted down in a few words: to keep them to yourself is unfair to your patient and your colleagues.

Clarity

The second basic principle of documentation is that it must be clear. This has always been important in medical care, but has now become absolutely essential. Physicians no longer practice in the relative isolation that used to characterize solo or small group practices, where the principal reason for documentation was communication with one's self or a few colleagues. Now even solo physicians are responsible for supplying information to multiple third parties. Plaintiff attorneys are pursuing any questionable medical action even more aggressively, and patients know they have a right to a copy of their own records. Often attorneys have been heard to request, "you are going to need to read these notes into the record; it's typical doctor's difficult handwriting." Doctors have even commented, "this was the way we were taught to write in medical school" in a sarcastic tone. Or before the deposition, "Well, if you can't read it, it makes it a lot easier for me to explain what it means!" Such comments may be hazardous to your success in court.

To dispel any potential misunderstanding, clear documentation is essential. There is no advantage to being evasive in your documentation. You may need to explain yourself in the unfriendly atmosphere of a courtroom. Nurses at times are unable to interpret orders or do so in an incorrect fashion because the handwriting could not be deciphered. Doctors give several plausible explanations for this. They are too busy, therefore their handwriting suffers. Or they honestly believe that other caregivers should learn to read their handwriting. Neither explanation is sustainable. A note that cannot be read is dangerous. It is not a health care time-saver since the nurses often have to pore over the handwriting, ask each other to help decipher, or page the doctor for clarification. On balance, it does not save time. One can no longer expect that other caregivers will recognize your writing.

In a recent case involving a general internist, who was alleged to have misdiagnosed a myocardial infarction, which led to a patient's death, the doctor was being questioned extensively about his office notes and the chart generally. The plaintiffs' attorney noticed in the chart that there were several old records, and he asked the doctor what these were and why they were included in his chart. The doctor carefully explained that it was the practice in their office to obtain prior records from patients for whom they were going to provide ongoing comprehensive care. He spent time explaining how important prior history can be as well as symptoms that were reported to doctors over the years and how it can help them understand the patient better. He went on to explain that this particular patient, who was elderly, like many in his practice, was not a good historian, and therefore the records became even more important because they painted a more accurate picture about the prior medical history. After this thorough explanation about the importance of these prior records, he was asked to read some of them that seemed pertinent into the court record. Unfortunately, the physician was only able to pick out a few words and phrases, but could not read the entire record and could not even glean what was done by some of the notes. The doctor realized, too late, that lack of clear documentation, especially after his thorough explanation, may have cost him the lawsuit. If he could not read the information when he received it, and such information is important, the plaintiff's attorney argued, why did he not try to find out what was written?

The use of dictation or the electronic record are excellent remedies when feasible, but in lieu of these, the first step is to break bad habits of poorly written notes. The amount of time that it takes to be clear in actuality is moments (see Figure 7–1). Setting aside patient care for a moment, although recognizing its paramount importance, in a litigation context, clear handwriting is also essential. Many plaintiffs' attorneys use indecipherable writing to their advantage. The note will be greatly enlarged and placed prominently in front of the jury. The explanation may be given by the plaintiff's attorney that the nurse or another caregiver could not decipher your note. You will be asked on the stand why you did not take the time to write more clearly. A facetious response that this is just "physician's handwriting" will not be accepted. The explanation that you are "too busy" will not be accepted when, in retrospect, the lack of a clear note allegedly caused harm to the patient. Jurors are angered by the explanation of health care providers that they are "too busy." Jurors perceive physicians as high income earners and thus the claim that they are "just too busy" is equated by the plaintiff's attorney as the physician's desire to see more patients and earn more money. In a managed

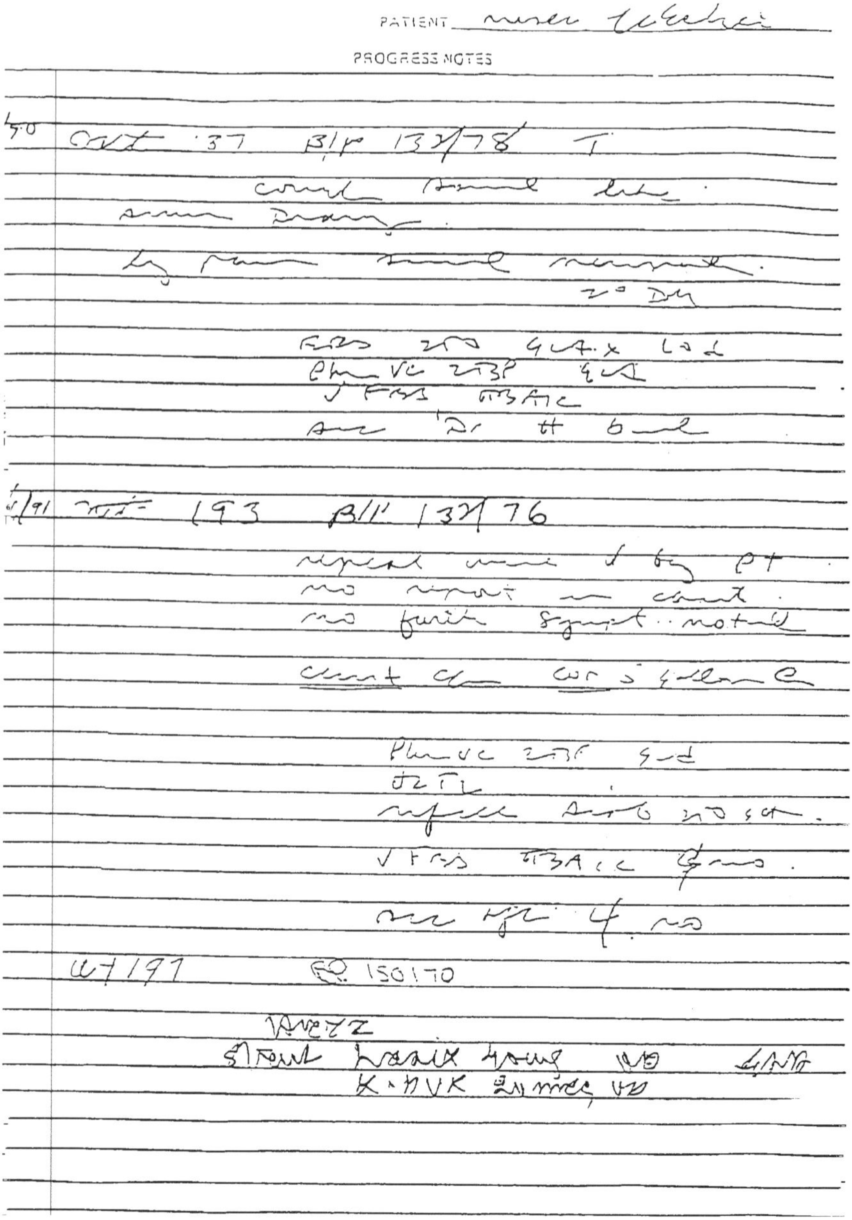
PATIENT

PROGRESS NOTES

Figure 7–1

care setting, of course, this all begins to fit together for the plaintiff's lawyer. If the physician is in a capitated system the only way to increase income is to increase the number of "covered lives." So what if a little less time is spent with each patient, so what if the writing is a little more hurried, argues the plaintiff's attorney.

A 1996 British study attempted to answer the question as to whether doctors do have worse handwriting than other professionals.[2] The investigators, Berwick and Winickoff, analyzed the handwriting of 208 professionals, 82 of whom were physicians. They found that the handwriting of physicians, in general, was no worse than that of other professionals. They concluded, however, that poor handwriting by physicians is much riskier than for non-physicians. Mediocre writing in medical circumstances may not be acceptable.

Therefore, at the most basic and fundamental level, documentation must be understandable. On balance, the time it takes to be clear is not significant. Being clear also means being concise; extraneous comments can be distracting and confusing. Busy people tend to scan or ignore long commentaries. It is not necessary to write long explanations, or even to use complete, grammatically correct sentences, when short descriptive phrases will do.

Appropriateness

The third, and easiest basic principle of documentation, is to keep it appropriate. Any information about a patient may be appropriate if one condition can be met: "Will I feel OK about sharing this information with my patient?" This means, of course, being quite careful to avoid any pejorative comment or any comment that could easily be interpreted by the patient as pejorative.

It is also important not to editorialize in your notes, always keeping in mind that your patient has an absolute right to the information in the record—all of it. One physician was very disappointed when a favorite patient moved to another geographical area and asked to have her records transferred. However, the patient's extended family were still located nearby and were under his care. The family was a large one and since the doctor was a primary care physician he saw many of her brothers and sisters and their children, and his former patient's parents. One day, shortly after the move and the transfer of copies of his patients records, he received a series of angry notes and requests to transfer all of the records from every one of the relatives. He was dumbfounded, but when he reviewed his notes in the patient's records, he understood. Several times he described the patient as a "whiner." In one place, probably in frustration since the patient was a challenging one, he had a notation that said, "patient comes in and again feels she has the problems of the world on her shoulders." He really did not understand why he had done this since she was a patient who did have multiple problems, many related to the stresses she was experiencing at different times in her life. He was quite embarrassed when he realized what happened. The patient must have shared her anger with all of her family. What made him feel worst was not only the loss of these longtime patients, which was bad enough, but the feeling that he had really hurt his patient deeply. All that is needed is clear, concise, to the point, objective notes. The chart is not the vehicle for venting one's feelings of the moment.

Sticky Documentation

There is another sticky area in documentation. How do we record information that a patient does not want recorded. What if the man who was hit on the head were your partner? Or the butcher's wife were your partner? The answer to this enigma lies in negotiation with the patient. It is probably a mistake to record any information that the patient expressly does not want recorded if you are able to do so within the limits of good medical practice and, of course, the law (e.g., admission of a felony, suspicion of domestic violence). If, for example, you believe your patient is addicted to pain medication, you will need to record that information for the benefit of other health professionals who may treat that patient in the future. Explain to your patient the reasoning for your opinion and the reasoning for recording it. If the patient objects, you must still record it of course, but be sure to document it very carefully.

Your male partner with the lamb problem might be content with the record entry, "struck on the head from behind by a blunt object." This begs the question of potential family, personal, and legal problems, but these are clearly between you and your patient at this point. If your partner's blond friend, perhaps also a partner, comes to you for counseling, she might accept your note, "concerned about domestic violence."

While physicians would like to assume that their records are non-violable, as they might have been in a solo practice, they are not now. They are almost quasi-public, because of the number of people who need to see them. This means that any "sticky" chart entry should first be discussed with your patient/partner, except in unusual circumstances.

INTRODUCTION INTO YOUR PRACTICE—THE BROCHURE

Since documentation includes all aspects of a patient's encounter with you, it may be helpful to walk in the patient's pathway through your system and examine each of the interfaces.

No matter what kind of a practice you have, patients want more information about you initially; an introductory brochure can accomplish this for you. If you do not have some type of practice brochure, you should develop one. It is the beginning of your documentation. Beyond the real value it is to patients, it is the beginning of malpractice prevention. It establishes the ground rules, the extent and limits of your practice, your availability and coverage, and what you expect from patients. The major emphasis throughout your brochure should be on partnering, letting patients know that you welcome them as your partner in their own health care. You want them to be involved in all the decisions that must be made. You want them to know that, as partners, they have easy access to the various components of your health care system.

The brochure should help your patients understand more about your practice, how best to help you take care of them, how to interact with your staff. If your group is small enough, it will help them learn to know you as a person. In the brochure you might tell about yourselves, your background and training, what your specialty entails, and also introduce other members of the health care team. This is an important place to put information about your advanced practice providers: both the importance and description of their roles. It is also an opportunity for you to explain any initial instructions such as the need to bring medication lists, medications currently in use, and any old records or x-rays to their first visit. Ideally this request could be sent to them prior to their first visit so they can be prepared and get the most out of that visit. It is frustrating for patients to get to the physician's office only to find that they needed to request prior medical records, laboratory tests, x-rays, a list of medications, or need to fill out a lengthy health history that they may or may not have time to do while waiting for their appointment. Your brochure or an introductory letter could provide all of this information.

The patient should be told how your practice works and how the system can help them, in a very positive and informative way. There can be an explanation of how you try to stay on time but why, at times, the schedule runs late including an explanation of how emergency patient visits receive first priority, and that the schedule may, for a short period of time, be delayed. For the pediatrician's office there can be an explanation of when well-child visits are held and when sick visits are held, or special telephone hours. Your on-call schedule or after hours numbers can be highlighted. Your particular billing practices should be reviewed and a telephone number provided for any billing questions. The responsibility for following through with instructions and scheduled diagnostic tests should also be discussed. All of this simply adds to the information base for your patient.

In some specialty offices it may be important to give an explanation of certain terms, phrases, or diagnostic tests that are regularly employed. This adds to the patients' knowledge base, so that when you discuss it for the first time they will understand it more readily. This type of informational brochure can turn out to be a time-saver and make patient visits a little more understandable for the patient and easier for the provider.

Endodontistry is an example of a specialty that has done this quite effectively. There is a very small number of different procedures performed that constitute the great majority of the work of the endodontist. These are described in simple terms with colorful, non-threatening pictures. This is very effective in countering the popular fear of having a root canal procedure.

The brochure can also be an instrument to help your patient understand the meaning of the term, "managed care," one of the most important current challenges to the health industry.[3] Patients do not necessarily want their care managed. Perhaps this is because of the unfortunate image of untrustworthiness that has arisen about managed care. Since some form of managing health care is here to stay, and since many of the negative images are no longer accurate, a new image needs to be created. Remember, the image of the managed care organization may become your image of the future. From a liability point of view, it is often the physician who is sued when a problem occurs. Any hostility that is directed toward a managed care organization is almost always directed to the physician as well. You need to paint a different picture, and this picture can be initiated in your brochure.

THE HISTORY FORM

Most of the essential background data can be captured using a set of forms. Demographic data, past history, family history, allergies, lifestyle, preventive procedures, current medications, and history of the present illness, can most easily and completely be recorded in this way. Most patients can complete these forms themselves, if they are constructed in lucid, plain language. Those who have difficulty with the language used, or who have reading or perceptual problems may need the assistance of a staff member. Of course the physician will want to review these forms and ask additional questions, but this information can easily be written legibly on the forms. The use of such forms helps to assure that no essentials are overlooked. They also capture the information in an organized and standardized way, providing for easy communication within the team and to consultants. Equally important is the fact that these forms provide patients this initial means of becoming directly involved in their own health care. The use of such forms fulfills the requirements for concise but complete documentation for this kind of information.

You may also wish to send the patient forms to be completed, such as a comprehensive health history. It should be explained very specifically how important it is to fill those documents out thoroughly and accurately. We recommend adding a statement such as, "The following information is very important to us in understanding your health and in treating any medical condition you may have. Please complete this form fully and accurately." This should be placed prominently at the beginning of the history form. At the end of the form there should be some verifying language. This simply means a statement such as, "The above information is true and correct to the best of my belief." If patients sign this, they will have indicated that they understand that you are relying on this information and it would be hard for them to disavow this understanding, in the event that it becomes important later, in a litigation context. More importantly, from a patient care standpoint, it may cause them to pause and reconsider some of the information they have provided since they are now "verifying its correctness." There are many lawsuits in which patients, in retrospect, indicate that they either were not asked certain information or were led to believe that the medical history was not that important.

In a recent case in which a patient had breast cancer there was a question about the family history of breast cancer. The patient adamantly stated that yes, she tried to fill out the comprehensive health questionnaire with information about cancer in her family but had to do so hurriedly in the reception area since her name was called for her visit. She had the health questionnaire on her lap and was frantically trying to answer all the questions. She simply ran out of time and failed to complete it. No one ever said anything to her about it; even though she sat in that same waiting room on many occasions for subsequent visits, and she never thought of asking for the form again. Had anyone checked to see whether she had completed the form? Had anyone reviewed the form with her? To those questions posed by the plaintiff's attorney, the answer was, "no." The plaintiff's attorney then asked the doctor whether he noticed that the bottom third of the form was not filled out, or if there was any follow-up or system to make sure this information was obtained. The doctor simply indicated that during the first visit he asked the patient for a family history of cancer and, "to his recollection," there was none. Of course this all took place six years previously and the plaintiff denied this conversation. Doctors do not do well during these so-called swearing contests, the plaintiff's word against the doctor's word, in the courtroom. Jurors tend to think that important information will be documented in the chart. Plaintiffs' attorneys can often get admissions from the doctor to support that conclusion during cross examination.

THE MEDICAL RECORD

One good system for medical records is the Milcom® Record System by Hollister, Inc.[4] These forms are readable and easy to follow, and are available in several languages. They are well-organized and there are forms for most situations, including both child and adult health maintenance recommendations and schedules. They have been widely accepted nationally, enhancing ease of transferring information to consultants or when a patient moves. Especially important, from a malpractice prevention standpoint, most of these forms have been officially approved, or met the criteria of the appropriate academic specialty organization.

In a managed care setting, the history and health screening forms take on new meaning. In the case of primary care physicians, who are in the gatekeeping role (we prefer the term "coordinator" or "shepherd"), they are, in fact, the coordinators of care. As managed care evolves and matures, this coordination will become more important than ever. Managing health includes promoting preventive services and healthy lifestyle habits. It is becoming important economically to focus more on preventing acute flare-ups from chronic diseases or injuries in the first place, and then managing these ailments in an effective fashion. To do this, there must be enough information initially from the patient and then ongoing updates.

In a specialty office, such as orthopedics, obtaining the patient's history of presenting symptoms, for example a low back problem, is important to the surgeon's decision as to whether or not to use medical therapy or more aggressive surgical treatment. Have all non-operative modalities been exhausted, do the patient's symptoms warrant surgical intervention, was the patient given all of the options, did the patient understand the options and alternatives? These are all questions that are posed in retrospect by the plaintiff's attorney when the result from surgery is not as anticipated. Much of this can be covered in documentation with a history form tailored to an orthopedic practice. The document should be thorough, simple, and make it clear that it is the patient's responsibility both to complete the initial form and any requested updates.

IN YOUR OFFICE

Typically, a doctor's reception area has many different kinds of documentation, in the form of notices, signs, and bulletin boards. They are all non-traditional ways to document information you have provided to the patient. They are effective and, in some areas, essential. If you use radiology within your office, you need to have a sign prominently displayed alerting the patient to "tell us if you could be pregnant." Even though the radiology technician has a practice or protocol for asking patients this question, there should also be a sign. Many offices have a short form documenting that the question was asked and the response was "no." Another sign frequently used is a notice, required by certain state or federal laws, as to whether this practice group has an investment interest in a certain diagnostic facility to which patients may be referred.[5] Often there are also signs or certificates identifying the participating providers.

A simple sign in the reception area indicating "Let us know if you have waited 15 minutes" can serve as a pressure release for patients. Patients get to stand up, walk to the receptionist, and have an interaction with someone who can politely apologize for the tardiness and explain why they have not been seen promptly. Perhaps patients can be given a pager so they can run a quick errand, depending on the location of the practice, or they can be offered use of the phone to rejuggle their schedules if necessary. It makes patients feel that you do value their time.

Many offices, particularly in primary care and in orthopedics in which sports medicine is featured, have patient bulletin boards. Here, although being careful to protect confidentiality, they display articles about patients, accomplishments in school activities, and other important patient information. They post announcements about upcoming educational programs in which the physicians are involved. They add articles from newspapers about the physicians or advanced practice providers. Patients have some down time in the reception area, and it is a wonderful way for them to learn a more about your practice, your doctors or staff, or an important health issue. One comment about your practice bulletin board: it has to become someone's responsibility to keep it up to date and organized. You need to make it someone's job. There is nothing worse than a bulletin board that is out of date, beginning to look out of shape, or messy. It creates a negative image instead of a positive one.

Videotapes, audiotapes, health information, and practice brochures are often made available in the reception area. This is also a form of documentation. Some offices have even set up an area where there is a VCR and a set of tapes with instructional material that can be used either before or after the office visit. For example, there might be updates about hormonal therapy in an obstetrician/gynecologist's office, new medications for various skin disorders in the dermatologist's office, new types of surgery in the ophthalmologist's office, certain cosmetic procedures in the plastic surgeon's or dentist's office, a tape about the importance of wearing a helmet for bicycle riding and other safety issues in the pediatrician's office. Many tapes can be acquired through commercial enterprises or through professional associations. The same can be done with audiotapes, easily accomplished by using small cassette tape players with earphones. Of course, contemporary magazines or pleasure reading should also be available in the reception area, but if the educational information is on topics of interest, many patients will gravitate toward it. These extra services could be described in your practice brochure. All of this is viewing the patient's trip to your office as an entire experience.

There should also be a place in your office where the various diplomas and certificates are displayed, not only of your physicians but all members of the health care team. This is impressive to patients and also reassuring. As with all of these various forms of documentation, it is important that they be presented in an organized fashion.

THE CHART

The most important part of the overall documentation, of course, is the patient's chart. Remember that patients tend to have great expectations of their records and that they have a right to the information contained within their chart. They do not have a right to the original chart, which should not leave your possession. If the chart is being requested for transfer of care purposes, it is prudent to send the chart to the physician who is assuming care and not simply give the records to the patient directly. You certainly do not want patients to get the idea that, for one reason or another, you do not want them seeing "their chart." They may become quite suspicious. I often advise physicians to explain that it is their practice to provide it directly to the next physician, together with introductory letters recapping some of the patient's ongoing needs. When patients push, I suggest the doctor explain that it is better for them to sit down with their new doctor to review their chart with them rather than simply look at it on their own. Often there will be terms or phrases used that may be misunderstood and that you would not want misinformation to be given in that respect. An important point to remember is that information within the chart is, in fact, the patient's, and that if requested, providing a copy is mandatory.

ORGANIZATION

The way in which a chart is organized is important in meeting each of its purposes. The traditional purpose of an office chart is to collect all of the essential information for the doctor's use in ongoing care, and for the use of partners. Essential data was usually extracted and summarized for the information of consultants. Those are still the principal purposes, the ones that most affect patient care.

Now, with managed care, the uses of the chart, and the need for clarity and completeness, are magnified. There are likely to be many other members of the health care team who will need to use the chart, for information, and to add their own findings and viewpoints. Your managed care organization has a responsibility to audit the chart on a regular basis for comprehensiveness and quality of care. While this could be interpreted as an additional burden, it actually is one of the benefits of being part of a managed care organization, for both your patient and you. It may help insure that nothing important is overlooked; it may add the clinical opinion of other physicians; it helps to assure you that the work of all the other members of your health care team is also being monitored; and it provides you with great malpractice prevention. The chart is also an absolute necessity for reimbursement purposes, also to your distinct advantage.

If you choose an established system, such as the Milcom Record System referred to earlier, most of the organizational requirements will be in place automatically, and it has the advantage of widespread use and standardization. This is especially valuable when the record will be used by many members of the health care team, and portions will be copied for consultants.

In addition to a well-organized chart, it is essential to have a system in place to minimize errors and omissions. There is also a need for a method to assure that any required chart review is accomplished and documented. There should also be a carefully monitored system to be certain that no test results are filed before being reviewed and addressed by a physician, and that this process is documented. Failure to address abnormal laboratory or imaging findings continues to be a significant source of malpractice litigation.

These systems do require time and effort to establish, but it is no exaggeration to say that a patient's life, or your professional career, could depend on it.

Another system in use in many practices is automatic tracking. This technique has been used successfully by dentists for many years, to remind patients of maintenance visits. The needs are much more complex in a primary care or specialty practice with needs for screening procedures, testing, and immunizations varying in different age groups and in different risk categories. This can be managed quite well with appropriate software, however. A description of how to choose a computer program, where it may be purchased, and how to use it, was published by Bruce Block, MD, in the October 1996 issue of *Family Practice Management*.[6] He promises that "a carefully chosen system and well-planned installation and transition will increase the effectiveness and competitiveness of your practice, and most important, the well being of your patients, within one year."[7]

Consider the format of your notes. We recommend the SOAP note, as described earlier, for almost all medical practices, along with the index to these notes, the Problem List. We also suggest the use of an ongoing medication list, which can be updated at each visit, if appropriate.

CONSENT FORMS

Consent forms will be discussed in detail in the following chapter. The informed consent form is a way to document the level of information that was given to the patient so as to meet the informed consent requirements of your particular jurisdiction. The informed consent form can present an opportunity for coordinating all the various forms of documentation that your office provides, but perhaps has never really brought together. For example, the informed consent form can note the fact that the patient has been given an introductory brochure, a history questionnaire, a pre-op and the post-op instruction sheet, as well as a procedure brochure. All of these documents are in frequent use, but often their use has not been recorded. Although certainly not required by any jurisidiction's informed consent law, adding this information to your consent form can provide a good check on your system.

Sometimes there is a misperception that informed consent is for the operating room or just for surgeons. In the new health care environment, informed consent may need to be obtained in the home health setting or even in cyberspace, depending on what actions are being taken. It may need to be obtained by a nurse or an advanced practice provider if they are performing the type of treatment requiring consent in their jurisdiction. The legal technicalities of under what circumstances to obtain informed consent have begun to change, and are becoming more stringent. Informed consent should become a patient education, patient focused documentation process that adds to the fund of knowledge that your patient has, and serves as a check on your various office practices. Used in this way, it is a major advancement in malpractice claim prevention.

TELEPHONE TRIAGE

Telephonic communication, or telemedicine, has a major and growing role in the health care environment. It is an essential component, not only at the sophisticated level of providing telephonic consultations with academic centers, but also at the level of everyone's practice. Receptionists, nurses, and advanced practice providers are all expected to assume greater responsibilities and many of those responsibilities will, of necessity, be over the telephone.

Since physicians are responsible for what people say on their behalf, they will want to establish some guidelines and rules. These rules, in telephone triage, can be protocols, and these protocols constitute another form of documentation. First, there should be a protocol concerning the course that should be taken when a patient calls and speaks with a staff member about a particular clinical problem. That individual should have a list or some set questions to ask the caller. Enough clinical information needs to be obtained so that a determination can be made whether an emergency visit to the office should be scheduled, a trip to the emergency department, or a visit scheduled within the normal course, or whether another level of the staff should be contacted to take the call. Does a medication need to be prescribed, and can that be accomplished without a patient visit? If a referral needs to be made, does the patient need to make a visit to the primary care office first? Can the primary care visit be avoided by satisfying a list of clinical questions according to the various protocols and requirements of the managed care organization?

Many organizations are beginning to allow direct referrals to consultants under certain situations. Primary care physicians should be encouraged to work with the consultants to develop joint protocols on what circumstances will permit a direct referral. This is an effort to begin to streamline the encounter with the patient and make it as efficient as possible for the patient as well as for the providers. Patients get frustrated when they are seen in a primary care office and have a determination made that they need to go for diagnostic tests. But because a referral to a consultant is appropriate, the patient has to see the consultant, who agrees that diagnostic tests need to be made. After the test is accomplished, the patient has to set up another visit with the consultant to have the treatment regime initiated. This sounds like a nonsensical sequence but it is still occurring in many settings! A system, based on joint protocols, determined by primary care physicians and consultants, can be established, which will eliminate much of this redundancy and keep patients much happier.

Telephone triage is also important from a documentation standpoint since it is critical to record that interaction with the patient. The patient is providing clinical information upon which the receiver of the information will make certain decisions. Even when written protocols are being followed, the correctness of those actions will depend on the information received. Therefore, a system has to be set up whereby the clinical information provided by the patient is clearly documented by the receiver of the information, and the instructions to the patient are also documented. Although this sounds self evident, it is often not occurring and is the source of much litigation. In other words, you create a snapshot with your documentation so that someone who is evaluating your actions several years later, can see a true picture as to why certain actions were taken.

Documenting a telephone call is not only important for staff, but for all members of the health care team, and especially for the physicians. Even when the physician is on call at home, a documentation pad should be readily available so that a note can be made to be placed in the chart later. Many offices have a central dictation system so that after a telephone call, whether it is in the car, at home, or at any other location, the physician can quickly call the central dictation unit and document the call. Again, create a snapshot so that later, if your decisions are being judged, they can be seen in an accurate fashion. In a managed care environment where patients and their attorneys may jump to the wrong conclusion as to why the test or visit wasn't offered, or a referral not made, these snapshots are essential.

INFORMED REFUSAL

Another source of litigation is noncooperation with physician recommendations. This is also a critical area for documentation, and in many ways is similar to informed consent. If the doctor is giving advice and the patient is refusing to follow, it is prudent to have the patient sign an informed refusal form. The purpose of this document is to show that patients received clear information from you as to why you are advising a certain course of action. You have given them the risks associated with that course and the alternatives, and you have told them the implications of not following through. They have achieved an appropriate level of understanding, and they have made an informed decision *not* to follow through with your advice. The patient needs to know that they are accepting responsibility for the consequences. A simple form can be created such as in Exhibit 7–1. This is important not only from a documentation standpoint but from a patient care standpoint. Often patients (or their family members) do not realize the seriousness of your recommendation until they see it in writing. Further, if they see that they are accepting responsibility for their actions, a central theme in the managed care environment, they often think twice. Failure to go through this process may expose you to a claim that you did not completely explain the significance of their decision or choice. Defense lawyers' filing cabinets are filled with cases in which patients or family members, in retrospect, say that their doctor downplayed the necessity for a certain procedure or test. This is clearly an area in which physicians need more protection, and this can be accomplished through appropriate documentation. This is especially true in a managed care environment where the family may jump faster to the conclusion that the reason you downplayed the need for the test is because of some incentive which would accrue to your benefit.

CLINICAL PATHWAYS

The new managed care environment is strewn with clinical pathways, protocols, and guidelines. In 1996, there were nearly 1,800 clinical protocols issued by 75 national groups and many were being developed by individual hospitals and clinicians.[8] In fact, an association has been developed to track and organize these various pathways. These pathways are being developed to manage the care of patients with certain diseases or injuries, and they can also add an additional level of documentation. The printed pathway itself is a form of documentation, describing recommendations of how a certain disease should be treated. Presumably these are based on research and outcome data and are developed as a collaborative effort to determine how to treat a certain disease more effectively, achieving better outcomes, being conscious of the use of resources and patient satisfaction. However, there are concerns about how they are used and about how their use is documented.

In any pathway, protocol, or guideline there should first be a clear statement of its intended use. Is the physician expected to follow these defined steps, or use personal clinical judgment, regarding these steps as suggestions? In a recent telephone interview, Kathleen M. Roman, Director of Risk Management at the Medical Protective Company, a national professional liability insurer, voiced her concern about clinical pathways and how, at times, they are used against physi-

Exhibit 7–1 Informed Refusal

I, I. M. Stubborn, have been told by Dr. Try-So-Hard of the need for ______________________________.

The doctor has explained to me the basis for the recommendation and why the treatment is important to me. These include, but are not limited to, ______________________________ . My doctor has also explained to me the risks associated with not having this medical treatment. These risks include, but are not limited to, ______________________________ .

I understand that I have the right to make judgments about the medical treatment and care which is rendered to me. I am taking responsibility for this decision and understand that it is contrary to the best judgment of my physician.

I am acknowledging by my signature below that I have had a full explanation of the reason for the treatment recommendation, what would be accomplished by accepting the treatment option and the risks associated with failing to accept my doctor's recommendation. Having all this information available to me as well as having all of my questions answered, I am making the decision to refuse the medical treatment recommended.

I have carefully read this form ❏.

I understand this form ❏.

All of my questions have been answered ❏.

______________________ ______________________

Date Signature of Patient

______________________ ______________________

Date Signature of Witness

*This is an example of a format. The text would have to be changed to reflect the specific facts in your case. State law should be reviewed.

cians. She urged that a new type of nomenclature be accepted for these pathways. "Couldn't they be viewed as 'considerations,' providing the doctor with guidance and making it very clear that these were not strict directions for care?" she asked. This concept has merit because physicians may get caught in the trap of not following a "clinical pathway" when it does not fit the clinical situation, in the doctor's judgment. Pathways were never meant to be the standard of care but are meant to offer guidance. Often plaintiffs' attorneys, however, have been able to capitalize on the physician's decision not to follow them rigidly. Unfortunately, demonstration projects utilizing practice guidelines as an affirmative have not yielded overly positive results. A recent study showed that clinical guidelines were more often used by plaintiffs as inculpatory evidence than defendants as exculpatory evidence.[9] This does not mean that there is not promise in this area, only that one has to be careful in how these guidelines or protocols are used, and how their purpose and use is documented.

Risk management assessments of proposed pathways should be made by someone well versed in risk issues, who can determine which points in the decision tree may be critical from a liability standpoint. Those are the areas in which it is most urgent to have clear documentation as to why the decision was made.

There are increasing efforts to manage diseases differently, and the standard of care may be in a state of flux. This makes documentation of treatment decisions in these critical clinical decisions essential. The important point is to look at the protocols with an eye toward determining where documentation will become key, and then noting that part of the decision tree as "documentation imperative."

DOCUMENTATION AND ADVANCED PRACTICE PROVIDERS

Advanced practice providers are becoming increasingly important in the new health care systems. They are regulated differently in various jurisdictions, generally by the state nursing board and/or the medical board. Authority as to who can practice medicine is often found in a particular state's medical practice act. Documentation is especially needed here since there are various requirements pursuant to these acts for both supervision and collaborative agreements. It is important for the practice to take great care in the hiring, credentialing, monitoring, and supervising of these advanced practice providers. Done appropriately, there is a great opportunity to enhance the practice by adding them to the health care team. However, failure to abide by the various statutes could result in medical negligence per se, if an untoward event were to occur. This means that negligence is assumed and need not be proven, since the statute on that point was violated and harm occurred. Close adherence to these regulatory provisions is essential.

Documentation here should include a check list as to your hiring, credentialing, monitoring, availability of supervision, and your collaboratory agreement.

Having a check list will not only help you in the event of litigation, and an assertion of corporate responsibility for failure to comply with appropriate credentialing, monitoring, or supervisory responsibilities, but it also acts as a good check on your system. These documents are not dissimilar to check lists that hospital medical staff offices use for credentialing purposes. If you are in the hospital setting, coordination with the human resources department will be both helpful and necessary.

WHERE TO START—IS YOUR DOCUMENTATION ADEQUATE?

A documentation system that was quite adequate in the past, even five years ago, may not be suitable now. A documentation check list, for use in an initial and periodic audit, is described in Chapter 9. As always, the essential component of this entire process is education: of the physicians, as to the new importance of documentation in a managed care environment; and of the staff, so they understand why it is important and so they have the tools they need to help you from a documentation standpoint. Without verification of the good care provided, the physician is constantly in a vulnerable position. Now it is more important than ever to document the level of care that you are providing. It has not only patient care implications but reimbursement, regulatory, credentialing, and risk management implications as well.

OTHER FORMS OF DOCUMENTATION

Other written information is created by your office that also needs to be added to the list of important documents.

Collection Letters

If a portion of your practice is fee-for-service, you will still have the problem of overdue accounts. Often nonpayment of a fee may be a request for additional information, a concern about the care that was provided, or a symptom of a new problem, or a financial crisis. Don't start an adversarial process until you first find out. Even if an agency is being used, the physician should maintain control of the situation so that some type of thoughtful process can take place prior to a patient being contacted for collection. An example of a well-balanced letter is presented in Exhibit 7–2.

Recall Letters

Recall systems are part of the managed care environment. Whether you are a primary care physician or a secondary or tertiary care specialist treating an injury

Exhibit 7–2 An Example of a Collection Letter

Mabel B. Jones
224 North Seventh Street
Gotham City, NY 10000

Dear Mrs. Jones:

We at Conscientious Family Practice take our responsibilities very seriously. We recognize that we have certain obligations to you and of course depend on your realizing that you have certain responsibilities in return to us. One of those responsibilities is payment for services. We note that you have an outstanding bill which has now existed for over 30 days. It might be that you have already sent a payment in and, if so, please disregard this letter and thank you.

We are also concerned that this may indicate that you have some unanswered questions about your care with us, or that you may be experiencing a personal crisis of which we are unaware. If so, please call us at once.

However, if payment has not been made, we would appreciate your doing so. If you need additional information or have any questions, please do not hesitate to contact us at 555-5555 and speak with Nancy Davis.

We look forward to hearing from you.

Conscientious Family Practice

*This is an example. The text would obviously depend on your particular situation.

or chronic illness, you will often need to remind patients of a follow-up appointment, a diagnostic test, or a yearly visit. Not only is it important to have a system in place under these circumstances, but also to have a properly drafted letter letting patients know that following up with your instructions about the visit or test is their responsibility and is important to their health. This is part of the process of letting patients know they are responsible in the managed care environment. These letters need to be firm but friendly. They need to provide enough information and make it very clear that the responsibility is theirs. The letters also need to talk about consequences and, most importantly, make it clear what the patient has been advised to do next.

Discharge Letters

Discharging a patient from the practice is always a difficult dilemma. In a managed care setting you need to look at the contractual arrangement that you have entered into and see what your responsibilities are when you find it necessary to discharge a patient. Involve the managed care organization and explain the circumstances. Patient discharge should always be a last resort. If you do have a situation where the patient needs to be discharged, the letter that you draft will be critical. Failing to discharge a patient appropriately could lead to a claim of abandonment which could justify punitive damages in many jurisdictions. Punitive damages usually are not covered by your professional liability insurance and therefore your personal assets may be exposed. It is recommended that you explain that you believe the discharge to be for the patient's benefit which, actually, it truly is. For whatever reason, you and the patient are not compatible. The patient may not be cooperating with your advice, may be disruptive with your staff, or may not be meeting his or her financial obligations. Under these circumstances it is very difficult to have a healing patient-physician relationship. Perhaps the patient will find another provider more compatible. Actually, patients who are discharged from a practice tend to behave better in the next practice. An example of what we call an anti-abandonment discharge letter is presented in Exhibit 7–3.

WHY DOES GOOD DOCUMENTATION WORK?

Managed care credentialing, and the potential of full disclosure of the information contained within the National Practitioners Data Bank, are making physicians wary. Physicians feel more strongly about the need to fight malpractice allegations instead of settling them out of court. This means that plaintiffs' attorneys must be much more cautious in the cases they choose to accept. Their income is generated on a contingent fee basis, and all of these cases take an

Exhibit 7–3 An Example of a Discharge Letter

Joan M. Dappointment
4204 East Tree Lane
East Gotham, NY 10002

Dear Miss Dappointment:

The patient/physician relationship is very important to us. We feel it is the cornerstone and foundation of good medical care. Unfortunately my relationship with you has been greatly hindered. I have made several attempts at offering you treatment modalities and yet our chart clearly reflects that you have refused my advice. More recently you have missed several appointments, notwithstanding the fact that my staff has taken the time to call you at home. It is clear to me that you and I have not been able to develop the appropriate patient/physician relationship and therefore I need, unfortunately, to terminate the same.

I will certainly see you if an urgent medical problem arises. However, within 60 days I would expect a request for a transfer of your medical record.

There are several fine primary care physician offices in our community, and I am told many are in your health plan's panel. If you need help in locating one, please do not hesitate to call our local medical society at 555-555-5555 and of course check with your health plan for coordination.

It saddens us to have to terminate the relationship at this time, but we feel it is far better for you to find a physician with whom you can connect than for us to continue.

Sincerely,

Dr. Care-So-Much

cc: Dr. Wright
Comprehensive HMO

*This is an example of a format. The text would have to be changed to reflect the specific facts in your case. State law should be reviewed.

investment of time and resources. Even with a 35% or 40% contingent fee, the percentage of zero is zero, if the verdict is for the doctor. The medical record is their primary source of information, the basis for the suit, and the basis for the defense.

Good documentation can prevent the initiation of malpractice claims in another way. At the patient level, informational documentation will help patients have more realistic expectations. In a managed care setting expectations are at an all-time high, so this effort becomes more important than ever. Informed consent is a form of documentation that can prevent a claim at the patient level. Many patients, or their families, after a complication has occurred, will review their copy of the informed consent form or the informational brochure that was given and see if they had been warned of the possibility of the unfortunate outcome. If patients have been both told and have documentation of the same, they are less likely to consult an attorney. However, if the damages are significant enough, or the patient is angry enough and seeks an attorney, the first thing the attorney will do will be to get a copy of the chart. The attorney will review it and see if the patient's story is substantiated or rebutted by the record.

A Request for Records

When you receive a letter from an attorney requesting copies of your records, with a properly signed authorization from your patient, don't delay or refuse. This could raise a level of suspicion on the part of the attorney. Provide a full copy of the chart, including everything that you used to make clinical decisions. Often the release or the request will ask for literally everything found in the patient's chart, including the billing information and any telephone notes or notices that you have in the chart. All of this should be provided. You want the plaintiff's attorney to be able to see the whole picture (especially when you know that your records are in good order), and it is quite embarrassing at best, devastating at worst, if portions of the chart are withheld only to appear later in the discovery process. Further, you want the expert who will be doing the initial review of the chart to have the whole picture.

Alterations

Perhaps it goes without saying, but no discussion about documentation is complete without reiterating and emphasizing how important it is not to change anything in the chart. You would be surprised how easily this can occur when a provider, now in retrospect looking at the records, realizes that something that happened never found its way into the chart. What is wrong with simply putting in what actually happened? In fact, if you want the plaintiff's attorney to get a full picture, don't you have to put it in? Aren't you duty bound to put it in? There are all sorts of ways to talk yourself into providing more information. The answer is, you *may not change* anything that is recorded. Adding something to a margin or in between two lines can be made by a plaintiff's attorney to look quite defensive, even if you date it. If you add or alter anything, and don't date it, you're headed for even more trouble. Plaintiffs' attorneys often obtain handwriting experts to review charts when such a suspicion arises. When this occurs, the physician's credibility is undermined, and the jury becomes hostile toward the physician, if they believe that something "fishy" happened to the chart. As one insurance claims executive recently expressed it, when an alteration to the chart is detected, "we open up the checkbook."

Once an attorney gets the chart and has it reviewed by medical experts, if the good care that you provided is well-organized, clear, and is contrary to the plaintiff's assertions, the attorney may refuse to take the case. When things aren't documented, plaintiffs' counsel argues that it is because the task, tests, instructions, or referral simply wasn't done. "If it is not recorded, it was not done."

Experts

There is an additional way in which documentation can prevent claims. In almost all cases, expert testimony is required to establish the applicable standard of care under the particular circumstances of the case. However, the rare exceptions may be *res ipsa loquitor* or some informed consent cases. Expert testimony is often needed for causation and damage questions as well. Having an appropriate expert is an extremely important part of your case. A true expert will look at the chart in good faith and see if the physician's care is documented and well-reasoned, and if there is an indication that the examination was done, and there was thoughtful treatment—even if there was a bad outcome. Good experts understand that the practice of medicine is not perfect and that a less than desirable result does not mean that there was malpractice. However, if your chart is silent on these issues or if your documentation is poor, many experts see that as a reflection of the quality of your care. It tends to affect their decision-making, and the emphatic allegations by the patient may be believed. Good documentation will make it harder for plaintiffs' attorneys to obtain experts and make it harder for these experts to form opinions against you.

It is unfortunate that today it is easier than ever to obtain expert support of plaintiffs' allegations of medical negligence. In many legal journals there are pages of advertisements by experts for hire. Some of them are quite professional and offering an appropriate, and perhaps needed, service. However, many of the ads appear to go too far, enticing plaintiffs' attorneys to seek a review. Consider the following list of sound bites: "free initial consultation within 24 hours;" "15%

off of second review;" "well-traveled expert has won millions for plaintiffs;" and "attractive to jurors, experienced in the courtroom." We have seen many reports from the physicians who advertise like this, experts willing to testify that any misdiagnosis in radiology is evidence of malpractice, that any infection in the hospital is evidence of a breach of the standard of care, or that failing to document any finding is a breach of the standard of care. These cases, fortunately, are usually won by the physician, but at the expense of an enormous amount of time, energy, and money. However, good documentation is your best protection against such experts and will, more importantly, make it unlikely that a true expert would take your case in the first place.

Jury Expectations

Jurors expect that all important information will be documented. They expect that you have made sure that the history and physical examination is recorded, as well as your instructions, any patient noncooperation or refusal of treatment, all telephone calls, and an informed consent. When they are not, it is very hard for the jury to have credence in your recollection, especially after the three to eight years that malpractice cases usually require to reach the courtroom.

Testimony often goes as follows:

> Question: Doctor, you say that you recall Mrs. Smith having told you about the fact she had breast cancer in her family history?
>
> Answer: That's right.
>
> Question: Doctor, how many patients do you normally see during the course of a week?
>
> Answer: I see approximately six patients an hour for six hours and am scheduled five days a week with one Saturday per month. I would say on average, on balance, perhaps 180 patients or so per week.
>
> Question: And how many weeks during the course of the year, since I am assuming you take some vacation, do you think you would be seeing these patients?
>
> Answer: Well, it may be, again as an average, I guess 49 weeks or so.
>
> Question: So, can we even assume 48 weeks? If we multiply the 48 times 180, you would see approximately 8,640 patients over the course of the year.

Answer: Yes, that is probably true, on average...this is not exact you understand.

Question: And, of course we all know this event took place nearly seven years ago, so if we multiply that out, you have seen 60,480 patients since then.

Answer: Well...uh...I guess that's one way to look at it.

Question: And you're telling the jury that you remember this uneventful first visit with this patient 60,000 patients ago.

Answer: I guess that's one way to look at it.

STILL MORE REASONS TO DOCUMENT

There are two additional reasons to do accurate documentation: billing and quality control. Inadequate billing in the past meant that you might lose money, a risk that you might have been willing to take. In managed care it may be that you have already been paid for the care. You now need to document it. Inadequate documentation could also lead to claims of fraud by third party payers, including the federal government. Quality control gives a third-party reviewer an opportunity to review the charts and truly understand how the physician is approaching the patient from a clinical standpoint.

Recognize that the principal reason for good documentation is still good patient care. Other reasons:

- sharing information with your patient/partner
- meeting accreditation standards
- reimbursement
- promoting your practice, and perhaps your referral base
- malpractice prevention.

HOW TO DOCUMENT BETTER

Review your entire documentation system. It should include:

- practice brochure, which could:
  - introduce a patient to your practice, including hours, emergency arrangements, coverage
  - introduce your health care team
  - help to explain the principles of managed care
  - explain common procedures

  - identify patient responsibilities
  - welcome patients as partners.
- patient chart:
  - initial health history including demographic data, past history, family history, lifestyle, allergies, health maintenance procedure records, history of present illness
  - recommend using SOAP style notes, with Problem List and Medication List
  - choose a system which is easily understood both within and beyond the practice
  - consider a system which meets professional society standard.
  - information check list to document in the patient's chart the information they have been given
- check office signage for completeness, clarity, and friendliness
- telephone message forms
- protocols for telephone triage
- patient informational materials, in various media
- complete coverage for your specialty
- recall letters to remind patients of follow up visit or procedure.
- special forms
- informed consent forms:
  - should be usable as another patient information tool
  - must meet requirements of your jurisdiction
- informed refusal forms, should be educational and clear
- discharge from practice letter, needs to be tailored to each individual situation
- collection letters:
  - initially should seek causes for delayed payment, and not be adversarial
- documentation audit form - to monitor all of above (see Chapter 9)
- congratulate your "Designated Nag" for making it all happen! (see Chapter 9).

CONCLUSION

Strong reasons are needed to justify all of this expenditure of time, effort, and money, and there are plenty. Good documentation:

- is essential to good patient care
- is necessary for reimbursement
- is required for accreditation of managed care organizations
- prevents lawsuits
  - by decreasing the chance of a patient initiating a suit

- by decreasing the likelihood of a plaintiff's attorney accepting a suit against you
- by decreasing the chances that an expert witness would testify against you

- provides a strong defense in the unlikely event of a lawsuit.

Inaccurate documentation is even worse. In the event of an audit, there could be serious legal consequences for the physician. Managed care organizations must maintain good quality control in order to meet the standards of quality control organizations, such as the National Commission for Quality Assurance (NCQA) and the Joint Commission on Accreditation of Healthcare Organizations (described in Chapter 9), or they may lose their accreditation. Both of these organizations require a certain level of comprehensive documentation, and that level is likely to continue to rise. The documentation, after all, is the only tool by which quality can be measured. Therefore, the reasons to refocus on documentation have significantly increased.

There is more to documentation than just the chart, and there is much more to documentation than preventing lawsuits. In managed care, a discussion about documentation has to include the information that is sent out by you or the managed care organization about you. It has to include your patient education materials, the brochures, pamphlets, audios, and videos that you have in your reception area. It has to include both the hard copy of your chart, the computerized medical records, the letters that you send out as reminders to patients, reminders concerning billing, and even your collection letters. It includes your consent forms, your documentation check lists, and even the letter used to discharge a patient. Good documentation involves setting a tone that is caring and making sure the substance is clear, concise, and appropriate. It involves making sure that your safety net, which is your chart, does not have the classic holes or new holes that are being created in the new environment. It involves setting up an auditing system so that you can monitor how you are doing from a documentation standpoint. It involves being conscientious about the requirements of managed care and credentialing organizations such as the Joint Commission and the NCQA. It means using your documents so that they not only achieve the goal of improving patient care but also document the great care that you are providing.

The use of all these forms, brochures, letters, and check lists does require more work initially, but each one is ultimately a great time saver. They permit your staff to look after the routines, and you to focus on patient care.

REFERENCES

1. L.L. Weed, Medical Records, Medical Education and Patient Care: The Problem Oriented Record as a Basic Tool (Cleveland, Ohio: Case Western Reserve University: 1969).

2. D.Berwick and D.Winickoff, "The Truth about Doctor's Handwriting: A Prospective Study," *British Medical Journal* 331 (December 1996): 1657–8.
3. The Picker Institute, *Eye On Patients* (American Hospital Association, 1996) 9.
4. Hollister, Inc. publishes a variety of medical record systems that meet professional society standards. The Milcom (R) system for primary care was developed in conjunction with, and has the approval of, The Society of Teachers of Family Medicine. Address: 2000 Hollister Drive, Liberty, IL 60048. Tel: (847)680-1000; fax: (847) 680-0414.
5. D.C. McGraw, "Financial Incentives to Limit Services: Should Physicians be Required to Disclose These to Patients," *The Daily Washington Law Reporter* 83 (1995): 1840.
6. B. Block, MD, "Using an Automated Tracking System to Improve Patient Care," *Family Practice Management* 3(9) (October 1996): 47–55.
7. Block, *Family Practice,* 54.
8. J. Firshen, "Measuring Progress Toward Practice Guidelines," *Business & Health* 14.5 (May 1996): 38.
9. A.L.Hyams, D.W.Shapiro, and T.A.Brennan, "Medical Practice Guidelines in Malpractice Litigation: An Early Retrospective," 21 Health Pol. Policy & Law 289 (Spring 1996).

CHAPTER 8

Using Informed Consent as an Offense Strategy

"Forasmuch as the lawe of God... allowes no man to touch the life or limme of any person except in a judicyall way, bee it hereby ordered and decreed, that no... physitians, chirurgians, midwives, or others, shall presume to exercise or putt forth any act contrary to the knowne rules of arte nor exercise any force, violence, or cruelty upon or towardes the bodys of any... without the... consent of the patient or patients (if they are mentis compotes...).

Law passed in the Massachusetts Bay Colony, May 3, 1649

Informed consent needs to be re-evaluated in the new health care environment. Once thought of only as a cumbersome legal requirement, it should now be considered as a patient-focused educational process that can be used for both the patients' and providers' advantage. Informed consent has its roots in the premise that the physician must obtain permission prior to performing a surgical or invasive procedure.[1] Prior to such a procedure the patient needs to know not only of the nature of the procedure but the risks as well as the other options or alternatives. Only then can the patient be said to be "truly informed" enough to give permission. Thus, informed consent.

STANDARDS

States or jurisdictions vary on precisely what standard they use; in other words, to what extent risks and alternatives need to be explained. Essentially, there are two standards. Many states adhere to what is commonly referred to as the professional standard. This means that the risks and alternatives that must be explained are those which a reasonably prudent physician, under similar circumstances, would explain. In these jurisdictions expert testimony can be used to help guide the jury as to what the physician would have been required to explain under the particular circumstances. In other jurisdictions, a prudent patient standard is used. The risks and alternatives that need to be explained are those that a reasonably prudent patient would want to know under the circumstances. In these jurisdictions it virtually becomes a question for the jury only, one that needs to be resolved by the jury as to whether the information that the physician communicated was reasonable in their collective minds in that particular case. The question is always ultimately for the jury, but with the professional standard, jurors are guided by experts, where in the prudent patient standard, typically they are not guided as to the question of what risks or alternatives would be considered material to their decisions. From time to time jurisdictional laws concerning informed consent change or evolve, so when creating a form or changing an informed consent process, make sure you review your particular jurisdiction's law. Some informed consent laws are found in statutes, others in the case law created by judicial decisions.

In addition, each state has its own description or requirement for which procedures or treatment the physician must obtain informed consent. Often these descriptions are part of a tort reform package designed to make the process less restrictive for the physician. In some jurisdictions case law has developed in such a fashion that informed consent is required only for surgical or invasive procedures.[2] In other jurisdictions it is required for any type of medical treatment.[3] Some jurisdictions have tried, legislatively, to mandate specific requirements for which informed consent must be obtained.[4] However, regardless of the standard there is often a case by case analysis in the gray areas. For example, if the standard is that informed consent must be obtained for any invasive procedure, does that include radiation therapy, general anesthesia, blood transfusion, setting of a fracture, and casting of an extremity? At times, within the same jurisdiction courts have gone both ways on these examples.[5] Providers are advised to err on the side of obtaining consent when in a gray area. As will be explained further in this chapter, there really is not much of a downside to obtaining informed consent, and many advantages.

Howard Brody, Director of the Center for Ethics and Humanities in the Life Sciences, and Associate Professor of Family Medicine at Michigan State University, has conducted a thoughtful inquiry into the informed consent process in this country, from a medical, legal, and ethical perspective. He reported his conclusions and ideas in a Hasting Center Report.[6]

Brody notes limitations to both of the legal standards currently in use. He believes that the prudent physician standard sends the wrong message because it may tend to promote physician paternalism. The prudent patient standard is more acceptable, he believes, but may convey an undesirable message to physicians. They may feel that with this standard they must identify all of the risks, benefits, and alternatives of the proposed procedure. He notes, "If one remembers to discuss the fifty possible risks, and the patient in a particular case suffers the fifty-first, the physician might subsequently be found liable for incomplete disclosure. Since lawsuits are triggered when patients suffer harm, disclosure of risk becomes relatively more important than disclosure of benefits. Moreover, disclosure of information becomes much more critical than effective patient participation in decision-making."[7]

Instead, Brody suggests a "transparency standard," meaning that adequate informed consent is only achieved when a reasonably informed patient is permitted to participate in the medical decision to the extent that patient wishes. The physician's reasoning is "transparent." "Reasonably informed" is interpreted to mean that the physician explains the basis for the choices recommended and the possible alternatives, and that all of the patient's questions are answered to that patient's satisfaction.

It seems unlikely that this could become the standard for informed consent in the future, since laws concerning informed consent are fairly well-established and from an evidential standpoint this standard would prove impractical. If anything, it appears that the trend may wll be to make them more closely akin to the prudent patient standard. It does, however, present a stimulating challenge to all physicians and reinforces the point that informed consent should be about patient involvement. Again, when in doubt, obtain an informed consent, since there is usually no downside as explained by the next section.

WHY INFORMED CONSENT?

Patient Education

Obtaining informed consent can do more for a physician than just meet the legal requirements that are set forth in state statutes, in hospital policies, in Medicare and Medicaid regulations, and in the common law.[8] Informed consent, when used appropriately as both an educational process and a documentation process, can bring patients' expectations more in line with reality. As explained in previous chapters, particularly in a mature managed care environment,* patients' expectations are higher than ever before. They have seen, heard, read all about the new, wonderful advancements in medicine. Now, when they or their loved one need this same medicine or treatment, they believe in it with all their heart and know that it will help them. They want the procedure promptly, conveniently, painlessly, inexpensively, and of course, without complications.

Many doctors are reluctant to tell patients of significant risks because it may frighten them unnecessarily and keep them from having the treatment that they need. Often patients are surprised at the serious complications that can occur. When this is considered, however, you see that this perception just fortifies the importance of having such a discussion. If a patient does not know that paralysis can occur following a laminectomy, or that a Stevens-Johnson syndrome could result from using certain medications, it is no wonder they are shocked if those

*A mature managed care environment is one which has been in existence for a lengthy period of time and market penetration is significant.

complications do occur. Telling patients of these potential outcomes is an important part of the informed consent process and is equally important to good patient care. The frightened patient syndrome can be handled by having a process that includes putting risk in context as to probability and related to the patient's particular condition.

Informed consent is a requirement of managed care and is one of its core concepts. Many managed care organizations have funded continuing education programs on informed consent to help their health care providers.[9] These organizations have realized that it is critical to achieve greater levels of patient involvement in a managed care setting. Patients, or consumers, are crying out that they feel uninformed and uninvolved, a natural prelude for litigation. This has been one of the principal findings of the recent American Hospital Association sponsored study by the Picker Institute (presented in Chapter 6).[10] This study showed that nearly 24% of all patients surveyed felt they were underinvolved in their care and in decisions about their care.

Prevention of Informed Consent Claims

When complications do occur, there is a strong possibility of preventing an informed consent claim if these discussions actually did occur and are documented. There once was a situation in which a patient had cervical neck surgery, followed by quadriparesis. She was of course devastated, as was her family and her surgeon. Obviously there was concern that a lawsuit would ensue. The woman was young and had been active and a major wage earner for her family. Imagine the surgeon's surprise when the patient pre-empted one of their post-operative conversations with, "You know, you told me this precise outcome could occur. You described it exactly as it happened. However, I never thought I would be the one it would happen to; the percentages were so small. I only hope you will do whatever you can to make my situation better." Of course he did everything he could to help her situation and, with time and therapy, her condition did improve, although it never returned to her pre-operative level of function. No lawsuit was initiated. This case is unusual in that, in the face of such severe, permanent damage, a family would not contemplate a suit. It shows how a proper consent, coupled with good rapport with the patient, can make a difference. If the consent process had not been accomplished, is there any doubt that the patient and family would have at least visited a lawyer, no matter what the relationship was? Once the lawyer reviewed a case with such damages, is there any doubt he or she would not have at least initiated a lawsuit based on a lack of consent and then, perhaps, filed a negligence claim as well? The consent form and process are essential.

Obtaining informed consent will not prevent all informed consent claims, but it creates an initial hurdle for the litigation-minded patient to get over. As noted in

Chapter 6, so many of these problems start with a breakdown of communication. The informed consent process should start long before the invasive procedure or treatment is recommended. Sometimes patients fail to recollect these discussions, and sometimes may even have a vested interest in forgetting. But others, particularly when family members are involved, will remember and this discourages patients from initiating the legal process or even visiting legal counsel.

There was a study performed by the University of Pennsylvania trying to gauge how much information patients recalled after such discussions. Patients only recalled a fraction of the information provided. This led some physicians to jump to the conclusion that providing the information really did not make any difference in the first place. Such thinking is flawed. Actually, the opposite conclusion should be drawn. It means that physicians need to do a far better job of explaining the risks and alternatives so as to increase that fraction. It means involving family members, where appropriate, and that documentation is critical.[11] Patients who do understand are least likely to initiate the litigation process.[12]

The first reason to obtain informed consent, therefore, is not because it is a requirement legislatively, statutorily, institutionally, or through the common law, but that it brings patients' expectations in line with reality. Most patients appreciate the process, and it can prevent an informed consent claim if a complication were to occur. Many doctors cite the fact that complications are so rare, and informed consent lawsuits so infrequent in their particular specialties that it is not worthwhile. However, such rationalization is naive, and must be set aside. That rare case will happen. They are like rare diseases: a physician may only encounter one case of kala-azar in a practice lifetime, but there are so many equally rare ailments that physicians may see one of them every month. A good informed consent process is an effective, although not perfect, immunization against those rarities.

In an informed consent claim, the procedure can be adequately prepared for and performed in a flawless fashion, and seem to be completely without incident. Later in the day, however, the patient develops a complication. It can be a known and reported complication, and even if 100 experts testify that it happens even in the "best of hands," the surgeon can be held responsible for all damages flowing from that complication, unless an informed consent had been obtained. It does not matter how well the procedure was performed. It does not matter if the procedure was highly difficult. If informed consent was not obtained, and there is a causal relationship with the damages, the physician can be held responsible.

Prevention of Negligence Claims

Obtaining an informed consent can also prevent negligence claims. Negligence claims are separate from informed consent claims. The difference is significant, and within it lies the reason for a great deal of frustration with informed consent claims. In a negligence claim, among other things, it must be shown that there was a breach of the applicable standard of care. Expert testimony in almost all circumstances must be used establishing the standard of care and how the conduct fell beneath that standard. In essence there is no case for medical negligence without wrongful or neglectful conduct. There has to be some degree of culpability on the part of the defendant.

A claim of negligence or medical malpractice means that the plaintiff must prove three points: that the particular physician or other health care provider owed a duty, i.e., that they had a patient-doctor relationship; secondly, that the physician breached the applicable standard of care under the facts and circumstances of the case;[13] and thirdly, that there was causation, i.e., that the particular breach of the standards of practice was the legal cause of the damages suffered. Legal causation differs in certain jurisdictions, but essentially it means that the injury was the proximate cause of the harm to the patient. In some jurisdictions, this causation standard has been loosened and a plaintiff can prevail if they show only that the breach of the applicable standard of care increased the risk of the harm occurring and was the substantial legal cause.[14] Obviously damages must be proven as well and all of the above must be proven by the "preponderance of the evidence." The preponderance of the evidence is the standard used in civil cases and differs from the standard used in criminal cases, which is "beyond a reasonable doubt."

Obtaining an appropriate informed consent can reduce the likelihood of a negligence claim because patients' expectations are more in line with reality. If patients know of a particular risk, they are less hostile and angry when a complication occurs. Patients and their families are less likely to jump to the conclusion that something "went wrong" when the specific complication that occurs had been explained as a possible complication of that particular procedure. Usually this will keep a patient from visiting a plaintiff's attorney to initiate the process. On another level, it can affect the attorney's evaluation of the claim. If a patient asks an attorney to evaluate the case, admitting that what happened was a risk that they were told about, the attorney will be less inclined to take on the case. That is not to say that the plaintiffs' attorney would refuse to take a case, especially if the damages are high.

Plaintiffs' attorneys are involved in malpractice litigation, to a great extent, for economic reasons. The rewards can be high, but so is their financial risk. Therefore, business decisions must be made before the initiation of these claims. Although not the primary purpose, one of the goals of the informed consent process is to affect those decisions. The thorough informed consent process can help in that regard, both with the patient and the patient's family, and with the attorney. Another reason to obtain informed consent therefore is to prevent negligence claims, either at the level of the patient who decides not to file a claim, or of the plaintiffs' attorney who decides that the chances for remuneration are not worth the effort.

In Court

Although one goal of this book is to help physicians prevent claims in the first place, having a strong informed consent is also the physician's best friend in the courtroom if a case were to proceed to trial. In many cases, in the courtroom, the defendant physician will insist that the complication that occurred was not a result of negligence, but simply was a known complication that can occur in the best of hands. Skilled and authoritative experts explain this in detail to jurors who, if the informed consent process is well-documented, are likely to be very accepting of this explanation. The contrary is true as well. If informed consent is not obtained, jurors can be very unforgiving. In some jurisdictions a lack of informed consent is considered a battery,[15] meaning an unlawful touching or unauthorized touching and can also give rise to a claim for punitive damages.[16] Remembering that discussions about your informed consent form may be the focus of attention in a courtroom, you need to consider carefully the document or form you choose. This will often be the key piece of evidence, and may be blown up to three feet by five feet and constantly posted in front of jurors. It will be highlighted, portions of it circled, and will actually go out with the jurors during deliberations. In the courtroom this form will take on special significance, either positive or negative, depending on the quality of your form.

In Managed Care

In the managed care environment, informed consent has become even more important. Managed care organizations want patients to understand fully their treatment plan or proposed procedure. They want patients to be involved in the decision-making. Providers are often questioned, evaluated, and rated on the extent to which they involve patients in their own care. The Picker Institute study, cited earlier, supports this conclusion.[17] The results were based on the findings of surveys sent to over 36,000 patients recently discharged from hospitals, to Medicaid and Medicare populations, as well as those enrolled in premier plans, and focus groups in a dozen states. The results were consistent throughout and showed that patients did not feel that they, nor their families, were involved in their own care and that there was actually a lack of respect for patient preferences. The patients also felt that insignificant information was given to them prior to their discharge from the hospital. In fact, 24% of all patients surveyed felt that there was a lack of information and education about their procedure or treatment; approximately the same percentage felt there was a lack of involvement of family and friends, and of coordination of care. As reported in a January 28, 1997 *Wall Street Journal* article, the American Hospital Association's Senior Advisor on Clinical Affairs, Jack Lord, conceded these findings were "ugly" and that institutions should view the results as a "road map" for steering their way out of this mess.[18] William Speck, MD, President of Columbia Presbyterian Medical Center in New York, was reported to agree, regretfully, with the conclusions. He traces part of the problem to the rapid rise of managed care but also indicates it started long before, when the focus began to turn to costs and stated, "A lot of decisions have not been made in the best interests of the patient, but on financial imperatives and that is a shame."[19]

The point is that patients are not getting enough information and this will cause problems from two standpoints: litigation and patient satisfaction. Patient satisfaction is becoming more and more important in the health care environment since it affects how consumers make their decisions about care; and dissatisfied patients are most likely to turn to litigation to resolve their complaints. Most patients want to be informed about their care, treatment, and proposed procedures. There are still a few who would rather not know and will say, "Hey, you're the doc, you decide—I don't want to hear about it." This sort of response is most likely to come from people who have a long-standing and trusting relationship with their doctors, or from elderly patients who recognize that their ability to comprehend complicated health issues has diminished. Ideally, family members could then be invited to participate, with the patient's permission, of course. Regardless, of who is involved, or not involved, or the strength or length of the patient-doctor relationship, documentation is essential. Documentation that an informed consent was obtained is what will be your best protection both from a suit and in court.

Not only is informed consent legally required and, from a risk management standpoint, prudent, but the process is important to your patients and something which they, through studies and surveys, have indicated concerns them greatly. Informed consent will increase patient satisfaction and reduce liability exposure. So the reasons to embrace informed consent include:

- patients want it
- it reduces informed consent claims
- it reduces negligence claims
- it helps you if you ever have to defend a claim in the courtroom
- managed care organizations require it
- the law requires it
- you will sleep better.

A NEW LOOK AT AN OLD PROCESS

Because of the importance of informed consent, and more so in a managed care environment, we ought to take a new look at this old process. Informed consent is actually an opportunity for the health care provider. It is an opportunity both to reduce the likelihood of liability exposure and to increase patient satisfaction and patient cooperation. The physician should wrap informed consent into a patient educational process. Rethink how you obtain informed consent in your practice and determine whether more information can be provided to the patient through this process.[20] Consider how you might use a multimedia approach as a springboard to increase the amount of information patients receive.

Consider an example from a surgical office. Often, in years past, and even presently, the informed consent process in a surgeon's office would consist of letting a patient know about the proposed procedure and having a brief discussion about its risks. The depth of discussion usually varied, depending on the surgeon, but it is probably fair to say the discussion often was not comprehensive. The patient would be given an opportunity to ask questions, but the whole process quite often was at a fairly brisk pace and the conclusion seemed apparent. Surgery was needed and, in all likelihood, it would help. Frightened patients are often told that surgery is standard and is performed successfully numerous times or that "it's no big deal." These statements are often made to try to allay patients' fears, appropriately enough, and to reassure them, but may have the effect of giving patients a false sense of security and, even worse, negating the informed consent process.

A surgeon we know always took a significant amount of time to discuss the risks associated with a coronary bypass with a patient. He was conscientious about it and wanted the patient to have a full understanding of the procedure, risks, and alternatives. The surgeon even explained that a myocardial infarction could occur in a small percent of these cases. In this particular instance, the patient, in the surgeon's opinion, badly needed the procedure and there was ample objective clinical and diagnostic evidence to support that it was indicated. In spite of the symptoms the patient had been exhibiting and the lack of improvement through medical therapy, the patient was quite distraught. He was upset about the risk of a heart attack and wondered if he really needed the surgery. In an effort to console his patient for this needed procedure, the surgeon explained, a little frustrated, that the chances of a serious heart attack happening were "like being hit by a Mack truck outside my office." The surgeon was trying to convey a sense of rarity, that it would be highly unusual for this complication to occur. The surgeon knew the patient very much needed the procedure and did not want this legal informed consent requirement to frighten the patient out of having it done. The patient, however, as recorded in deposition testimony several years later, felt the physician was telling him that it essentially would not happen. The doctor's office was in the outskirts of a residential area; Mack trucks were never found in that area and certainly not found in the doctor's parking lot. The message the patient heard was that it was not going to happen. This statement became the focal point in subsequent litigation.

Unfortunately with this particular patient, a major infarction did occur. Everyone involved was devastated. The procedure was indicated, the performance was technically correct, but the myocardial damage was substantial. A plaintiff's attorney evaluated the case and decided to pursue solely an informed consent claim, not a medical negligence claim. Documentation was there but was scant. A generic form had been used. However, the most important factor became the comment that the chances of infarction occurring were "like being hit by a Mack truck outside my office." The plaintiff testified to this at his deposition as did his wife. The doctor admitted during his deposition that he made the statement but tried to explain that he was just trying to console the patient. As trial approached, the doctor decided to pursue settlement of the claim as an option. He felt that the jury would be extremely sympathetic to this man, now in heart failure, and in a wheelchair. The statement he made about the "Mack truck" plagued him. Was this going to be blown up on a chart and marched into the courtroom? He thought the risks were too high and a substantial settlement was negotiated. All of the doctor's good work and conscientious effort was erased by his own "backpedaling." Adhering to his good informed consent process and then documentation of the same could have prevented the claim.

In the past, patients were told of the risks and alternatives, and at some point, generic forms were given to them to sign. The name of the procedure was often scribbled on the form and of course the patient signed it. The signature was witnessed and the doctor certified that the patient completed the process. This is a rather standard description of the old, traditional process and it is not adequate for today's health care.

The doctor discussed the planned surgery beforehand, but often there was no real education process, not enough information to allow patients to be informed about that which they were being asked to sign. The process was not treated seriously and the patient was left to think the process and the form was simply, "just another form," "a legal requirement" or, worse, used by the doctor to "cover one's backside." The form was generic and did not give nor document any specific information. The witness only witnessed the signature, which rarely becomes an issue. These holes in the process are the reason why physicians have often lost, or decided to settle, informed consent cases.

If we consider what patients would need prior to a specific surgical procedure, a total knee replacement for example, it would not be hard to assemble a package of useful information. This could include the risks of the procedure as well as the alternatives, clearly listed, and also the pre-operative instructions, what to expect on the day of surgery, what to expect post-operatively, and the type of rehabilitation that will be needed. It could emphasize how important patient involvement is, commonly asked questions with short understandable answers, and telephone numbers where additional information can be obtained. All of this could be presented as a patient information brochure, which could be printed professionally or simply typed. (The latter may seem more personalized.) An informed consent form could also be created, listing these same risks and alternatives. This informed consent form could become part of the package of information the patient receives.

Often an issue is raised as to whether all risks need to be listed. This in part will depend on your jurisdiction, but is an almost impossible task. Usually listing the six to eight most common and serious risks on your informed consent form and making it clear that the risks "include but are not limited to..." strikes a good balance. For some procedures it may be necessary to list more on the form. For others you may want to list more in the information brochure. One option is to have the patient information brochure incorporated by reference into the informed consent form so that the patient would not only acknowledge the risks on the form but acknowledge that they have received this patient information brochure.

This does not replace the time needed with patients to help them be truly informed about their procedure and to answer all of their questions. This is still essential and fundamental. It doesn't take much more time to incorporate a process that provides patients with more information, using a combination of written materials, perhaps involving other clinical personnel in your office, to help you truly inform your patients. Every office and specialty is different. The challenge is to look at what information patients need, what are the best ways or points in the process to communicate it, and from a documentation standpoint, incorporate verification by the patient that it has been received, understood, and that questions have been answered.

The difference in results between the two processes discussed above are phenomenal. In the second process you will achieve the goal of clearly reducing liability exposure while, at the same time, achieving greater patient satisfaction and patient cooperation. Many offices have found that this process reduces the time spent on the informed consent process, not increases it. One reason is that it is followed by fewer telephone calls requesting information, answering questions, and expressing unresolved concerns. That is apart from the time one would have to spend in defending the lawsuit if that occurred. The number one reason we hear why the informed consent process is not used within an office is that, "It takes too much time. Our resources are shrinking. We can't spend the time providing more information to patients." However, many groups have found that it doesn't take more time in the end. On balance, it can create greater levels of efficiency. There does need to be an investment of time to put the process together; however, once that is accomplished, it will actually promote efficiency. The positive benefits are just too significant to allow "it will take too much time" to inhibit you from implementing this important concept. If you prevent one lawsuit over your career—and you will—it will be well worthwhile.

A NEW LOOK AT AN OLD FORM

The traditional informed consent form was very generic, and in the hospital setting, this may have been appropriate at one time and necessary, since that same form was used for multiple procedures and in multiple areas of the hospital. These forms are being replaced and many institutions and physicians in office or outpatient settings have begun to use procedure specific forms instead. In many specialties physicians can pick four or five office procedures that make up a substantial part of their practice and create procedure specific forms for each of them. They can then use a more generic form for the remainder of procedures with enough space to describe the details of the particular procedure.

A procedure specific form should list the name of the procedure at the top together with a description in lay terms. The form should be written in a straightforward fashion, at an eighth grade reading level,[21] and almost always can be put on one page of paper. No sophisticated language or process is needed for the creation of these forms. We recommend that you try to look at the forms, both through your patients' eyes, and with the two goals in mind of truly informing patients and reducing the potential litigation exposure.

A study performed at the M.S. Hershey Medical Center of the Pennsylvania State University reviewed existing informed consent forms to see what educational level would be most appropriate. Hopper, et al., reviewed 160 existing consent forms from private practitioners, groups, and academic centers. They discovered that most required at least a high school level of education to comprehend, and 10 (6%) even required a college level to understand. The authors of the study recommended that consent forms be designed to be able to be understood by people at an eighth grade level, and they provided examples in the article.[22] We have recommended to groups who are creating forms, that they ask a focus group of patients to review them. They are the ones who are going to use it. Usually patients are very cooperative and are happy to give suggestions on what they understand, what needs to be clarified, what additional questions could be answered, and how they interpret the form. Sometimes their suggestions are impractical, but most of these focus meetings generate a great deal of useful information. They will not be able to tell you what information needs to be in the form or how to explain information, but will give you a sense for whether or not your form is understandable. It is essential that the form is understandable, yet clearly documents the explanations that have been made and, of course, meets legal requirements.

One suggestion is presented in Exhibit 8–1. The procedure is named at the top with a short explanation in lay terms. The remainder of the form was designed to address the many reasons that informed consent cases are often lost or settled. In reviewing multiple informed consent suits nationally, it appeared that patients would often say that they just read "too many forms," and just signed "on the bottom line" as requested. They described the process as a time of confusion and nervousness and that they were not truly aware of what they were signing. They knew that they had to sign many different documents, so they could have whatever it was the doctor said they needed. Therefore, they simply glanced at every form and signed as asked. Often patients would compare it to a settlement on a house, when you sit at the table and just review numerous documents and sign the bottom line. This is hard to imagine as a credible argument, but has been accepted by jurors in the courtroom. Patients also say that it was not impressed upon them that the informed consent form was important or that this was an essential process. It seemed like nothing more than a standard procedure to allow the surgeon to perform the operation.

In light of this, the consent form should include an introductory paragraph that establishes that this informed consent process is important and not merely routine. You should inform your patients that you do not want the form to be signed unless they truly understand the risks and alternatives, and the risks associated with the alternatives. There should be a place for the patient to initial and date that paragraph. This prevents the argument that this was just another process and that the patient was simply given many forms to "sign on the bottom line." It sends a clear message to the patient that this is an important form and an important process.

The next significant change is that risks are listed on the form itself. Physician preference and judgment must be used here since some may want a substantial list of risks and others only the six or seven most significant risks that they want the patient to understand. By doing so they are probably covering 95% of the problems that do occur. The written list doesn't have to cover every risk described during your conversations, but should include both the most common and most serious. However, some contingency language such as "the risks include, but are not limited to," should be placed in the form. The reader of the form will know then that not all of the risks discussed during the conversation are listed. Often physicians will go through a laundry list of concerns and describe them with one short phrase. For example, before a laparoscopic procedure, a surgeon may say that "there could also be damage to other structures in the same anatomic area." There are many ways physicians can describe groups of risks to patients, and not

Exhibit 8–1

AUTHORIZATION FOR TREATMENT OF ____(fill in procedure)____

(description in lay terms)

It is very important to the physicians of ____(name of group)____, that you, our patient, understand the treatment we are rendering and any invasive procedure which we may, with your agreement, perform. We want to involve you in any and all decisions concerning invasive procedures which you may need to have. We take "informed consent" very seriously in our office. Therefore, we only want you to sign this form when you understand the procedure that is to be performed, you understand the risks, alternatives, the risks associated with those alternatives, and all of your questions have been answered.

__________ __________

Initials Date

I, ____________________, hereby authorize ____________________ and any associate or assistant, to perform a ____(put name of procedure)____.

I also authorize any further procedure which, in the doctor's judgment, needs to be done because of any unforeseen condition which arises during the procedure.

I also authorize the administration of and maintenance of sedation and anesthesia and any other therapeutic procedures that in the doctor's judgment may be necessary or advisable for my comfort, well being and safety.

The doctor has explained to me the risks inherent with this procedure which include, ***but are not limited to,*** ____(put in 6 or so most common and most serious risks)____.

Alternatives to this procedure have been explained to me, along with the risks of those alternatives. Alternatives include, ***but are not limited to,*** ____________(fill in)____________

____________________________________.

I understand that medicine is not an exact science and that no guarantee or assurance has been given to me that the proposed treatment will be curative and/or successful to my complete satisfaction.

I have had an opportunity to read and fully understand the terms and words of this authorization and I have had an opportunity to ask the doctor all questions concerning risks, complications, alternatives, and risks of those alternatives.

	Yes	No
I have carefully read this form	❑	❑
I understand this form	❑	❑
All of my questions have been answered	❑	❑

__________ ______________________________

Date Signature of Patient

__________ ______________________________

Date Witness

Certification of Physician: I certify that I have discussed and explained the procedure described in this consent form with the individual granting consent.

__________ ______________________________

Date Signature of Physician

This is a format. Jurisdiction laws should be reviewed.

every one has to be mentioned individually. That is not to say that specific risks should not be given, only that common sense must be used, too. It is important that the patient be given information as to the risks, so that a reasonable decision can be made. Obviously, the standard that your particular state uses must be considered as well. The area in which physicians often seem to be getting caught is not mentioning a rare but very significant risk, such as death. The argument is that the risk is remote and may well frighten the patient. However, plaintiff's attorneys argue that this is precisely the type of information patients must have. We feel it is important to mention the most serious risks but in a balanced fashion.

This same process should take place for alternatives, which is often much easier. The alternatives for any type of surgical procedure or treatment are frequently few. In the case of a surgeon performing an operation, the alternative of doing nothing at all should also be described. In the case of using a certain therapeutic medication, in a jurisdiction where informed consent must be obtained for medications,[23] other medications and their advantages and disadvantages should be described. As always, explain the consequences of the alternative of doing nothing at all. As will be explained further in this chapter, the alternative portion of the form may become a great deal more important with greater penetrations of managed care, since alternatives for patients, at least from a reimbursement standpoint, are shrinking. This is important since you do not want to be accused of not offering a reasonable alternative because of utilization concerns.[24]

A lot more help could be obtained from the witness too. It is often thought that the witness is verifying the fact that the patient is signing the form, or in other words, the patient's signature. This is often true but not very helpful, since it is rare that patients disavow their own signatures.

In an office setting where the witness is a member of your staff, it is very effective to have the witness ask three questions as a matter of protocol and have them included on the form. These questions are:

	Yes	No
1. Has the patient read the form?	❑	❑
2. Does the patient understand the form?	❑	❑
3. Does the patient have any further questions?	❑	❑

These questions are not ambiguous and the response, assuming the process has gone well, will normally be "yes," "yes," and "no." The witness can check off the appropriate boxes and sign as a witness. You now have a true witness, not only to the signature, but to the entire process. This does not mean the witness literally had to oversee the entire process, which would be impractical, but if your form has been well drafted, the witness will be able to attest to the fact that the patient understood all the very specific risks listed. If complications occur, the patients have verified that they understood the risks and alternatives and had no questions about them. In two recent cases, this type of form was referred to in the courtroom—both were quick verdicts for the defendant doctors. Jurors in one of the cases asked, after the conclusion of the court session, "Why was the patient even allowed to sue given the fact that he acknowledged the risk right on the form!?" This is the type of response that we want from jurors. These forms have gone a long way toward discouraging claims in the first place.

In the hospital setting, the use of a witness on the form may need to be set up a little differently. Informed consent is the non-delegable obligation of the physician or provider performing the procedure, and hospital counsel may be concerned about interjecting nurses too much into this process. This concern can easily be alleviated by revising the questions on the form and having the patient check them off. You will have similar legal protection since you will have substantiation that the patient read and understood the form and had no questions. (See Exhibit 8–1) The questions would simply be asked a little differently:

	Yes	No
1. Have you read the form?	❑	❑
2. Do you understand the form?	❑	❑
3. Do you have any further questions?	❑	❑

These questions are important for several reasons. The witness, observing the patient's answers to these questions, becomes a true witness to the process. From the patients' standpoint, they will have a greater level of understanding that this is more than just one more form, but an important process. These questions also act as a check on the entire system. If the form has described the risks specifically that may occur, and the questions are asked and answered in an appropriate fashion, you have verification that the patients understand that complications could occur and that their questions have been answered. A physician once asked at a medical staff retreat where the process was discussed, "What if a patient answers one of the questions wrong?" Of course there is no wrong answer, per se, but if the patient does not answer as expected, it means that further information is needed by the patient. This may be accomplished by the nurse or an advanced practice provider only if it is within their knowledge base and understanding; but it would be more appropriately addressed by the physician, since the patient evidently has some serious concerns. Any patient who truly does not understand the risks associated with the procedure puts you at the greatest risk. These questions can help to drive home the important points of informed consent and catch those patients who need more information.

In this type of form you could also incorporate additional educational material. Some groups have referenced patient information pamphlets from an academic society or other professional association, or companies that specialize in publishing such educational materials. Video or audiotapes may also be used and could be referenced. One cautionary remark: In some specialties, such as plastic surgery, educational videotapes may have a certain element of promotion, which may not fully identify the possible risks, complications, or less than desirable results. If patients saw only the pamphlets and the videotape, they might get a lopsided, or at best an incomplete, picture of what could occur. Shown in front of a jury, without the information on the "other side of the coin" as usually supplied by the physician, it could be very detrimental to the physician's case.

In a recent case involving an unfortunate complication associated with a rhinoplasty, the jury was shown all of the professionally prepared brochures and videotapes. They clearly painted a picture of a procedure that was easily accomplished and that its goal was to create an esthetically pleasing result. Risks and complications were minimized. In view of a very significant complication, this would have made the case very difficult to defend had it not been for the outstanding consent process of the plastic surgeon which mirrored the above discussion. A verdict was promptly rendered for the defendant. Discussions with jurors after the verdict yielded some important information. Jurors felt that the brochures and videotapes painted an unrealistic and misleading picture. They observed simple things like the noses of all the individual actors in the rhinoplasty videotape. They indicated they all seemed to be perfect and did not represent reality. They said the brochures seemed to portray the same type of picture. They said even the discussions of the procedures and minimal discussions about risks seemed to downplay the possibility that a problem could occur and that if it did, how serious it could be. They viewed the whole videotape and brochure process as one which was overly reassuring and led them to the conclusion that one would not think seriously that a problem, such as the one that did happen, could occur. On the other hand, the particular surgeon involved made it very clear to the patient beforehand that complications could occur that could even require additional surgery, hospitalization, expense, and time off work. In his form, he mentioned that one of the risks was additional surgery. In a long letter written to the patient, he addressed the possibility of an external deformity developing. The jurors felt that the surgeon made it very clear to the patient that a bad result could happen and that the patient, wanting the procedure badly, simply never "heard" the doctor on this point or, if she did, never believed that she would be the one to whom it would occur.

FURTHER DOCUMENTATION

As mentioned in the above example, under some circumstances, it makes sense to go a step further and to write the patient a standard letter following a consultation for a specific procedure. Cosmetic surgery is a good example of the type of procedure for which this could be appropriate and very helpful both to the patient and in an effort to prevent liability claims. Cosmetic surgery presents extra challenges, because these patients' expectations are often at a very high level. Many plastic surgeons have a standard letter that reviews the patient's history, goals, the procedure in lay terms, the pre-operative tests needed, a description of the procedure, description of the risks and alternatives, as well as an opportunity to ask additional questions. This can be prepared in a standardized fashion and then tailored to each patient. Letters such as this, in high risk procedures, can be very effective, are appreciated by patients, and enrich the informed consent process. An example of a letter sent by a plastic surgeon, actually from the example described above, is presented in the Appendix at the end of this chapter. Asked whether this was overly time consuming, the surgeon stated, "once you have the process down in your office, it is not something that takes a great deal of time. It becomes part of what you do for each particular case. It becomes more or less automatic. Actually, the time it takes is nothing compared with these claims. I don't want patients to feel that I'm selling any procedures. It is simply not worth it." Ronald P. Gruber, MD, Clinical Assistant Professor of Plastic Surgery at Stanford University and one of the founders of the American Rhinoplasty Society, author of multiple textbooks on rhinoplasty surgery, and Director of instructional courses on rhinoplasty for the American Society of Plastic Surgery from 1987 to 1997, who was an expert witness in the case, said that this exemplified "the best informed consent process I had ever seen."

BACK TO MANAGED CARE

In a managed care environment doctors need to be even more aware of informed consent, not only because greater levels of patient involvement are important, but because the reasoning behind a decision whether or not to conduct a certain procedure may come under close scrutiny. A pre-printed form listing the pros and cons of certain recommendations may be helpful to both the patient and to the physician in the event of litigation.

As the roles of physicians change, so do their responsibilities. It has been claimed that managed care changes the alternatives that are offered to a patient to include only those that would be reimbursed according to that particular organization's guidelines and protocols. That is simply not the case. A physician's first responsibility is still to the patient. The so-called "gag rules," once prevalent, which would prohibit a physician from discussing procedures not offered within a managed care organization, are contrary to good judgment, and have been either legislatively prohibited[25] or voluntarily withdrawn.[26]

The informed consent form of the future may include language stating that there may be alternatives recommended by the physician which would not be reimbursed by the managed care organization. It might also state that discussion concerning whether or not a procedure is reimbursed is outside the scope of the physician's responsibility and that patients should understand and acknowledge that it is their responsibility to discuss the same with the managed care organization. In a capitated system it becomes even more difficult. Patients may feel that certain alternatives were not explained because the physician who was capitated did not want to send the patient for an expensive diagnostic test, since it may be to his/her financial disadvantage. The hazards of this perception may make the alternatives portion of the form very important in the future. Physicians will want to make sure they describe all the alternatives recommended to the patient so that the patient is fully informed and will not feel that a useful alternative was withheld. In the past, the alternative portion of informed consent was infrequently the subject of much litigation. Claims were usually based on the occurrence of unexpected complications and patients claiming that they were never told of the risk of complications. In the future there will likely be more claims in a capitated system that certain alternatives were not mentioned because it would be financially disadvantageous to the physician. It has become very important to have all alternatives included in the informed consent form so as to block a claim, at a later date, that your advice was economically motivated.

UPDATING YOUR INFORMED CONSENT PROCESS

Recognize that the purposes of this process are multiple:

- patients appreciate it
- the law requires it
- it will minimize your risks for informed consent litigation
- it will minimize your risk for related medical negligence claims
- in the event of a lawsuit, it provides great protection
- managed care organizations and accrediting agencies will require it
- you will sleep better.

Consider the informed consent process as part of your patient information package:

- it is a prime means of communication
- it permits patients to become actively involved
- it helps to build close patient-doctor relationships.

Teach your staff the whys, wherefores, and hows of the informed consent process. Create your own individualized informed consent forms:

- use the form provided as models
- consult your practice attorney
- consult your managed care organization.
- consider having the forms critiqued by a focus group.

Develop a procedure specific form for your most frequent procedures, and develop a more generic form for all other uses, allowing space for particulars:

- In both, include a statement at the beginning stating the importance of this form, to be signed by the patient.
- In both, include three questions for the witness to answer, certifying that the patient has indicated that he/she read and understood the form and has no unanswered questions.
- In both, be sure to discuss the alternative of doing nothing.

Develop a brochure, or information sheet, which includes a description of the procedure and the risks involved, and any pre- or post-procedure instructions—you should consider referencing this in your form. Note on your Information Check List that your patient has been given both of these documents. Review all of these procedures with your staff and assign responsibility.

CONCLUSION

This area of your practice might be greatly enhanced by spending time on the process of informed consent and tailoring it to your particular specialty, institution, and setting. Create or revise your forms so that they reduce your liability exposure and increase the level of communication with your patient. All of this will be time well spent. It could increase efficiency by providing more information at the outset for the patient so that follow-up phone calls and questions are minimal. As additional information is wrapped into this educational process, it may help to assure your patients' cooperation with any instructions you give them, which will, in turn, produce a better health outcome. It will most certainly have the effect of reducing your liability exposure and increasing the level of understanding and satisfaction of your patients.

REFERENCES

1. H.J. Bursztajn, L. S. Saunders, and A. Brodsky, "Medical Negligence and Informed Consent in the Managed Care Era," *Archives of Internal Medicine* 156 (October 14, 1996): 16.
2. "Lack of Informed Consent Can Open Door to Law Suits," *Medical Staff Reporter* 11 (1994): 11.
3. "Lack of Informed Consent," 11.
4. Bursztajn, Saunders, and Brodsky, "Medical Negligence and Informed Consent in the Managed Care Era,"16.
5. K.D. Grant, "Informed Consent: Medical Legal Update for the Practitioner on Recent Judicial Opinions Applying to State Laws," *The American Surgeon* 58.2 (1992): 146.

6. H. Brody, "Transparency: Informed Consent in Primary Care," *Hastings Center Report* (September/October 1989): 5–9.
7. H. Brody, "Transparency: Informed Consent in Primary Care," 6.
8. Bursztajn, Saunders, and Brodsky, "Medical Negligence and Informed Consent in the Managed Care Era," 16.
9. Bursztajn, Saunders, and Brodsky, "Medical Negligence and Informed Consent in the Managed Care Era," 17.
10. American Hospital Association, "Eye on Patients," (Internet presentation, available at http://www.amphi.com/eyeonpatients/charts.html.)
11. "Eye on Patients."
12. B.R. Cassileth et al., "Informed Consent—Why are Its Goals Imperfectly Realized," *New England Journal of Medicine* 302.16 (1980): 896.
13. Grant, "Informed Consent: Medical Legal Update for the Practitioner on Recent Judicial Opinions Applying to State Laws," 146–47.
14. Hamil v. Bashline, 481 Pa. 256, 392 A.2d 1280 (1978).
15. J.A. Gold, MD, "Informed Consent," *Archives of Ophthalmology* 111 (1993): 321.
16. Bursztajn, Saunders, and Brodsky, "Medical Negligence and Informed Consent in the Managed Care Era,"16.
17. "Eye on Patients."
18. L. Lagnado, "Patients Give Hospitals Poor Score Card," *Wall Street Journal* 28 Jan 1997: B1.
19. L. Lagnado, "Patients Give Hospitals Poor Score Card,"B1.
20. K.D. Hopper, MD, H.A. Lambe, and S.J. Shirk, "Readability of Informed Consent Forms for Use with Iodinated Contrast Media," *Radiology* 187.1 (1995): 279.
21. Hopper, Lambe, and Shirk, "Readability of Informed Consent Forms for Use with Iodinated Contrast Media," 282.
22. Hopper, Lambe, and Shirk, "Readability of Informed Consent Forms for Use with Iodinated Contrast Media," 282.
23. Grant, "Informed Consent: Medical Legal Update for the Practitioner on Recent Judicial Opinions Applying to State Laws," 149.
24. "Rationing by Another Name," *New England Journal of Medicine* 336.23 (1997): 1668.
25. Bursztajn, Saunders, and Brodsky, "Medical Negligence and Informed Consent in the Managed Care Era," 16–17.
26. Bursztajn, Saunders, and Brodsky, "Medical Negligence and Informed Consent in the Managed Care Era," 16–17.

APPENDIX

Ms. Vera Lucky
135 North Road
Southtown, PA

Dear Ms. Lucky:

It was a pleasure to meet with you and your mother in my office on 6/16/97 to discuss the possibility of you having surgery to change the appearance of your nose. You stated that you are on no medications, have no known allergies to medications, and have never had any past surgery requiring general anesthesia. You denied having any diabetes, hypertension, asthma or other respiratory problem and do not smoke. There is no history of hepatitis, heart murmur, irregular heart beat, chest pain, or any history of bleeding disorder. You do use aspirin products at the time of your period.

You denied any injury to your nose and have no difficulty breathing. You do have seasonal hayfever in the fall, which you treat with a decongestant. Specifically, you stated that you did not like the profile of your nose and felt that it was too long and too wide.

Physical examination reveals that the nose is a little long and wide. There is no dorsal hump. Internal examination of the nose revealed the septum is slightly buckled but nearly straight and of no concern. I did mention that we saw large bilateral inferior turbinates. The airway was good on both sides and on deep inspiration through your nose, there was no evidence of any internal nasal valve collapse. You do have a short upper lip.

If any of the above information is incorrect, please contact our office so we may correct our records.

In addition to all the other information that you were given I would like to review some additional points with you. Before one considers any elective surgery such as this you should not only be familiar with the procedure but also the possible risks and complications of such surgery. In order that you make a truly informed decision, it is the policy of this office that no patient is allowed to schedule surgery until all of their questions have been answered to their complete satisfaction and that they understand the operation, its possible risks and benefits, as well as alternative therapy.

Surgery can be performed either as a Day Surgery patient at the hospital or at an outpatient facility such as the Southtown Surgery Center. The operation is performed under general anesthesia which as you know carries a certain risk in itself but this risk should be considered minimal in someone who is otherwise healthy.

I described the surgical approach which is known as an open rhinoplasty that is there will be no incisions on the columella which is the portion of the base of your nose between your two nostrils. We have found, in general, that these scars tend to heal quite nicely but there will be a permanent scar the exact appearance of which cannot be preoperatively predicted. The open approach allows us to better visualize the underlying structures with which we work to create the new structural system of your nose. I feel that direct visualization of these structures as we are working on them allows us to be more precise with the surgery trying to meet your objectives for having the surgery. As I told you in as many as fifteen percent of all rhinoplasties secondary surgery may be necessary. I hope that this percentage would be lower using the open approach. The cartilaginous and bony framework is re-shaped and then your skin must redrape over this newly created framework. It takes about one year to see the final result from such surgery on the nose. The skin must drape over this new framework and shrink. As we discussed various skin textures drape differently. For instance, somebody with fine skin can expect that the skin would drape very nicely whereas somebody with thick, oily skin may not have the skin drape as well and take longer to heal. Because the skin is elevated at the time of surgery, it is also denervated and the tip of the nose becomes numb for several months and has an unnatural, woody hard feeling. This generally goes away and you get return of feeling to your nose. One must be careful to protect against sun or frostbite during this time as there could be injury from either one.

Bleeding is always a possibility, and I would ask that you take no aspirin or aspirin containing products such as Anacin or Bufferin for at least two weeks prior to surgery. Your only pain medication you should take without consulting me would be Tylenol.

It is unusual to get an infection in the nasal area because of the good blood supply to the area, but it could be possible, therefore, we do use a broad spectrum antibiotic at the time of surgery in an attempt to reduce this risk. Following surgery, you will note that there will be swelling around your eyes which will turn black and blue. This normally lasts for a period of a few weeks.

In order to try to reduce the possibility of bleeding from your nose after surgery, we place packing in your nostrils at the time of surgery. It is not unusual to have some ooze in the immediate post op period but certainly any frank bleeding should be reported to us. It may be necessary to return you to the operating room to control this bleeding. You will find that your nose is swollen for a few months following surgery. In order to have the swelling go down as soon as possible, I would ask that you refrain from any activity that raises your blood pressure or do much in the way of bending over which would also tend to retain the swelling in your nose.

You will have a splint on your nose which is worn normally for one week. The packing in your nostrils is usually removed the next day.

Whenever one considers cosmetic surgery it is important that you have a clear understanding of the procedure to be performed and also a thorough understanding of the possible risks and complications of such a procedure as well as alternative treatment which is to do nothing.

I invite you to return for additional consultation at no additional charge should you have any unresolved questions. Remember that I stated that there must be a balance for you between the risks and the rewards and that you must have clearly communicated your desires to me so that there can be a meeting between your desires and my surgical ability to fulfill these expectations.

My surgical fee for the rhinoplasty is $2,750. This procedure is not covered by your insurance, therefore, the fee is due in full two weeks prior to surgery. The surgery takes between one and one and one-half hours to perform and I would estimate that there would be costs of $800–900 for the use of the operating room if done at the Surgery Center. The anesthesiologist's fee is in the realm of $600. I would estimate that should you choose to have surgery done at one of the local hospitals you could add an additional $1,000 to these approximate fees.

If you have any further questions please do not hesitate to contact me. If you desire to schedule surgery you may do so by contacting this office and arrangements will be made for you to return to have photographs taken, a history and physical performed, and the necessary forms to be completed for your surgery.

Sincerely,

M.A. Goodman, M.D.

CHAPTER 9

Patients as Partners

"This is my vow:. . . to love the sick, each and all of them, more than if my own body were at stake,. . . not to collect any money without earning it,. . . not to guess, but to know."

Paracelsus (1493? – 1541)

A controlled environment is another means of communication between the creator of the environment and the "consumer." To the extent that you manage your patients' surroundings, you are responsible for their milieu. You have another opportunity to insure that your patient has an optimal health care experience. The converse is a liability to both of you: to the extent that your patients perceive that they are not receiving optimal care, they are less likely to heed the advice you give them, and (assuming your advice is great), will be less likely to have a good outcome. And, of course, you are at greater risk for a medical malpractice claim.

Communication is a pervasive concept. It's how each member of the health care team, the receptionist, the telephone operator, the billing clerk, and the office nurse, relates to the patient. It's how the office communicates with the patient through the educational materials, instruction guides, reminders, and signs and notices in the office. The environment in which your patient is seen is also a form of communication. In managed care you will be rated for the environment you create. These ratings will be used for various purposes, potentially including accreditation, compensation, and marketshare. Creating the right environment is fundamental to good patient care, increases patient satisfaction, provides a competitive edge, and reduces liability risks.

As we have shown earlier, communication breakdowns are often the culprits in malpractice claims.[1,2] In part these miscommunications occur because the right environment for the patient was not developed in the first place. Patients are not made to feel that they are listened to, or believed. The Picker Institute study of hospitalized patients revealed some startling perceptions. Almost 24% of patients felt that their concerns and thoughts were not attended to.[3] This means that the major cause of lawsuits—miscommunication—is happening at a more prevalent rate than anyone realized. Preventive action has now become mandatory. Creating the right environment can also create a conducive atmosphere for patients to feel better about the practice, to become more involved, and to be more cooperative, more active patient partners.[4] This is the essence of a co-active practice.

Accrediting agencies, such as the Joint Commission on Accreditation of Healthcare Organizations (Joint Commission) and the National Committee for Quality Assurance (NCQA), look closely at the environment that is created for patients. All patient satisfaction surveys include questions designed to evaluate the environmental component of the practice as viewed by consumers. There are multiple pressing reasons to be concerned about the environment you create for your patients. A healing atmosphere:

- helps achieve a co-active practice, which means greater patient cooperation, and therefore can improve outcomes
- increases patient satisfaction
- is important for accreditation
- reduces the potential of a medical liability claim
- enhances employee satisfaction.

WHAT IS THE RIGHT ENVIRONMENT?

The right environment is a healing environment. This means a milieu in which patients perceive that they are being cared about, respected, believed, and involved in their own care, and that you are listening to them. To do this, it may be helpful to reexamine the environment, through the patients' senses, as they would go through each step in your practice; this is often referred to as the "ten points of contact." Your practice is changing with the greater restrictions of managed care. Even if you have not recently merged, networked, or hired an advanced practice provider, it still has changed significantly because the perceptions and expectations of your patients have changed. This is an area fraught with the danger of having a false sense of security: "My practice is very friendly," "My patients like me," "I've always been close to my patients," or "I've never had a lawsuit." A reexamination is necessary, looking at how each member of the health care team interacts at each stage. A more thoughtful and serious evaluation is necessary as your practice adapts to the new environment.

THE FIRST CONTACT

What is the first contact the patient has with your office? In managed care it may be the marketing or promotion that is being done on your behalf. It is prudent to find out by reviewing the promotional or educational materials that are being provided to the organization's members (your patients) and see what they are being promised. This will help you understand what their expectations may be. If you see information that appears to be erroneous, or inconsistent with reality, you need to start a dialogue with the managed care organization in an attempt to make sure false expectations are not created. There is often conflict and stress between those who need to market a managed care plan, and risk management and legal departments.

In a recent case of an alleged misdiagnosis of breast cancer, the plaintiff focused on a promotional marketing piece that proclaimed in bold letters, "the most comprehensive health care from our doctors—quality care without the worries." Another section indicated, "Our doctors believe their time with the patient is the most important time they have." These all make for very appealing slogans, but when put in the context of the particular case, they created a troublesome picture. In this case there was an alleged misdiagnosis of breast cancer. The patient was seen over the course of a year by a nurse practitioner who carefully examined the patient, but did not detect a lump. A mass was found later and grew rapidly. The patient insisted that there was a delay in diagnosis, which increased the risk of metastasis which had, in fact, occurred. A review of the records and of the deposition transcript of the nurse practitioner describing the careful evaluation, made it apparent that the care was prudent. However, when set side-by-side with enlargements of this marketing material, additional questions arose. Why didn't the marketing material mention nurse practitioners instead of focusing on doctors? If the most important time for the doctors is seeing patients, why were nurse practitioners seeing the patients instead of doctors? If this was the highest quality care without the worries, why was this lump not detected? What standard of care would this nurse practitioner be held to? Was it going to be the highest quality of care provided by a doctor, as promised in the marketing materials?

Creating the right environment means creating the right expectations as well. When reality and expectations are inconsistent, problems will occur.

THE INITIAL VISIT—SCHEDULING

The way in which the scheduling of an appointment is handled is very important, since first impressions are often lasting ones, whether positive or negative. How the telephone is answered, whether it be by a smiling "hello" or a rushed "hold please" can make a big difference. Neil Baum, MD, a New Orleans urologist and author of several books on marketing in physician practice, puts a mirror by all phones as a reminder to his staff to "smile through the phone."[5] Considerations include how promptly calls are answered,[6] whether they are answered electronically or personally, whether callers are immediately put on hold or asked if they can be put on hold, whether the person receiving the call extends a demeanor of warmth and helpfulness, or is rushed or communicates a sense of being put upon. Finding an acceptable appointment time, in a fashion that will let the patient feel that the office is sincerely trying to cooperate, can be challenging. It is the challenging patient you most need to satisfy, and when you do, it will decrease your liability risk, since these are the patients who often put you at the greatest risk.

Consider whether the individual you have using the telephone has the right skills. You should have a systematic way to monitor how these telephone calls are being received and determine whether the individual responsible for these calls continues to maintain the professional poise that you want, even when the schedule becomes hectic. Many of your staff will be able to process these calls and have the even temperament to do so; others do not. Make sure that your receptionist or telephone operator understands how important it is to you, the physician, the practice manager, and the practice as a whole, to maintain a professional demeanor even in the most trying of circumstances. Is this considered in your interviewing process for new employees? Is it part of the employees' training and is it brought up during their periodic evaluations? Is there a section in the employee handbook devoted to the level of professionalism and service that needs to be maintained during these telephone calls? Too often this is an overlooked area. Anger generated by mishandled telephone calls to the doctor's office is frequently expressed in plaintiffs' depositions and in patient satisfaction survey results.

THE FIRST 30 SECONDS

Every office has a personality, a tone, a culture, although it is often unintended and goes unnoticed by those who work there. It often starts with a strong personality at the top. Staff will mirror the attitude and personality of the physician or physician leaders within an office. Gladys detected that Dr. Smith was quite frustrated with the managed care arrangement. She heard him grouse about it numerous times to her and others on the staff. However, he would always end his comments with "but we're more or less stuck with this situation and we need to make the best of it." Gladys wouldn't remember that. She would only remember the frustration and the bit of hostility in Dr. Smith's voice. That frustration and hostility was then reflected in many different ways when Gladys was interacting with patients. Often this kind of attitude is apparent to patients in the first 30 seconds.

This overall personality or culture of your practice is not something you can hide, or even disguise, at least not for long. It's something which patients can often tell almost immediately when they enter into your practice. These first 30 seconds are often the most telling interactions with the patient. Does the receptionist greet the patient with a smile and a "hello?" or is the receptionist too busy on the telephone to notice that a new patient has walked in? Unfortunately, some offices simply have an impersonal notice, telling patients to sign in (and inadvertently potentially breaching confidentiality, especially if there is a column asking for the problem or presenting symptoms). Having the right individuals with the right skills serving as receptionists is paramount. They personify your practice personality. They represent you to the public on the front line and to do their job well requires a tremendous amount of energy, compassion, enthusiasm, and discipline, even under trying circumstances. Especially in a managed care environment, this individual is a key player. It is essential that this person is not alone in responsibility for answering the telephone, so that back up is readily available and every patient is greeted promptly.

Much depends on setting the tone for your office in that first 30 seconds. You either set the stage for a good relationship or, potentially, for a hostile one. Remember it may not even be 30 seconds—it could be just the 3 or 4 seconds it takes the receptionist to smile, connect, and to extend warmth. It takes no more time, but is critical. It takes having the right person and making it a priority.

YOUR OFFICE SETTING

Your office setting tells patients a lot about your practice. Obviously it needs to be scrupulously clean and well-organized. It ought to be comfortable but it need not be fancy. Patients should have enough room to be seated comfortably and to view any educational material or current periodicals that you have in your reception area. In managed care, the volume of patients that you see will probably increase. You may need to reassess whether or not your reception area is still appropriate. Remember that the patients coming to your office are already stressed, feeling ill, and uncomfortable. The little efforts that you make to attempt to make this wait for their visit a little more comfortable will go a long way.

THE WAIT

Waiting is still the number one complaint that is consistently voiced by patients. When patients are waiting, they feel that the doctor values his or her own time more than theirs. Almost everyone is involved in a fast-paced life, and schedules are often tight. Patients have additional responsibilities and other appointments to keep; almost everyone would rather be somewhere else. Expectations are high and the managed care industry often promises to see patients promptly and on schedule. Tension begins to build up in a reception area when no one is moving. While waiting for a doctor's appointment, I once heard a patient say to another, "Hey, I'm 9:15, who are you?;" the other patient replied, "I'm 9:00." Imagine my surprise, since I was sitting there since 8:30 and it was already 10:00! Some strategies to help with the wait include employing advance practice providers, starting exactly on time, allowing more time per patient, or even expanding your hours. The important point is to first find out about the waiting time in your office (discussed later in this chapter). If you have a problem in this area, even the fact that you are doing a study helps to assure patients of your concern.

Chronic waiting can be avoided. Strategies can be incorporated such as adding a slot which is open and not filling the last scheduled slot. In the managed care environment, where achieving greater levels of patient education and patient involvement is a major goal, this time could be used to ask patients to update their medical history, update a health status form, review additional health promotion information, or even various health policy and procedure matters. There is no reason that this time in the reception area should be viewed as down time. The visit should be scheduled and coordinated so some time can be given to obtain these updates and to provide more information. The more information that is exchanged between your patients and you, the more those patients will recognize that they really are partners in their own health care.

THE CALL BACK

Next, review how your patients go from the reception area to the inner sanctum, the beginning of the loop. Are they summoned, commanded, or invited? Patients often complain that the call back is more like having your number called at the butcher shop or bakery. Many practice groups have endeavored to make changes in this process, some with success and some not. The staff of one of my client practices excitedly told me that they had cured what they perceived to be a call back problem. They simply called patients by their problem instead of their name; they felt that confidentiality was protected since names were not used. And this was a urology practice! This is not acceptable, of course, but the point is that the call back can be made more comfortable.

DO THE LOOP

Every doctor should, occasionally, wait in the reception area and then walk the loop that the patient walks, perhaps on a day off and unexpectedly. Only then can you truly hear, see, smell, and feel what your patients do. You may be surprised how much confidential information can be seen or overheard. This is worrisome to patients because, although they are hearing someone else's confidential information, it makes them wonder if their personal information is being seen or overheard as well.

Are there bottlenecks that put people close to a telephone or dictation alcove? Do people go past the staff lounge on the way to the examining room, where they might observe the casual chat and discussion taking place? Are there charts that are left exposed? Many of these things can be easily remedied as soon as you know what takes place during the "loop."

THE VISIT

While all of these other facets are important, the visit with the physician, or health care provider, is still paramount. Patients often feel that doctors are, or appear to be, rushed when the visit occurs. If you put this in the context of patients who have taken time away from work or other activities, waited in the reception area for perhaps 30 minutes or more, waited in the examining room, and then felt rushed through a visit, you can understand why they may feel hostile at times. These patients feel cheated even if they aren't paying the bill directly. Remember that the marketing material they were sent promised they would receive the highest quality of care, in a timely, comprehensive manner, "without the hassles." The number two complaint uniformly voiced by patients is that when they finally see their provider, he or she appears rushed.

Much of this has to do with communication, as discussed in Chapter 6. The medical literature has an abundance of information on how doctors can improve communication or interactions with patients. This plethora of studies, as well as the continuing frequency of lawsuits based on miscommunication, is evidence that there is still a great need. Patients want their doctors to sit down. They want their doctors to look them in the eye and avoid looking at their watch. They want to review why they're there and to be given time for questions. They don't want to be interrupted and they want empathy for their problem. Most patients do not have the medical sophistication to be able to judge our clinical skills, but every one of them has the skill to judge how they feel we are communicating with them. They also obviously want answers and they want help. In the University of Chicago/Levinson Study, cited in Chapter 6, which audiotaped many physician visits, it was found that a very short amount of additional time made a difference in the interactions with patients.[7] Those physicians who spent that additional time were the ones who had many years of practice with far fewer malpractice claims against them.[8]

SECONDARY AND TERTIARY CARE—SPECIAL PROBLEMS

The focus of a specialty practice often causes lopsided expectations. The specialist needs to focus on the particular problem for which the patient was referred, often to the exclusion of other concerns, which, although quite appropriate, patients may not understand. Many specialty visits tend to be short and to the point; yet the wait for the appointment in the reception area, and in the examining room tend to be longer. No wonder there is a bit of resentment toward the specialist who doesn't take the time to hear all of the patient's other concerns. In part, this can be handled through patient education material, or personal explanation, so that the patient understands the particular role of the specialist. Those other complaints or concerns by the patient should never be simply disregarded, however, but duly noted and referred back to the primary physician. Above all, patients need to know that they're being listened to and that their concerns are being heeded.

COMPLETING THE LOOP

The visit really is not over after the interaction with the clinician. The patient needs to be ushered to the area in which other business and clinical matters may be handled. If it's not a capitated arrangement, there may be financial information that has to be exchanged. There may be some confusion as to what is or is not covered by the patient's insurance. There could be co-pay or other financial arrangements that need to be made. Having an individual who is knowledgeable in these business areas, as well as being cheerful, patient, and a good communicator, is essential. Often there is a bottleneck at this area and patients can have an otherwise positive interaction with the physician spoiled by a prolonged wait to settle the account, or schedule the next visit. Since many patients are completely befuddled about the workings of various types of insurance, gap insurance, deductibles, co-pays and the like, someone has to have the time to help patients. Much of this information is confidential, so if there is a bottleneck at this area, great care should be taken to arrange the way this aspect of the patient's visit is handled so that confidentiality is maintained.

Arranging consultations and referrals smoothly is another critical area. Systems can be developed to create seamless levels of care. Using patient satisfaction surveys, described later in this chapter, will help in understanding where there are glitches in the system. Addressing these areas will pay large dividends.

If patients at check out still voice clinical questions, this feedback needs to be given to the provider. Patients should not leave your office without understanding what the next step is. A check out clerk once said that patients, especially those from one particular physician, often asked her clinical questions as they were leaving—questions that she was not equipped to handle. After being urged to talk to her physician, she said, "I could never do that! He would be so upset." (It is disturbing to learn how physicians can, inadvertently, intimidate their staff members.) The check out person agreed, however, that she could write, or e-mail, a short memo to the doctor, saying something like, "I am sure you would want to know that Mrs. Q has some more questions about her medication. Her telephone number is…"

STILL NOT OVER?

You are not finished creating the right healing environment for your patient. In many specialties, particularly after a procedure or a major change in medication, there ought to be a follow-up telephone call to find out how someone is doing and if there are any further questions. Doing so not only increases patient satisfaction but helps to assure patient cooperation and a good outcome. This is more important than ever in a capitated environment where some patients believe that corners are being cut and that, because there is a set fee, the physician is no longer willing to spend additional time after the procedure. That simply is not true, for many reasons, including the fact that complications are costly, not only to patients, but to the providers. Making sure the patients truly understand their post-procedural course is essential. Follow-up phone calls are being made in many practices with wonderful results.

The same is true for the reporting of test results. In the past, many patients have been told that they will not be contacted unless their test result is abnormal. Patients are traditionally uncomfortable with this but, if that is the office practice, often will not voice concern, although some will call their doctor's office regardless. Some even receive an explanation that, "if you've not heard, you should assume that there is not a problem." This is not comforting to the average patient and it certainly does not portray a practice that cares about the whole patient, including the level of anxiety. Systems can be created where all test results are reported back to patients. Failure to obtain and make patients aware of test results may lead to late diagnoses and is a significant cause of malpractice claims.[9] It is also a major source of patient dissatisfaction.

WHEN THERE IS A PROBLEM

Patients have learned that they need to be assertive and inquisitive; otherwise they may lose out in the health care shuffle. This tension fosters anxiety, fears, and doubts, and this rainbow of emotion is a breeding ground for claims. You will get complaints. The way in which you handle those complaints is a key element in creating a healing environment. Too often the reflex response is to become defensive. Loyal staff members, like Gladys, intuitively try to protect their doctors. Patients are ready for an argument and the situation quickly can become adversarial, instead of a partnership. A complaint should be viewed as a call for additional information, additional communication. Even though some patients are chronic complainers and some of these complaints are without justification, the initial response should be one of finding out the source of the complaint, and why the patient feels it is justified. After this, ways can be explored to resolve or defuse the complaint, which may simply be listening. Some problems cannot be resolved, but patients feel better if they know they have been heard. The patient who is mishandled through the complaint process puts you at tremendous risk, not only for a complaint to your managed care organization but for a medical negligence claim.

SENDING THE BILL

Billing, including the way in which attempts are made to collect outstanding balances, is all part of the patient care environment, a form of communication. An unpaid balance may be a subtle call for more information. It may be a not-so-subtle expression of anger. It may be the symptom of another item for the patient's Problem List, an impending financial crisis. Always it is worth an inquiry before resorting to any adversarial action. Looking at the way your 30-60-90 day letters are written is also advisable to make sure they are firm but not too quickly adversarial.

WHAT TO DO FIRST

Detailed planning is required to create a healing environment, and could begin by reevaluating each of the points of contact, with a view to increasing the probability of the interaction becoming a positive one instead of a negative one. This environment provides an opportunity to create a caring partnership, which is good for patient care and for you, the most enjoyable way to practice. Do not assume that your practice is already doing all of these things perfectly. We have found that there is a false sense of security among many physicians, who believe that their patients already feel appreciated and that they have already achieved an optimum healing environment. There is a spectrum of success in this area.

Start with the premise that all of us could do better. The delivery of health care services has changed and physicians, both in office practice and in hospitals, are finding that the use of resources is being squeezed. Changes in the environment are insidious and often not discovered until a problem has occurred. One of the symptoms of such changes is an increased number of patient complaints, which all too often are ignored as simply unreasonable. In reality, patients often do have unreasonable expectations, but in part, we as the health care industry, are responsible for those expectations. Those expectations have been driven by the successes of health care providers in the past and are being fed further by managed care marketing. The reasonableness of those expectations is irrelevant; still, physicians need to try to bring those expectations in line with reality. Regardless of the expectations, we must address all of the various points of contact with patients in order to create an optimum healing environment.

DOCUMENTATION: A PART OF THE HEALING ENVIRONMENT

Creating a healing environment also means good documentation. Although primarily intended for the welfare of the patient, good documentation also helps to create a healing environment for the physician, removing much of the dread of a malpractice suit. Good patient care has always required good documentation, but the need and importance of these recordings has greatly expanded. Records were always needed for communication within the practice, but are now required for communication with other professionals beyond the practice, with peer review bodies, with managed care for utilization review and for billing, for the patient, and perhaps, even for the patient's attorneys.

Revising one's record system can be a daunting process, but does not need to be if done incrementally. Physicians' responses to these revisions regularly seem to fall into three categories. One group says, "I'm not sure where to start." When you have that feeling, the danger is that you don't start at all. You are overwhelmed by the task and at times feel frustrated. Others will say, "I haven't had a suit. Things couldn't be that bad." These individuals may have the same feelings as the former group, but latch on to a false sense of security. The last group is the most interesting and probably the largest. These are individuals who say, often sarcastically, "Oh, I've heard much of this before... be nice... care, this is all common sense garbage. Of course we're doing that. Tell me something new." What is interesting about the last group is that while they may have heard it before and they may know it, many physicians certainly do not practice it.

Try to set all of those feelings aside no matter in which group you find yourself. Instead of just riding on your past history, or assuming your systems are at least adequate, first find out. Scrutinize every aspect of your practice as thoroughly as a plaintiff's attorney might. Look for any weaknesses or omissions in your documentation systems. In part, this also means finding out what concerns your patients might have. It also means finding out if there are holes in your documentation systems which will be of concern to managed care organizations and to accrediting agencies. In order to avoid feeling overwhelmed, focus your energy on any systems that need work, make incremental changes, and allow yourself and your staff to measure and appreciate the progress you make. This can be a time saver. It allows you to focus on your problem areas, which are probably aspects of your practice which prevent you from being efficient.

Many physicians have become frustrated, and even bitter, that the practice of medicine is simply *not* like it used to be, when doctors just did good clinical work and the patients and payers appreciated the quality of care provided. Those days are gone. Fundamental changes have occurred to the industry, mandating reexamination of many basic practice issues.

WHERE TO START—IS YOUR DOCUMENTATION ADEQUATE?

A documentation system that was quite adequate ten years ago almost certainly is not suitable now. A documentation check list may be helpful and can provide an effective working guideline for the person you assign to conduct a periodic documentation review. This review should include an assessment of the completeness, clarity, and quality of your entire documentation system. Health care providers, especially physicians, whose focus of attention is on the immediate concerns for the well-being of their patients, often do not take kindly to being reminded of their documentation shortcomings. The position of the staff member who is appointed to be the reviewer could be assigned as the "Designated Nag" and the role explained explicitly to everyone involved.[10] Hopefully, any anger generated will be directed to the role, and not to the person.

The following is an example of a documentation check list:

- Does your managed care organization's advertising promise more than you are delivering?
- Is your practice brochure adequate and up to date?
- Are the signs in the office helpful and courteous?
- Is the initial history form complete? Is there an explanation of its importance at the beginning and do patients sign it at the end?
- Is the chart being kept up to date, including demographic data and preventive procedures?
- Are all the basic components of the chart filled out?
- Do the notes follow the SOAP format? Are they keyed to the Problem List?
- Is the Problem List current?
- Are all notes legible? Are they dated and signed?
- Is there a current medication list?
- Is there a current preventive procedure check list?
- Do the notes on the physical examination address all of the findings checked as abnormal?
- Are the telephone triage protocols adequate?
- Are telephone calls documented? Do the notes contain the essential information: complaints and recommendations, time, date, and initials?
- Is every diagnostic procedure filed in the chart initialed to show that it has been reviewed by a clinician?
- What patient information materials do you have available?
- Does the chart include a patient information check list? Is it used appropriately?
- What is the length of time that the chart remains out of the file after a visit?

- Are informed consent forms adequate? Are they completed whenever indicated?
- Are informed refusal forms adequate? Are they used when indicated?
- Is there a documented recall system, for "no shows" and for follow up visits?
- Is there a follow-up mechanism for referrals?

This list is not complete, nor suitable for every practice, but is intended as a starting point and a list of threshold questions.

Alternately, you may want to consider asking someone from outside the practice to do your initial documentation audit. Most of us have a natural tendency to be somewhat blind to the defects or omissions in systems that we have created ourselves. We also develop shortcuts and abbreviations, which everyone in the practice understands clearly, but may be foreign to the other people who will need to read the records

It is very tempting to ignore a record system defect, even when it is clearly identified, because, "that really never caused a problem in all my years in practice," but the practice of medicine is vastly different from what it was five years ago. A documentation glitch or deficiency is often overlooked until a catastrophe happens. A diagnosis is missed, a patient is harmed, a medication error occurs, and a problem ensues. That problem could be a medical liability claim, an audit that uncovers document deficiencies, a problem with managed care credentialing, a report to the National Practitioners Data Bank if there is a lawsuit that needs to be settled, and a whole cascade of negative outcomes that could affect your practice.

FIRST FIND OUT WHAT YOUR PATIENT/PARTNER THINKS

The health care industry has finally recognized the primacy of the patient. The patient is our reason for being, not the art or science of medicine. This is not to say that pleasing our patients is our total raison d'être; it is not, but serving our patients' best interest is. These goals are often, but not always, synonymous. There are certainly times when physicians need to make decisions that are not pleasing to their patients, that they do not agree with, and do not want to hear. In these situations all the physician can do is discuss and explain, and occasionally even apologize or cajole, but adhering to what he or she believes is right for the patient. And, of course, document. Fortunately, this kind of interaction is the exception, not the rule. Usually our aims are the same.

Physicians need to find out how well they are meeting their patients' wishes, how they might serve them better, how they can ease their distress or add to their comfort. Every patient has an opinion, a belief, and a feeling about each physician and the practice group, and, in managed care, the organization. This is useful data: without it, physicians are deaf people playing violins. The music on the score is beautiful, but how are they playing it?

There are many ways to obtain this information: you can ask patients directly; use a suggestion box; gather patients in focus groups; hand them a questionnaire or send one to them, use follow-up telephone calls, or even use the "Standardized Patient" technique. Alternately, you could just count the patients who do not return.

Ask Your Patient

Asking patients directly is very useful if you know your patients well enough to know who will give you a thoughtful, honest answer, and who will just tell you what they think you want to hear. It is time consuming, however, and you certainly do not want to take time away from your other patients. It is also a difficult way to gather data that can be compiled, compared, and shared with your colleagues and staff. It is not likely to give you much useful feedback about yourself. It can be most useful in gaining some impressions about problem areas to be studied in more detail and more objectively.

Dr. Smith apparently relied heavily on this kind of assessment, in an informal way. He prided himself on his good relations with his patients, and expected them to tell him if they were dissatisfied. The problem (one of many) for Dr. Smith, however, was that those patients who were not pleased that he had not joined The Plan, simply went elsewhere. This is a kind of feedback, but not useful. It is too much like trying to see how close you can get to the edge of a cliff without falling off—you can't tell until you take one step too many.

Suggestion Box

Suggestion boxes have been around for a long time, probably not because they are so useful, but because they are easy. How useful are they really? They seem to solicit negative comments. No one ever "suggests" that everything is perfect, although there may be occasional compliments. They do provide a small outlet for a dissatisfied client to vent anger. They do not generate any statistically valid data, but they sometimes provide innovative and useful ideas.

Suggestion boxes are most useful when they are displayed in a prominent place, with signs inviting their use. They must be emptied regularly (what could be more oxymoronic than an overstuffed suggestion box?). To be most effective, the suggestions should at least be acknowledged, and answered, if possible. This can be done by using the bulletin board, or a newsletter, or, if signed, by a letter.

Focus Groups

Another way to gain information is to have a focus group. This means you can bring in a group of patients, either a cross section of your practice or a subgroup, to talk about how your practice could satisfy them more. How are their initial visits, how is the telephone handled, how long do they wait, what is their initial impression? Having the right facilitator for a focus group is critical. Patients may be uncomfortable about saying some things to doctors, but when there is a person there with the right skill to bring out this information, it can be an excellent way to find out how well you are satisfying your patients. It can be as simple as your office manager inviting patients in for a pizza lunch, posing certain questions and starting the ball rolling with discussion. Soon a great deal of information about all areas of the practice are covered, and you will have a wealth of information to consider.

For specialty practices, it may become important not just to survey your patients but also to survey your referring practitioners as well. This may include surveying employers, or payers, such as managed care organizations, and should also certainly include any advanced practice providers with whom you relate. Find out what makes their job easier. Find out how things in your practice can be done, organized differently, communicated better, to make your practice a stronger resource.

Patient Surveys: General

Patient surveys can be global, asking about every area of your practice; open-ended, asking patients to address any area of interest to them; or quite specific, focusing on a defined problem. Patient surveys have become a way of life in managed care, an indispensable management tool. Patient satisfaction surveys are here to stay. Accordingly, agencies and payers will more often be requiring surveys.

As described by Anne-Marie Nelson, et al., in their book, *Improving Patient Satisfaction Now*, the patient survey is a "collective assessment of patient expectations; it is also a way to monitor their satisfaction, behavioral intentions, and practice problems and trends."[11] In this age of consumerism, especially in the health care industry, making sure that patients are satisfied with their visits is critical. "Managed care organizations know that patients have feet; when things go on that do not satisfy them, they choose another health plan."[12] In other words, the rate of members who leave the plan or do not enroll for successive years will increase, an important marker for managed care organizations. The Medicare and Medicaid population will also have very sophisticated mechanisms available to show their dissatisfaction as provided in the new Medicare legislation. In many organizations, compensation agreements with physicians, advanced practice providers, and nurses is based, in part, on patient satisfaction, as measured by the surveys.[13] You will need to have patient satisfaction surveys to help you understand how patients are perceiving your practice. It makes sense to survey your practice, and uncover and improve weaknesses, before a third party does and uses it, perhaps, to determine the distribution of a bonus pool.

There are many different designs for patient satisfaction surveys and many different ways to accomplish them. This is an area that can feel overwhelming, but it doesn't have to be. When you do a survey, you will want to do it in a professional and complete fashion, and you need to be committed to sharing the survey results with both your staff and your patients. This may be done with a follow-up letter, if you have asked people to sign their questionnaires, or through a newsletter or the patient bulletin board. When you survey your patient base, remember that you are going to bring some concerns and problems to the surface. Failing then to address them would actually put you a step behind instead of a step ahead. Your follow-up should thank your patients for their efforts, describe the major findings, both good and bad, and your plans to remedy any problems. An initial survey will give you a baseline; but plan on repeating it on a regular basis so that you can continue to be aware of the changes in your practice and both you and your staff can see the results of your efforts.

Initially you may wish to contact a consultant for assistance in developing survey questions. The Patient Satisfaction Survey (see Exhibit 9–1) is very comprehensive, but would, of course, need to be tailored to your particular specialty and practice. This example is reprinted from the book mentioned above, *Improving Patient Satisfaction Now*, which is full of practical ideas and examples, and has an additional reading list. Many practices would start with a survey such as shown in the example, with permission, and then focus it to get more specific information.

When you compile your questionnaire, note that questions should be short, to the point, and posed in such a fashion that the patient has an equal opportunity to express positive or negative feelings. You need an honest appraisal of how you are doing in your interactions with the patient and how they are interpreting those interactions. You need an honest appraisal of how they're viewing all the various aspects of your practice. A good patient survey will allow you to get feedback on all the environmental areas that have been discussed in this chapter. Some commonly asked questions include:

- How long did it take to get an appointment when you called the practice?
- How convenient was the appointment time for you?
- How helpful was the telephone receptionist?
- What was the comfort or discomfort level of the reception area?

Exhibit 9–1 Patient Satisfaction Survey

We value your opinion! Will you please tell us how we're doing so that we can improve if needed? Your answers will be kept strictly confidential.

Who is your physician or care provider in this practice? ______________________

We would like to know how we are doing and where we may need to improve. For each question, place an X in the column that best describes your opinion of our care, services, and facilities.	*Needs no improvement*	*Some improvement needed*	*Much improvement needed*	*Not applicable*
1. The length of time between your call for an appointment and the day of your visit.				
2. The convenience of your appointment day and time.				
3. Days and hours we are open for appointments.				
4. The comfort of the reception area.				
5. Amount of time you wait in the reception area.				
6. Amount of time you wait in the exam room.				
7. Exam room temperature and appearance.				
8. The amount of time your physician spends with you.				
9. The amount of time nurse or other provider spends with you.				
10. The doctor's interest in you as a person.				
11. Courtesy of the office staff.				
12. Professionalism of the office staff.				
13. Courtesy of your doctor.				
14. Your doctor's medical knowledge and judgment.				

continues

Exhibit 9–1 Patient Satisfaction Survey *(continued)*

	Needs no improvement	*Some improvement needed*	*Much improvement needed*	*Not applicable*
15. How well your doctor listens to your concerns and answers your questions.				
16. Your doctor's willingness to refer you to a specialist when necessary.				
17. Doctor's explanation of your condition, diagnosis, tests, and procedures.				
18. Doctor's explanation of prescriptions and information about medications and side effects.				
19. Information provided about recommended treatments and options.				
20. Explanation of fees, co-pays, or payment arrangements.				
21. How promptly your phone calls are returned.				

Please answer a few questions below about our office, using a scale of 1 to 5, with 5 indicating greatest satisfaction.

22. Overall, how satisfied are you with the quality of care you receive in this practice?	1	2	3	4	5
23. How satisfied are you with how well organized and smoothly functioning our office seems when you call or visit?	1	2	3	4	5
24. How satisfied are you with the way our office staff and providers work together as a team?	1	2	3	4	5

Please circle your answer for the following questions:

25. How likely are you to refer family or friends to this practice?	Definitely would refer	Unsure	Definitely would not refer

continues

Exhibit 9–1 Patient Satisfaction Survey *(continued)*

26. How long have you been a patient in this practice?		1st visit	Less than 1 year	1 to 2 years	2 to 5 years	More than 5 years
27. Please check the boxes that indicate your age group and gender.	M ❑ F ❑	under 18 ❑	19 to 34 ❑	35 to 49 ❑	50 to 64 ❑	65+ ❑
28. How would you describe your physical health?		Excellent	Very good	Good	Fair	Poor
29. Please indicate education level completed.			Grade school	High school	College	Post-graduate
30. How would you describe your mental health?		Excellent	Very good	Good	Fair	Poor
31. What is your marital status?			Married	Divorced	Widowed or separated	Single

32. Please list any serious or chronic medical condition(s) you have.
____

33. Approximately how many times in the past 12 months have you seen the doctor or other provider in this practice? None 1 2–3 4 or more times

34. Who is your insurer, health plan, or HMO?
____

35. Based on your satisfaction with the care and service you receive, do you intend to remain with your physician in this practice? Definitely yes Not sure Definitely no

36. What is the one thing you like best about this practice? ____________________
____

37. What is the one thing you like least about this practice? ____________________
____

38. Do you have any comments or suggestions for improvement about which we have not already asked? ____________________
____
____

Source: Reprinted from A. Nelson, et al., *Improving Patient Satisfaction Now,* pp. 315–317, ©1997, Aspen Publishers, Inc.

- How long did you have to wait in the reception area?
- How long did you have to wait in the exam area?
- Describe the practitioner's interaction with you.
- Were the office personnel courteous?
- How well did your doctor listen to your concerns?
- Were all of your questions answered by your doctor or other practitioner?
- How involved were you with your treatment?
- Were the telephone calls you made to the practice returned promptly?
- Overall, how satisfied were you with the practice?
- Would you refer a family member to the practice?
- Please indicate your physical health, indicate who your insurer is, and any additional comments:

Patient Surveys: Specific

One of the specific problems that almost every practice needs to survey, because it remains a huge problem, is waiting time. Especially in a managed care environment, patients are finding waiting absolutely unacceptable. Starting from a "first find out" basis, you will want to find out if your patients wait and, if so, how long. Over the last 20 years, patients' expectations about waiting have changed significantly. In 1988 about 60% of patients thought that 15 minutes was an acceptable waiting time, but by 1995, 75% said they expected to be in the examining room within 15 minutes.[14] To find out, a simple surveying instrument can be used, which has the double advantage of giving you information and letting your patients know that you are concerned about their time. You should measure the time of the scheduled visit (not when the patient comes) to when they are seen in the examining room and then when the doctor actually sees the patient.

Some interesting things will happen when you audit the waiting time, especially in a larger group, and make the study physician-specific. One business manager related the following story: During their second year of doing an annual physician-specific wait survey, she was upset at something she saw. She happened to find one of the doctors erasing one of the recorded waiting times and changing it. She was surprised and was not quite sure what to do, thus the call to me. I told her not to worry, but thought it was wonderful that the doctor cared enough to try to change the results. I also told her to start recording it in pen!

By documenting the waiting times, you will know exactly what is happening, and reports can be provided to each of the practitioners. Otherwise it is just something that doctors are aware of because they know their schedules, but have no idea of the magnitude of the problem. Doing this audit on a regular basis can benchmark whether there is improvement or not. There are many systems of scheduling to improve these waiting times and to get patients' expectations in line with what the approximate time will be. There are also many techniques available for making the perceived time less. First find out.

Telephone Follow-up

There are other ways to do a survey than to have a complete patient satisfaction form or specific problem form. Much can be learned by having someone follow up with a telephone call after an initial visit and asking about the patient's experience. If you do this, it should be done promptly and someone should be assigned to the task, given instructions, and should have a format to follow to promote consistency. The findings should be tabulated and summarized so that you can understand the results.

The Standardized Patient

Another technique that has recently been gaining acceptance, is the use of the Standardized Patient. An example of this method was published by McLeod, et al., in *JAMA,* in October 1997. Their purpose was to test whether this technique would be useful in studying inter-physician variability in ordering tests and referrals, in prescribing behavior, and in total visit costs. This kind of information can be of vital interest to a managed care organization.

In this method, people were trained to act as patients, to present their history, symptomatology, and physical findings during a scheduled appointment with a physician. The physicians had all volunteered to participate, but did not know when, during the course of a year, the Standardized Patient (SP) would appear. McLeod, et al., chose four people to become SPs. They were all given the diagnosis of osteoarthritis of the hip, a past history of peptic ulcer, and all were also under treatment for type II diabetes mellitus and hypertension. Two of them had histories of treatment with non-steroidal anti-inflammatory agents, which had aggravated their gastrointestinal problems, and the other two had received alternate therapy for their hip disease. The training program was intensive, requiring from seven to fifteen two-hour sessions. The training was conducted by a physician from the research team and a psychologist, and the actor's performance was monitored by videotape by members of the investigating team.

There were 112 physicians who agreed to participate (63% of those who were invited) and each was visited by a Standardized Patient from two to four times. The physicians were asked to report any encounter in which they were able to detect that the patient was an SP; they were able to do so on only 11% of the visits. Following each visit the SPs were required to complete an extensive questionnaire concerning their observations of the encounter.

The results of the study were that the investigators were able to gather reliable data on physicians' services, tests ordered, referrals, and data that they considered to be moderately reliable on total visit costs. They found extreme variations in total visit costs, but these were found to be due to a very small number of physicians. The authors concluded that, "the Standardized Patient technology provides a reliable, feasible method to assess variations in resource utilization between physicians."[15] Although this study was conducted in Canada, they believe it to be equally applicable in the United States.

There are obvious drawbacks to this method; it cannot be used with many diagnoses, it is quite expensive and time consuming, and the mechanics are difficult. Also, the authors of this book fervently hope it would never be used without the physician's consent, which, of course, limits its usefulness, since those who know they are "outliers" may not participate.

Just as in any other diagnostic process, all of the possible techniques have their own specificity and reliability, their positive and negative aspects. You, your colleagues, your staff, and your managed care organization, should all work in concert, identify the information you most urgently need, as a first step. Then choose the option or options with which you are most comfortable. While it may be appealing to try to do everything at once, resist the temptation and stay with what is comfortable. The only option that is counterproductive, and may soon disappear anyway, is to do nothing.

ACCREDITATION

Another potent reason for all the concerns about creating a healing environment, monitoring your documentation, and finding out about patient satisfaction, is the need for accreditation. Your managed care organization needs to maintain a good approval rating in order to be competitive, which, in the business world, means survival. Two national bodies have been formed and generally accepted for the purposes of assessing many of the essential aspects of managed care organizations and/or providers.

The National Committee for Quality Assurance (NCQA) was developed in 1991 for the purpose of assessing the quality of managed care plans. The committee is a private, not-for-profit organization that is governed by a board of directors consisting of employers, consumer and labor representatives, health plan administrators, quality experts, regulators, and representatives from organized medicine. The standards that the NCQA follows were developed by health providers, employers, and union representatives to provide purchasers and consumers of managed care with more information about their health care choices. The ideal objective of the NCQA is to force managed care organizations to focus on the quality of care rather than on the cost issues surrounding health care. Consumers have shown their support for the NCQA accreditation with the fact that "more than 75% of all Americans covered by HMOs are in HMOs that have been reviewed by the NCQA."[16]

To receive accreditation from the NCQA, fifty different standards are used to analyze the health plan. These standards are divided into six broad categories. The six categories are: quality improvement, utilization management, physician credentialing, members' rights and responsibilities, preventive health services, and medical records. After these six categories are examined, the NCQA applies one to four possible accreditation levels. The four levels are: full accreditation, one-year accreditation, provisional accreditation, or denial of accreditation. The accreditation level of each of the managed care programs analyzed by the NCQA can be accessed on the Internet.

NCQA accreditation places the most emphasis on the quality improvement category, making it 40% of the total score. This category analyzes the quality of care provided, coordination of all the parts of the delivery system, access to care by the members, and improvements that the plan will be able to demonstrate. The physician credentials categories represent 20% of the score for accreditation. This category examines the training and experience of its physicians, history of malpractice suits, and periodic evaluations of the physician's performance in the plan.

Members' rights and responsibilities is assigned a 10% emphasis as a category in the accreditation process. This category examines how well plan members are informed about the plan in terms of access to services, choosing a physician or changing physicians, and making a complaint. In addition, this category considers how responsive the plan is to the member surveys.

Fifteen percent of the accreditation score is based on preventive health services. This category focuses on the plan's encouragement to members to have preventive tests and immunizations, and how successful these programs have been. The utilization management category is assigned 10% emphasis on the final score. This category considers the plan's process in determining the appropriate health services for its members, including denial of payment, the appeals process, under-utilization, and expertise of decision-making. The final 5% of the total score is focused on the medical records category, including how medical records are kept. An example in this category is physician follow-up on patient care.

Full accreditation is established when the health plan achieves the standards set by the NCQA in each of the categories or no additional action can be taken by the organization to place it into compliance with the standards. If an organization receives full accreditation, it will maintain that status for three years at which time the organization will be reviewed again under the standards that exist at the time of renewal.

This entire analysis and accreditation process is used to insure that the health organization plan is fundamentally capable of providing acceptable health care to its members. To make the accreditation process easier, the NCQA has also developed the HEDIS program to determine how well the organization actually provides the care to its members. HEDIS is a computer program that compares health plans by using 71 performance standards. These standards are amended periodically to keep them current with technological advances. These standards have been used to provide organizations with "report cards" to show achievement by the managed care organization. Through this program, the NCQA has been able to provide consumers with a standardized way of comparing and evaluating the various health plans that are available to them.

The development of the NCQA has also offered physicians many opportunities to cope better with the changes managed care has had on the health care environment. The NCQA provides critical information about the various plans with which a physician will have contact. This information allows the physician to make an educated choice as to the plan chosen. In addition, physicians will know which areas of the plans can be improved upon and cooperate with the plans to provide better health care.[17]

The NCQA creates a competition among various health plans. There is an incentive for the plans to make the improvements suggested to them so that they will receive the national recognition that will be appealing to plan members. Ultimately, the "NCQA's mission is directly aligned with the practicing physician's mission, which is to ensure that patients get the best care and service possible."[18] It is quite evident that inadequate or inaccurate documentation would make NCQA accreditation very difficult.

The Joint Commission on Accreditation of Health Care Organizations (Joint Commission) was created in 1951 as an independent, not-for-profit organization for the purpose of providing information to consumers and accrediting medically affiliated organizations. The Joint Commission has provided accreditation to more that 15,000 health care organizations, which includes 5,200 hospitals and almost 10,000 other health care organizations.[19] In addition to hospitals, the Joint Commission provides accreditation for long-term care facilities, ambulatory health care organizations, home care agencies, hospices, health care delivery networks, and organizations offering major mental health services.[20]

Through the accreditation process, the Joint Commission concentrates on the performance of the various organizations that it is reviewing. To do so, it has developed four general performance standards to analyze performance expectations of activities that will affect the care given to the members of the plans. These standards were developed by health care experts, providers, measurement experts, purchasers, and consumers. After these areas of performance are evaluated, the Joint Commission issues the health organization with one of six possible accreditation levels.

When the Joint Commission evaluates an organization, it examines four areas of the performance of the health care organization. These areas include patient care, hospital staff, infection control and safety, and organization leadership and management. Specifically, the evaluation of patient care involves patient assessment, medication use, operative procedures, patient/family education, and patient rights.[21] In addition, the Joint Commission offers educational programs to provide information to the health care organizations to suggest ways to improve the operation in each of these areas.

When the Joint Commission analyzes the four areas of a health organization, it considers eight aspects of the operation. The analysis reviews: rights, responsibilities, and ethics; continuum of care; education and communication; health promotion and disease prevention; leadership; management of human resources; management of information; and improving network performance. The health organizations can provide proof of compliance with the standards through organization or department documents; interviews with leaders, staff, patients, and families; patient unit visits; and medical records reviews. The guidelines for these standards are updated on a frequent basis, reflecting the changes that occur in the health care field.

After the survey is conducted, the Joint Commission issues a "report card" to the organization evaluating the level of compliance. The level of accreditation is determined by answering questions appropriate to each standard in order to evaluate performance expectations. There are six levels of compliance that each health plan can receive.[22]

The Joint Commission is heavily relied upon across the nation by federal and state governments to insure that the health care that is being provided is acceptable to its constituents. It is widely accepted as the organization that grants licensure and certification of health care providers. In addition, it serves as a monitoring body due to the fact that the health organizations that receive certification from the Joint Commission must be re-evaluated at least every three years and under certain circumstances more. This process is considered valuable because it insures that consumers of health care are receiving high quality and technologically accurate care. As in the NCQA accreditation, having a good documentation system is critical to this evaluation.

HOW TO CREATE A HEALING ENVIRONMENT

Recognize the importance of your practice environment, knowing that:

- it increases patient satisfaction
- helps achieve a co-active practice, with your patients as partners, which can improve outcomes through better cooperation
- is important for accreditation
- improves employee satisfaction

- reduces the potential of a medical liability claim.

Reexamine each of the points of contact:

- The first contact: does the advertising match what you are delivering?
- The initial visit, scheduling: is your telephone handled promptly, cheerfully, and helpfully?
- The first 30 seconds: is your patient welcomed promptly and pleasantly?
- Your office setting: is it comfortable, clean, organized, and user friendly?
- How long do your patients wait? Are you doing all you can do to make the wait seem shorter?
- Have you done the loop recently?
- Entering the loop: are your patients summoned, commanded, or invited?
- The visit: do you make direct personal contact with each patient? Can you allow them enough time to ask their questions? Do they perceive you as being rushed?
- Completing the loop: are there any bottlenecks?
- Follow-up: are follow-up calls made after a procedure or whenever appropriate? Does your system for reporting test results work well?
- When there is a problem: are complaints recognized as calls for more communication, rather than a signal for defense?
- The bill: are outstanding balances considered first as a possible call for information or a symptom of financial distress?

Assume that it is possible to improve your healing environment. Invite someone from outside the practice to walk through your patient care system. At a very minimum, sit in your reception area, then walk through the loop, waiting in line when necessary, and try to sense everything that your patients see, hear, smell, and feel.

Recognize that documentation is another aspect of a healing environment:

- Begin by compiling a document check list, including every aspect of your practice.
- Consider asking someone from outside the practice, with the appropriate skills and experience, to conduct your first documentation audit.
- Assign a “Designated Nag” to conduct continuing audits.
- Share the information obtained with colleagues and staff.
- Identify any areas which need immediate attention.
- Designate people to make needed changes.
- Repeat audit of specific areas after changes have been effected.
- Find out what your patients are thinking.
- Consider asking selected patients, but allocate time to do this.

- Consider inviting patients to meet in focus groups.
- Institute a suggestion box, publicize it, empty it regularly, and post or publish especially helpful ideas.
- Conduct a general patient survey.
- Identify the information that you want.
- Obtain help to formulate questions, from a consultant, or from the literature, such as *Improving Patient Satisfaction Now*.
- Share results with staff and patients, along with plans for correction of deficiencies.
- Re-survey at appropriate intervals.
- Conduct a specific patient survey to address known problems and monitor progress, and share efforts and results with patients.
- Consider other techniques, such as the Standardized Patient.

Congratulate yourself on having the courage to find out and expose any blemishes in your healing environment, with the help of your patient/partners, and making efforts to correct them.

CONCLUSION

Creating a healing environment for your patients in a managed care setting is far more complex than in a private fee-for-service practice. While these changes in the practice environment do add to the burden of the practitioner, they are also absolutely essential to a managed care organization and, therefore, equally essential for the physicians. There are also many benefits. For your patients, there is the protection of systems to minimize errors or oversights, continuing peer review, and in-depth coverage. For you, there are exactly these same advantages, plus help in establishing the systems that assure this protection and, once established, minimize your paper work. There is also the advantage of the malpractice liability protection that these systems provide.

REFERENCES

1. C. Vincent, et al., "Why Do People Sue Doctors: A Study of Patients and Relatives Taking Legal Action," *Lancet* 343 (1994): 1609–1613.
2. G.B. Hickson, et al., "Factors that Prompted Families to File Medical Malpractice Claims Following Perinatal Injuries," *Journal of the American Medical Association* 267.10 (1992): 1359–1363.
3. American Hospital Association, "*Eye On Patients*," (Internet presentation, available at http://www.amphi.com/eyeonpatients/charts.html).
4. D.L. Shelton, "Bridging the Gulf," *American Medical News* (4 September 1995): 10.
5. N. Baum, *Marketing Your Clinical Practice Ethically, Effectively, Economically* (Gaithersburg, MD: Aspen Publishers, Inc., 1992): 235.

6. A.M. Nelson, et al., *Improving Patient Satisfaction Now* (Gaithersburg, MD: Aspen Publishers, Inc., 1997) 217.
7. W. Levinson, et al., "Physician-Patient Communication," *Journal of the American Medical Association* 277.7 (1997): 553.
8. Levinson, et al., "Physician-Patient Communication," 553.
9. Physician Insurers Association of America and the American College of Radiology, *Practice Standards Claims Survey* (February 1997): 4.
10. T.L. Leaman and J.W. Saxton, *Preventing Malpractice: The Co–active Solution* (New York: Plenum, 1993).
11. Nelson, et al., *Improving Patient Satisfaction Now*, 64.
12. Nelson, et al., *Improving Patient Satisfaction Now*, 8.
13. D. Bellandi, "Prevention Inattention," *Modern Healthcare* (30 June 1997): 48.
14. D. Weber, "Convenience—You Still Have a Long Way to Go," *Medical Economics* 1972 no. 16 (21 August 1995): 68–83.
15. Weber, *Medical Economics*, 68–83.
16. "National Committee for Quality Assurance: An Overview," *America Online.*
17. "NCQA: It's Not Just Another Acronym," *Family Practice Management* (May 1996): 47.
18. NCQA, *National Committee for Quality Assurance 1997: Standards for Accreditation of Managed Care Organizations*. Washington, D.C.: National Committee for Quality Assurance, 1997.
19. Online: http://www.jcaho.org
20. http://www.nnlm.nlm.nih.gov/nnlm/jcaho.html
21. http://www.healthscope.org/hospital/accredit/index.html
22. Portions of the following level descriptions were taken from: http://www.healthscope.org /hospital/accredit/index.html. Information contained in this summary was taken from: JCAHO web page.

CHAPTER 10

Seven Risk Management Dilemmas

"It is a riddle wrapped in a mystery inside an enigma."
Sir Winston Spencer Churchill (1874 – 1965)

PREFACE TO DILEMMAS

Managed care today is a lot different from what anyone imagined it would be 20 years ago. The trends that have developed are different from what Paul Ellwood, MD, or Professor Alain Enthoven, two managed care pioneers, predicted as they explained in a recent article in *Modern Healthcare.*[1] Concerning managed care, Enthoven said, "some trends are different from what Paul Ellwood and I had in mind. We envisioned competing delivery systems and consumers who would have multiple choices in health plans." The article goes on to explain that the early developers of managed care thought fee-for-service plans would eventually fade away naturally; then consumers were supposed to migrate to more desirable and less costly managed care plans. This is what has happened in a few places such as the California Public Employees' Retirement System and Stanford University. Within both of those organizations, 80% of the employees joined HMOs, driven by consumer choice. However, now in most areas there is not a great deal of choice, and many employers simply replaced fee-for-service plans with one HMO.[2]

As explained by John Blum, Associate Dean, and Professor of Law at Loyola University Institute for Health Law in Chicago, the rapid acceleration into managed care has led to a potential collision course with quality.[3] The evolution into managed care was in part a result of the significant dissatisfaction among employers about the rising cost of health care. Managed care was not quickly embraced, and even after the HMO Act of 1973, still took until the late 1980s to catch fire. But catch fire it did and by 1995 over 45 million people were enrolled in HMOs. Soon, however, concerns began to rise regarding the quality of care provided by hospitals and physicians through managed care plans. A Commonwealth Fund study of 1,700 physicians found that nearly 60% of the physicians interviewed had serious concerns about health plans, particularly the external reviews, and the limitations that were placed on their clinical decisions.[4,5]

There continues to be an ongoing public outcry which has led to a massive amount of proposed legislation, often referred to as "patient protection statutes." These statutes normally address the perceived managed care abuses which include the so-called "gag clauses," limits for hospitalization for deliveries, mastectomies, rights of physicians, including due process rights when terminated, and their ability to belong to a plan. There has also been proposed federal legislation to try to protect consumers, such as the 1997 Kennedy-Dingel bill, referred to as the Health Insurance Bill of Rights Act.[6] This legislation is comprehensive, covering gag clauses, banning financial incentives from provider contracts, requiring HMOs to develop quality assurance as well as dispute resolution programs; prohibiting plans from denying emergency and specialty care; allowing women to select their own obstetrician/gynecologist as primary care physicians; requiring disclosure of managed care plan operational rules including co-payments, referral rules, utilization, and grievance; establishing a prohibition against coverage denials for medical care deemed necessary by the treating physician; and more. A working group met through 1997 to discuss patient/consumer rights in health care, and came to some conclusions referred to as the Patient Bill of Rights. President Clinton has announced that he will urge Congress to use their document as the basis for new Federal legislation.[7–9] One piece of legislation under consideration is the "Patient Access to Responsible Health Care Act" which would provide broad protections which some feel would be overly restrictive to health plans and could increase insurance costs.[10] States such as California have similar groups whose job will be to advise legislators on what reform is needed.[11] The panels are diverse so that different perspectives are heard, considered, and balanced. The issues are hotly contested and striking an appropriate balance will be the key.

PUT THE PATIENT FIRST

At the same time that legislation is being considered, the American Association of Health Plans, the organization composed of managed care organizations throughout the country, is attempting to create standards for the industry. One such effort is the "Put the Patient First" initiative, attempting to show that there was a good faith effort to respond to consumer concerns. Certainly, it is also an effort to start to rebuild their image. However, some people have sharply criticized it. Jerome Kassirer, MD, editor in chief of the *New England Journal of Medicine*, addressed this in an editorial in the *Journal*.[12] Kassirer stated that the "Put the Patient First" program does not go far enough, although he believes it's a good starting place. He criticized the fact that there are no enforcement methods, or teeth, and that most of the standards put in the Patient First program are recommendations and not requirements. Although it calls for informing health plan enrollees about utilization rules, drug formulary rules, and the process the managed care organization uses to determine coverage of experimental procedures and of financial incentives for physicians, it is only *if* the patient requests the information. In addition, it specifies that members do not have to release specific details of physician financial information.[13] Kassirer asked whether this can truly protect consumers themselves. NCQA President Margaret E. O'Kane does not think so. In the March 17, 1997, issue of *The AMA News*, she was quoted as saying, "Self regulation alone can't fully protect consumers. While many employers, especially large companies, use NCQA accreditation and quality reports to guide their health plan choices, others are unfamiliar with that organization. Regulation can serve as a back-up for private quality efforts. We think the market and regulators can work together to improve quality."[14] In that same article, Enis Fitzgivens, Deputy Staff Director for House Commerce Committee Democrats, indicated that the problem with self regulation is that it is unenforceable; health plans that do not belong to the American Association of Health Plans (AAHP) could "do quite well" while ignoring the group's policies.[15]

In a recent *Modern Healthcare* article entitled, "Patient-Protection Rift," this growing concern is reviewed in rather vivid detail. The article states that a group of not-for-profit HMOs, as well as consumer organizations, led by Kaiser Permanente has called for "an appropriate government entity" with the authority to enforce standards.[16] Some say that the California-based Kaiser, the nation's largest HMO with 8.7 million enrollees in 19 states and the District of Columbia, is simply trying to rebuild their own image. However, they should be applauded for at least this move, which is supported by other organizations such as Health Insurance Plans (HIP), the American Association of Retired Persons (AARP), as well as Families USA. Karen Ignagni, president of the AAHP has said, "Any significant changes in the current regulatory framework should be seriously and deliberately evaluated to understand their impact on voluntary employer based health coverage."[17] This point needs to be considered, since cost is in part what got us here, and studies have shown that as costs go up, the ability to afford coverage goes down. Further recent studies have shown that the public is less concerned about certain managed care reform, if the impact is to increase the cost of premiums or, worse yet, cause the employer to drop coverage.[18] In a recent telephone interview with Ignagni, she explained in a thoughtful way many of these issues:

> "Managed care recognizes that it is a little bit of a 'work in progress.' However, it is here to stay and is not a fad that is going to somehow go out of style. Physicians need to realize that their efforts and energies should go towards making the managed care system better. This can be done by physicians bringing their concerns, complaints, and innovations to health plans and beginning a dialogue. Health plans, now and

> in the future, will want to sit down with physicians and talk about which systems will work and which will not. This could include reimbursement, the way the appeal process can be streamlined, understanding their rights when contracting, innovative ways about delivering care, and resolving disputes when they arise."[19]

Ignagni indicated that she firmly supports the Putting Patients First Initiative. She believes that it is a concrete way for plans to restore trust with patients and physicians. She welcomes groups to look for the AAHP affiliates when evaluating plans.[20]

The following quotes, published in the *Modern Healthcare* article ("Patient-Protection Rift") come from several health care leaders and reflect the growing split over these issues:

> *"'Putting Patients First' amounts to little more than a thinly veiled attempt to ward off state and federal legislative actions to curb the abuses of managed care." – Journal of the American Medical Association* editorial by Jerome P. Kassirer, MD

> *"The 'Putting Patients First' initiative strongly reflects our support of patient-centered medical care."* – American Association of Health Plans

> *"There is a need for standards that will be legally enforceable [by] an appropriate government entity [with] adequate resources and sanction authority."* – Kaiser Coalition

> *"We want to make sure anything that is done does not disrupt the private-sector market."* – United HealthCare Corporation

> *"We intend to insist on even higher standards of behavior within our industry, and we are more than willing to see laws enacted to ensure that result."* – Anthony Watson, Chairman and Chief Executive Officer, HIP Health Insurance Plans

> *"A lot of this [Kaiser's proposed standards] is already embodied in existing regulations."* – Foundation Health Systems[21]

It appears that there are many approaches to this question of regulation, self-regulation, and what is the right balance, but all are a recognition that consumers, i.e., patients, are aware and concerned.

After reviewing the nation's literature on the subject, interviewing dozens of individuals involved in the industry, reviewing voluminous legal studies and legal decisions, we believe that it is clear that managed care can raise significant ethical and legal dilemmas. The resultant turmoil appears to be driven by the rapidity of the changes in the health system at significant and fundamental levels. The way that health services are being delivered is vastly different, and that has affected the care that is provided. However, patients are expecting that the difference in their care is that it will be delivered more promptly and more comprehensively. What a collision course: patients' expectations, which are being fed by mature managed care marketing; providers, who need to offer care at a very high level but conserve resources, often making what can only be considered as rationing decisions; and a legal system that holds providers accountable for the care consistent with those patients' expectations. What might be the result of all this?

1. THE SQUEEZE PLAY

Managed care, better described as the new health care environment, pushes expectations higher through aggressive marketing campaigns, which increase as markets mature. Managed care organizations have more commercials proclaiming "the highest standard of care," and "finally care you can depend on." One doesn't see commercials boasting that managed care organizations are excellent at conserving resources or reducing referrals or tests, or controlling costs. You have never seen a billboard that proclaims, "Good care…cheap!" Nor is it reasonable to expect that you should or will. The result is that expectations are higher than ever. Health plans are in part pushing like any industry in advertising, but they are meant to be sincere. The provider, however, in order to compete, must conserve resources to reduce costs. Whether it is a primary care physician who is capitated, a specialist who is subcapitated, a group of physicians who are involved in global capitation, or physicians who are involved in a PPO which controls utilization carefully, it doesn't matter. In close calls, in those gray zones, physicians are being encouraged to rely on their clinical judgment and postpone or avoid ordering the additional (albeit expensive) tests. Physicians are being prompted to see patients in their offices instead of the emergency department, or when seen in the emergency department, patients are discharged to their homes for observation ("call back if your symptoms get worse"), instead of being admitted to a hospital. Hospital admissions are declining and the amount of time spent in the hospital for observation is decreasing. Primary care physicians are referring to consultants later in the course of a disease and sometimes to a physician with whom they are not familiar. Practices are being told which laboratory to use and, in some cases, there are quality concerns. Volumes of visits and telephone consultations are rising, as is the use of advanced practice providers. All providers are being pushed harder.

This is simply the environment in which many physicians and other providers find themselves. In a survey which took place in a mature managed care environment in 1995 and 1996, only a third of the physicians surveyed would recommend the health plan that they were providing services for to a family member. Few believed that the authorization policies in place improved patient care.[22] In a recent study published in the *American Journal of Nursing*, two out of five nurses surveyed said they would not want a family member cared for in their institution.[23]

What if something goes wrong? What if a patient has a post-operative infection at home, or has a myocardial infarction on the way back from the hospital because he or she has been discharged instead of admitted for observation. What if a baby becomes dehydrated at home because the first time mother is unable to care for the baby adequately? A lawsuit ensues and plaintiffs' attorneys not only claim that the standard of care was breached, but that it was breached because economic motives preempted, or at least affected, clinical judgment. Experts are easily obtained and many are ready and willing to attack and lash out against this type of utilization control. We now have a profoundly injured plaintiff, a plaintiff's attorney ready to fan the fire that this physician made a utilization decision or an economic decision instead of a clinical decision, which harmed a patient, and an expert who indicates the standard of care was breached. The expert will go on to say that these are the types of problems caused by the strict utilization controls that managed care is using and something has to be done about it. Is it not hard to imagine why jurors become apprehensive and upset and that this has helped lead to an almost 14% jump in median malpractice awards from 1995 to 1996. It is one of the reasons that one-fourth of the verdicts in 1995 and 1996 were for $1 million or more.[24]

Recently in California there has been a claim made for "torture" in a denial of treatment circumstance against a West Coast health plan and the treating physicians. The case dealt with the alleged denial of treatment for a baby boy with congenital heart defects.[25] Would anyone have thought that claims could go this far?

This is the classic squeeze play. When expectations are rising, the use of resources declining, society is growing suspicious, and ready and willing plaintiff's attorneys are prepared to help "injured patients follow up with their rights," the conditions are right for an explosion. As Mark Hiepler, a noted plaintiffs' attorney from Oxnard, CA, stated in an interview with *Family Practice News*, "when you combine economics with care, you end up with conflict."[26] Hiepler explained further in a recent telephone interview: "The problem started when utilization became prospective. Then it began to affect people's lives, not just finances. From my perspective, when a doctor is involved in sharing financial risk with a managed care organization and he or she does not share or disclose that information, it is a breach of the fiduciary duty that a doctor owes the patient. Since that particular claim is not a medical malpractice claim, the doctor also does not have the protection of medical malpractice caps."[27]

The first step is to recognize that the environment has changed and that new risks are being created. You then need to get past the frustration and begin to sort through those risks and reduce your exposure.

How to reduce the risks:

- Recognize the potential conflicts between needs and costs.
- In practice err on the side of patient welfare.
- Discuss issues with patients and make joint decisions if possible.
- Rely on your clinical judgment.
- Document your decisions and your reasons for making clinically significant decisions: a snap shot.
- Act promptly if your decision was in error.

THE CHALLENGES INCREASE

The squeeze play is simply inherent in the rapid and fundamental change of the health care system. Employers and consumers wanted to pay less for health care for many good reasons. There was a lot of excess cost in the system perhaps, but squeezing that out wasn't going to be enough. Competition developed when consumers were told that certain organizations could, in fact, deliver high quality care for less. All of this moved forward at a very rapid pace and soon expectations began to climb at a rate faster than providers could meet in a cost effective fashion, without sacrificing quality of care defined in patient satisfaction, outcomes, and perceived quality. Patients became suspicious, and we have a legal system which is ready to hear those concerns. There is no easy way to resolve this conflict. Some observers say in time this conflict will resolve itself. Others believe that the quality of care may in fact be reduced. Still others wonder if the quality of care simply may be reflected by which contractual relationship is chosen. In other words, perhaps you will get the quality for which you pay. Will that mean there will be more cases for breach of contract or bad faith than actual tort claims? Patients will be able to enter into contracts with providers for a certain level of care. It will be specifically outlined in an agreement between the provider or managed care organization and the patient. It the patient feels that care provided does not meet the contractual terms, such as more in-depth screening, use of more sophisticated testing, specialty care provided at an academic center, they could sue on a breach of contract theory. In this respect, patients could "purchase" the level of care they desired.

Tort reform, although continuously on the horizon and enacted in some states, in all likelihood will not be the answer. A $250,000 cap, which has been proposed numerous times, is believed to have a significant effect from a cost standpoint. It is believed it could save Medicare from $480 million to $800 million over the next five years. (See the discussion of defensive medicine in Chapter 1.)

Efforts to reform the tort system should continue. Regulation, especially to establish some floor or to try to curb perceived managed care abuses, should also continue, as well as attempts by the managed care industry to analyze weaknesses and implement improvements. However, concurrently, we must begin to address problem areas that are already a reality on the front line, producing claims.

In trying to ascertain trends in liability areas which can be attributed to managed care activities, we asked for the help of the Physicians Insurer Association of America (PIAA). The PIAA is a trade association of physician/dentist-owned or operated medical malpractice insurance companies. The PIAA membership consists of 56 insurance companies representing over 235,000 physicians, 35,000 dentists, and 550 hospitals in this country and many abroad. The PIAA has considerable experience in conducting surveys aimed at identifying factors that lead to malpractice claims.

The member companies were queried and over 70% responded with data, sometimes in the form of research and reports, but more often in important anecdotal information, as to what problems providers were currently experiencing. In many parts of the country, managed care is just beginning. Many new claims were related to basic managed care tools, such as utilization restrictions, capitation, and closed provider panel selection. One senior claims analyst on the West Coast stated that many of these claims are driven by managed care utilization decisions but are often lumped together as "misdiagnosis cases." Claims overall are increasing, with the number of misdiagnosis claims being at the top. The value of claims is also increasing. Often claims representatives reported seeing lawsuits where it was clear that patients fell through the cracks and that their care was actually less coordinated in the managed care setting, or at least it appeared that way. There were reports of claims in which plaintiffs' attorneys were alleging a lack of financial disclosures on the part of the doctors and ones in which managed care organizations are co-defendants. One claims representative from Texas explained that it appears that plaintiffs' attorneys are eager to get the managed care organizations into the courtroom and perhaps attempt to bring the physician onto their side. We are not sure that is well-advised. We were also told that even in cases where a managed care system or organization had nothing to do with the claim, there is an attempt to inject economic motivations when possible. Certainly, this is to try to incite the jury. There are cases coming from early discharge without adequate instructions and many cases where a hospital admission for the emergency department was not recommended. In both these situations, again economic reasons were pleaded by the plaintiffs' lawyers.

What we have used, therefore, is the collective knowledge and experience of claims adjusters, and claims analysts not only from the PIAA, but from other large national companies such as the Medical Protective Company and the Catholic Health Initiatives, as well as many hospital and health system risk managers. These individuals are on the front line. They receive calls from physicians who are presented with these dilemmas. They receive information about claims and are in a position to resolve claims before they become a suit. Using that information, together with information gathered from a comprehensive review of the literature, we focused on the following specific dilemmas that are created with greater levels of managed care penetration.

It is important to note that no blame is being cited, nor is there a reason to point a finger. These are problems best characterized as inherent to the new health care environment. In many respects, and for the purposes of this book, it is not a question as to whether managed care is good or bad, but that it is here and that it is creating new risks for physicians, dentists, and other providers. *We believe that much of what managed care can bring is actually very good and that the next challenge will be to cultivate the good aspects of managed care, while addressing and reworking what is perceived to be bad.*

A risk manager's first step is always to identify a problem so that appropriate policies, procedures, and systems can be put in place to reduce the risk created by the problem. In part, that is what we are endeavoring to do here, setting aside any commentary, either from an ethical or political point of view. This expanded list of dilemmas is by no means all inclusive. There are multiple issues and sub-issues that flow from the dramatic changes that are occurring in health care. In parts of the country where managed care is more mature, the issues may be different. This is our studied analysis of problems that need attention.

2. THE GATEKEEPER

One form of utilization control implemented by managed care is designating a provider as a so-called gatekeeper. As mentioned earlier, we take issue with that description. It is a description that conjures up many negative implications and suspicions. This was never the intent, although in some sensational stories, it could be said that was, in fact, the effect.[28] The gate was meant to be nothing more than a system and the physician was supposed to provide guidance and direction within that system. Sometimes what appear to be rigid decisions have been made, and at times patients who are accustomed to receiving whatever care they want, feel offended. This concept was never intended to create a division in the patient-physician relationship. However, the way that plaintiffs' attorneys have used it in the courtroom is to explain that the gatekeeper's job is to keep the patient from needed care and that the gatekeeper is rewarded with financial incentives for doing the job well. This, of course, is precisely the opposite image managed care organizations and providers want to create. The gatekeeper is supposed to be more of a care coordinator, or a "shepherd" looking after the needs of their patients or "flock" on a continuing basis.

So-called gatekeepers have been in use in HMO settings, with different types of PPOs, and also in fee-for-service plans. They are paid a certain management fee, or coordinator's fee per month per patient. For this they are expected to see patients first, when they have a need, and make decisions about whether consultations or diagnostic tests are necessary. They are also expected to monitor and endorse certain types of preventive care and promote healthy habits. Their utilization is monitored, but there may or may not be any financial incentives or withholds connected to it. With capitation, the gatekeeper in a traditional HMO, of course, does have financial incentives to use resources carefully, albeit appropriately. The gatekeeping role with financial incentives, of course is subject to potential abuses.

Regardless, the so-called gatekeeper accepts additional responsibility and will have an inevitable patient perception problem. That additional responsibility has not yet been fully evaluated. If one reviews the literature that is provided to plan members, it will be noted that health maintenance, preventive services, and health promotion are all part of the primary care or gatekeeper's role. It will not be surprising to find a claim against them when someone's cholesterol is not kept in check, leading to an allegation of an undiagnosed cardiovascular problem, or even when something adverse happens to someone who has not been counseled appropriately on weight loss, tobacco use, or other adverse health habits. Perhaps the gatekeeper will be held responsible for an undiagnosed psychiatric illness that leads to a suicide attempt, or liability to a third party for failure to diagnose an HIV infection and to advise the proper precautions. Will the gatekeeper then be responsible or liable to third parties or other individuals with whom the gatekeeper's undiagnosed patient comes in contact? The gatekeeper must approve the need for tests and referrals to consultants as well. Therefore, under the heading of gatekeeper dilemma, one must first understand that the gatekeepers have an expanded role in general, and with capitation, the role and responsibility could be ever more expansive.

The perception problem is inevitable, even for those gatekeepers who are absolutely pure at heart. Patients whose primary care physician is capitated and is subject to strict utilization review often question, "is the gatekeeper refusing to refer to a consultant because of financial or other incentives?" Legislation has been proposed requiring that this type of information be made known to the patient. Many have suggested that this is an obligation that the managed care organization should fulfill. Others have suggested that informed consent encompasses telling the patient about financial incentives and often economic arrangements which may potentially affect clinical decisions.[29] Many frown on this as raising more flags than need be. The thought of physicians discussing whether a patient needs to see a consultant, then announcing that they have a financial incentive not to refer, seems very counterproductive and could undermine the patient-physician relationship. Of course, of concern are the same type of breach of fiduciary duty claims discussed earlier, which are already beginning to appear.

Physicians need to understand that they are going to be held accountable for failing to provide good clinical judgment in these situations and refer to consultants when they judge that it is necessary. Perhaps over time, physicians' judgment in the gray areas will change. Perhaps the standard of care will evolve. The law still recognizes that as long as physicians use good clinical judgment, their failure, in retrospect, to choose the appropriate avenue is not malpractice, assuming there is good clinical substantiation.[30,31] However, this remains an explosive area. Some patients and patients' attorneys will jump to the conclusion that financial motivation was pushing clinical decisions and that some form of *disclosure* about this potential conflict should have been made. This is an important issue since it goes to the heart of the patient-physician relationship. Will the physician continue to be the patient's advocate? Is the gatekeeper type role going to undermine the fundamental relationship with the patient?

One point of view is that not much has changed. In the past there were incentives to overtreat, which still exist in the fee-for-service environment, sometimes resulting in harm to patients. Does allegedly undertreating cause more harm? We live in a culture that is not used to being "undertreated," even if it may arguably be in our best interest. Part of the problem may be healed with time as images are rebuilt and trust is reinstated. However, in the interim, this is an area that needs attention.

Higher levels of patient education are needed. For example, within the patient brochure, as suggested in Chapter 7, you could include a section about managed care, and what it means. You could explain that patients in some managed care plans have a capitated arrangement and that, in order to keep patients' premiums at an acceptable level, all providers are asked to be efficient with resources. You can be proactive and explain that the doctors' decisions are always based on good clinical judgment. They are as concerned about unwarranted referrals to consultants, and unwarranted testing, as they are about getting patients in promptly for tests that are needed. These may not be the exact words or phrases, but the point is that you can put the information in the appropriate format and provide it in context. Some form of disclosure is necessary, but it ought to be at the beginning of the relationship, similar to the requirement that physicians disclose which facilities they refer to in which they have a financial interest.

Being a coordinator of care should be described in the positive sense as someone who will help the patient, be there to answer questions, and help make determinations about referrals and testing. This balances the need to know about incentives, with putting the information in perspective. It also gives patients the information at a more appropriate time—at the beginning of the relationship—not when the patient is under duress. If the law evolves to the point where disclosure has to be made about financial incentives, whether it is a capitated arrangement, a withhold, or a risk pool, as part of an informed consent process, the timing of giving this information will have to be reviewed. One would hope that this does not occur, and that providing this information at the beginning of the relationship will suffice. We believe making this type of disclosure would, on balance, be traumatic to the relationship. Clearly more information will need to be communicated to the patient, and when and how that information is communicated can make a big difference.

Also, the term gatekeeper should be dropped. It should not be used in contracts or in literature, with the term "coordinator" or a similar word used instead. Perhaps the primary care physicians could be the "medical home" of the patient. This is the term used for the gatekeeper in a primary care case management project in Lancaster, PA, for a Medicaid demonstration project with great success. Although not a capitative project, the primary care physicians helped direct and coordinate patients' care. The data showed that costs were reduced and satisfaction increased.[32] Patients understand the system better and had greater access to specialty physicians. Physician satisfaction with the project was also high, an important, although at times underemphasized factor. Many managed care organizations have already initiated many different changes. Perhaps such a change should be accelerated. Maybe we should not even refer to this entire concept as "Managed Care." How about "Coordinated Care" or "Managed Health?"

Because the clinical decisions that you make are going to come under scrutiny, clear and concise documentation as described in Chapter 7 is mandatory. Being able to obtain appropriate experts in the event that a lawsuit is initiated will be essential. An appropriate expert should be able to look at the documentation, a snap shot you have created that shows the patient's condition at the time when this decision was made, based in good clinical judgment and not on financial motivation. Having strong experts on this standard of care question is probably more important than ever. This is especially true for the danger points, such as a decision as to whether the patient should go to the emergency department, a decision not to refer at this time to a specialist, or a decision not to get a further diagnostic test; in other words, those decisions that could potentially be perceived as having a perverse economic motivation. Until we have resolved this particular dilemma, documentation—especially regarding the danger points— and strong expert support for clinical decisions become essential.

How to reduce the risks:

- Abolish the term "gatekeeper;" use coordinator or medical home or shepherd.
- Change the name "managed care" to "managed health" or "coordinated care."
- Understand the role of being a "coordinator."

- Explain yourself as a coach or coordinator of care in your patient brochure as well as in your interactions with patients.
- Start a dialogue with your managed care organization to have them explain your role as a coordinator, and to have discussions concerning financial incentives.
- Provide disclosures of financial incentives in the practice brochure in context, explaining that all decisions are based on good and appropriate clinical judgment.
- Discuss the issue with your patient/partner.
- Always be guided by clinical judgment and document reasons for referral plans, both reasons for referral and reasons for not referring a patient.
- Treat patients uniformly as to referrals, tests, admissions.
- Take a "snap shot" of clinical decisions, especially during danger points.

A related issue involves the multiple questions raised with the use of various utilization control tools. It is actually a combination of issues, which are described in the next dilemma.

3. UTILIZATION DISPUTES—IMPLICIT GAG RULES

Physicians have a duty to advocate on behalf of their patients. This precept has been upheld by law, based on the Wickline v. State of California and Wilson v. State of California[33]-type decisions. If physicians believe a certain course of treatment, a referral, or a test, is indicated clinically, and yet the managed care organization will not provide for the same, they need to attempt to work with the managed care organization to explain their position and support the patient in the appeals process. Legislation has been aimed toward pushing managed care organizations to have mechanisms in place to deal with these disputes. There will be more pressure on managed care organizations to resolve them promptly and fairly, with the careful consideration of an independent review panel.* Setting legislation aside, the answer is in striking a balance. The problem lies with the fact that physicians, both legally and ethically, have a duty to advocate for their patients. Yet if they do, will they hurt their chances of obtaining good contractual terms with the payer against whom they have to advocate, a potential negative incentive? Even if we acknowledge that there are no explicit contractual provisions referred to as gag rules, are there *implicit* gag rules?

In a survey in a very penetrated managed care area, in late 1995/early 1996, 16% of the physicians surveyed indicated they feared repercussions if they criti-

*In the future you will see different tracks, some are for urgent decisions and another for all others.

cized their plan. This statistic was reported as striking since it's in a particular jurisdiction that has a law that protects doctors from these so-called "gag rules."[34] The "gag rules" have fallen into disfavor. In fact, *American Medical News* reported that 14 states in 1996 and 4 states in 1995 passed laws prohibiting HMOs from "punishing providers for disclosing treatment options or for advocating on behalf of enrollees."[35] However, there still are implicit gag rules since physicians and physician groups need to negotiate with managed care organizations for various contractual or other reimbursement terms. As mentioned above, many are reluctant to take a position that is at odds with the managed care organization for fear that it could lead to an unfavorable bargaining position or, worse yet, termination. The rights of physicians who have been "deselected," or terminated, are in a state of flux. In the California case of Potvin v. Metropolitan Life, the physician gained the right to sue the managed care organization that terminated his contract without cause.[36] This case has generated a great deal of publicity and already additional jurisdictions have considered this position.[37]

In this case, Dr. Potvin, an obstetrician/gynecologist, had been terminated without cause, with 30 days notice from a panel in which he had participated for many years. Potvin respectfully asked for an explanation and allegedly was told that an explanation was not needed, but that a review of his malpractice history had shown that he did not meet the standard in that area. Potvin had three suits which had been dismissed and one settled in his 30-year career (an example of why it is important to prevent claims in the first place). Potvin sued alleging, among other things, breach of contract and bad faith and eventually, an appellate court agreed. Unfortunately, Potvin died in Fall of 1997, but his case still lives on, soon to be reviewed by the California Supreme Court. Physicians may well take the position that terminations that take place for no stated reason, yet are implemented after physicians have advocated on behalf of their patients, are against public policy. The courts will be more willing to accept the same. Nevertheless, resorting to a legal action is a long, time consuming and expensive process, a major threat in itself. The extent of advocacy that a physician is willing to take remains a dilemma.

The appropriate balance is in supporting your patient and your clinical decisions and becoming familiar with and following the appeals process set up by the managed care organization. Although this sounds as if it would be cumbersome initially, once there is a process in place, any disputes can simply be put through that system. If the patient does not obtain certain treatment for which there is subsequently a lawsuit, and you had made a recommendation and documented it, you will greatly reduce your liability. If in the lawsuit, it is alleged that the patient did not have a test or other service because reimbursement or medical necessity was denied by the managed care organization, yet clearly you recommended it, you will have a greater level of protection.

This type of utilization dispute will happen more and more and is inherent in a managed care system. In Texas and in some additional states, the courts or legislators have decided that a managed care organization can also concurrently be held liable for patients harmed through a course of treatment where utilization decisions were involved. Federal legislation has been proposed as well.[38] In this situation, having documentation of where you stood on the utilization decision will become extremely important. Further, if you should be terminated as the provider on a panel, without cause, your chances of having any type of recourse in the courts will be greatly increased if you have documentation that your interactions with the managed care organization have been on behalf of patients, were in support of good patient care, and were consistent with the managed care organization's own appeals process, policies, and procedures.

How to reduce the risks:

- When a clinical decision is made, make the recommendation to the patient, and document the need for the referral, test, or course of treatment, or the reason for refusal. In other words, let the patient know why or why not and take a "snap shot."
- When, through utilization review, a negative determination is made, document your attempts to advocate on behalf of the patient according to the particular managed care organization's policies and procedures.
- Understand the appeals process of the managed care organization and set up a system to comply with it.
- Do not participate in managed care bashing. Help the patient follow the appeal process and let the patient know your feeling that the test was needed and remember that the utilization decision does not take the place of your clinical decision.
- Do not have a big "HMO stamp" for patients in HMO plans and do not have different treatment protocols.
- Consistency is key, accept the fact that different authorization or referral patterns may have to be used, but your clinical practice should be consistent.
- Understand your contractual rights with managed care organizations from the beginning.

Another form of utilization control has begun to affect the length of hospital stays. This a change in the *where* reviewed earlier in this book (see Chapter 3). Some of these controls are simply changes to a different, more appropriate setting. However, systems need to be set up in these different settings to protect the patient. When harm occurs, retrospective analysis of why the patient was discharged will occur, and a claim may be filed for inappropriate discharge based on economic motivation. Change in the setting of the care, including lessening length of stay, is the next dilemma.

4. EARLY DISCHARGE

As managed care develops, the length of hospital stays decrease. In a recent article in the *American Journal of Occupational Therapy*, Charles Lundy and Joe Knox point out that services are delivered more and more on an outpatient basis and use less costly medical professionals.[37] They estimated that by the year 2000, 65% of all health care will be provided outside of hospitals and that 69% of nurses currently employed within hospitals will be working elsewhere.[38] They also predict that more will be expected from health care professionals as hospital operations are streamlined, and that nursing and allied health staff numbers will be reduced and patients will be discharged even more quickly.[39]

As patients are discharged from the hospital earlier, the importance of home health care discharge instructions and follow-up, increases tremendously. Most patients and their families are ill prepared for the amount of information that they are given on discharge. Although all of the information seems routine to providers, it is foreign to the patient who is recovering from a course of treatment. The present level of instructions used or what is usually used is often insufficient and frequently has led to litigation. Standard discharge instructions scribbled on a form are insufficient. The attorney/author has been involved in many cases in which discharge instructions were scribbled on the last page of the chart, a portion of which was preprinted and easily legible, but a portion of which was written by the physician and supposedly explained by the physician and nurse. At trial those discharge instructions became pivotal in the case. The discharge instructions were enlarged and jurors were asked whether or not they could decipher the writing (not the preprinted part, but the physician's handwriting). Usually they could not.

It becomes a "swearing contest" between the patient and the provider as to whether these discharge instructions were sufficiently explained. These credibility contests often result in verdicts in favor of the injured patient. Jurors remember that they have been patients themselves, and they become irritated with the hasty handwriting on the form. They feel it is indicative of the way that the discharge was handled and the way discharge instructions were given.

Discharge planning should start long before the actual discharge. Some of the care after discharge is generic and can be handled through carefully drafted preprinted information sheets. Some of the discharge planning can be taken care of pre-hospitalization, when patients may be in a better frame of mind to comprehend the instructions.

As we move more to home health settings we need to evaluate the risk management systems that are in place there. In the hospital setting there are many systems which have been created over the years. The simple forms of documentation, protocols, policies and procedures, credentialing, peer review, on-going quality assurance and continuing education programs will be essential with discharge planning. Family members should be involved when possible. Thorough discharge planning has many benefits and many positive implications. Patient cooperation will increase and understanding of the instructions will help in the overall care of the patient. This has important economic significance to the provider, particularly in a managed care capitated setting. The goal is not just early discharge; the goal is early discharge with appropriate outcome, without complications, and without readmission. More information must be provided, and more teaching done as the length of stay decreases. Documentation of this is essential, not only from a patient care standpoint, but also from a malpractice prevention standpoint.

Follow-up telephone calls are also important. Patients should be called as a matter of course post-surgery, especially when discharge has occurred soon after the procedure. A nurse, or someone else with clinical experience, should call to assure that discharge instructions, rehabilitation instructions, and medication orders are all clearly understood. Questions should be encouraged and answered. Physician reinvolvement should be facilitated where appropriate or necessary. All of this must be documented on something as simple as a check-off sheet.

In a globally capitated environment, where the physician, and the nurses who are working with the physician, may be responsible for home health personnel, it is essential that appropriate training for home health care be documented and ongoing activities monitored.

As more and more care is provided outside of the hospital setting, we must make sure that the same type of risk management principles found in the hospital setting are found in the home health setting, albeit in a tailored fashion. This includes making sure we credential the individuals who are providing the care in a home health setting, with regular evaluations and peer review, and making sure the home health nurses are documenting the clinical status of patients on an ongoing basis. Home health professionals must have the ability to obtain immediate physician and other emergency backup and be prepared to handle immediate post-operative conditions.

How to reduce the risks:

- Reanalyze your process for discharge planning and education. When appropriate, place discharge education in the pre-admission setting.
- Analyze the documents and information you provide to patients to be used during the post-operative period. Is it being provided in the right way and at the right time to patients? Can it be clearly understood? Do patients or their family members have opportunities to ask questions?
- A good check on discharge instructions is to have a "focused review" by patients and take suggestions.

- Have patients review your discharge education material to assure their understanding, incorporate any practical and pragmatic changes they suggest.
- Be sure that the individuals who are now seeing patients in the home health area are properly credentialed, have a sufficient amount of training and experience for the new problems that will be encountered, are monitored, peer reviewed, and have opportunities for continuing medical education. All credentialing activity should be documented in the event of a corporate negligence claim.
- Be sure that the documentation used in home health setting is adequate, showing the clinical progress of the patient, patient interactions, use of medications, and cooperation with treatment regime.
- Follow up with a telephone call to ensure instructions have been understood and to check the status of the patient, all of this being appropriately documented.
- Make sure the discharge is based on appropriate clinical judgment and that it is clearly documented so your judgment can be substantiated at a later date.

The next area is one which has always been high risk from a liability standpoint. However, in a managed care setting these risks must be recognized and risk reduction is essential.

5. THE EMERGENCY DEPARTMENT

It's not surprising that emergency department use is one of the first targeted areas for reduction in costs. It is fairly well-documented that emergency departments are overused for nonemergent health needs that could be cared for more appropriately in a primary care office. Studies have shown that as much as 49% of ambulatory emergency department (ED) visits are nonurgent on prospective triage.[42] Linda F. McCraig reports from the National Hospital Ambulatory Medical Care Survey in 1992 that 55.4% of the visits were nonurgent.[43] In a study of 190 ED patients, Baker, Stevens, and Brook (1994) found that 68% of all ED visits were classified as nonurgent. It was further reported that of the 89% of patients who said that they needed to be seen "immediately," more than 50% did not require care within 24 hours.[44–46]

The Baker, et al., study indicated that over half of the 89.8 million emergency department visits in 1992 were for nonemergent care. The most common complaints were stomach and abdominal pain, cramps and spasms, chest pain, fever, headache, and injuries to the upper extremities, according to the National Ambulatory Medical Care survey. The most common diagnoses were ear infections, open wounds to the head, respiratory and other chest conditions, and abdominal ailments.[47] There have been many different reasons for this high emergency department use, including lack of a primary care physician, transportation problems, and the need for after hours care.[48–50]

Emergency department care is expensive. Once in the emergency department, federal law requires a certain level of examination and stabilization. Early on the dilemma was that some managed care organizations, or their gatekeeping physicians, did not fully understand the comprehensive Emergency Medical Treatment and Active Labor Act (EMTALA), which led to exposure under the statute.[51] The law requires stabilization prior to transfer of any patient brought to an emergency department and sets forth certain requirements for transfer. Now managed care does understand, and armed with the above data, the industry argues that non-urgent conditions are better seen in an area other than in an emergency department. They have, therefore, paid more attention to making sure that only patients with true emergencies are treated in the emergency department.

Many managed care organizations use the primary care doctor as a gatekeeper whose job it is to oversee and control the use of the emergency department. In 1994, one large managed care plan sent to all of its members a patient care manual explaining that it regarded heart attacks, strokes, and poisoning as emergencies, but it considered twisted ankles with no open wound, minor burns, or abdominal pain lasting one day or more to be "non-emergent conditions." A true emergency involves severe symptoms, requiring immediate care, that "must occur suddenly and unexpectedly." It specifically directed participating doctors to "use the ER judiciously."[52]

Other managed care organizations literally told their members *not* to go to the hospital for urgent care (as distinguished from emergent care), but to call their primary care doctor and await instructions. This patient education needed to be more specific and more inclusive because it began to create a sense of confusion in both members and doctors. Utilization strategies were developed in other organizations with small co-payments or even as large as $50 or $100. As reported in the recent book, *Health Against Wealth*, a managed care executive called this "a hesitation fee." "If it's going to cost you to visit the ER, maybe you'll wait."[53]

The number of emergency department visits did shrink and probably many of them appropriately, since many of these visits clearly could be handled by the primary care physician. However, this was not improvement without pain. Many highly publicized cases focused on the ills of this system. In one case, a 78-year-old man awoke with severe precordial pain and his wife called their HMO health line, who apparently called an out-of-town ambulance service, who could not find their home. After 20 or 30 minutes, a local policeman arrived, after which the emergency medical crew arrived, but to no avail. Her husband had died.

Curtis Klimer, MD, a family practitioner in Silverton, OR, experienced a similar situation and reported it to the *American Medical News*:

"A patient of mine who had only mild asthma became depressed in the past three months. I was unaware of her condition. In an effort to lift her spirits, her husband took her to Los Angeles for her 30th high school reunion. While there, her depression worsened. She had lost 15-20 pounds and was unable to walk across the room. Her husband realized she was getting into serious trouble.

His first thought was to telephone her managed care plan and try to get her some help in the Los Angeles area. After several hours and numerous conversations with people, he called me. He described her as being in a condition I would characterize by phone as one of severe dehydration and impending circulatory collapse. I advised him to call an ambulance and have her transported to the closest hospital. He felt this might be a problem because he had been advised that the Oregon Health Plan had contracts with certain hospitals in the Los Angeles area, but neither of us knew where or who they might be. He wondered if he shouldn't put her in the car and drive to see me since I was her primary care physician. I advised strongly against this and told him to call an ambulance and we could sort this out later.

In about 45 minutes I received a call from an emergency room physician advising me that my patient had just come in full arrest and died. The next call I received was from the L.A. County coroner wanting to know if I had any idea why my patient had died. Would it be fair to say she died because the managed care plan had done such a good job scaring this family about the proper way to use the system that they were unable to actually access the care needed when it was needed?"[54]

Probably focusing on a few of these situations is unfair. However, they are real when they create a real life dilemma for primary care physicians, emergency department physicians, and, most importantly, patients. What is and is not a real emergency? When can emergency care be reimbursed appropriately? There is little doubt that there are huge costs involved. Inappropriate emergency department usage is thought to cost between $5 billion and $14 billion annually.[55,56] Another consideration is that the quality of care could be compromised when it is provided by the emergency department, under inappropriate situations.[57–59] So there is good reason to try to move some of these patients from the emergency department to a more fitting location.

Another problem unique to the emergency department touched on above was created by the enactment of the EMTALA in 1986. The EMTALA is a federal statute which requires certain action by emergency department physicians when patients present to their department. The physician must screen all patients to determine whether there is a need for emergency care and to stabilize such patients without regard to their ability to pay. Amendments to the statute have actually broadened EMTALA's applicability and has led to some very unusual results.[60] Here lies the dilemma. Managed care will want to keep patients from the emergency department who don't truly belong there for a number of reasons. Primary care physicians are asked to screen these visits. Emergency department physicians, once patients are there, will be required to do a full evaluation and to stabilize them, and they appropriately will want to be paid for their services. Patients are caught in the middle. If they go directly to the emergency department and it is later determined that it was not an "emergency condition," they may be left with a significant bill. When they call their primary care physician, they must go through a triage process that some patients (during depositions) have said discouraged them from seeking emergency department care. No patient wants to hear that an emergency department visit is necessary in the middle of the night. If their doctor seems to be saying that a visit the next day will probably suffice, they will readily accept that. Remember Dr. Smith's patient?

There has been a great legislative outcry concerning all of this. Statutes have been enacted in Maryland (1993), California (1994), Virginia and Arkansas (1995), with an additional 20 states since then.[61,62] Although there are obviously varieties within all of these statutes, one of the issues focused upon is under what circumstances must managed care organizations pay for an emergency visit? Some require payment for care in the ED if "a prudent layperson with the average knowledge of medicine and health and experiencing the same symptoms would have gone to the ED." Others require a managed care organization to pay if a reasonable person would have sought care at the ED. Another standard would require managed care organizations to pay for all emergency services. There are also consumer protection laws that preclude the requirement for prior authorization for screening examinations and stabilizing or emergency treatment.[63]

These legislative mandates were reviewed in an excellent chapter in *Achieving Quality in Managed Care: The Role of Law*, a monograph published by the Health Law Section of the American Bar Association, and authored by David A. Hyman, JD, MD.[64] Hyman concludes that such legislation should be looked at with a jaundiced eye. "There is no reason for the government to pick sides in the trench warfare that some providers are waging against managed care—let alone do so under the guise of 'consumer protection.'" He goes on to state that "consumer protection" legislation involves a high stakes encounter in the ED, and does not change his analysis. Indeed the higher the stakes, the more important it is to not make things worse than they already are, by opting for the wrong uniform solution.[65]

The emergency department dilemma probably serves as a lightning rod for other criticisms of managed care. Sensational stories are reported, patients are confused, and legislative involvements continue. The goal was always to fit the patient into the appropriate level of care by the right person at the right place. However, achieving that in the present managed care environment is easier said than done. There are risks for the providers involved. There is risk to the primary care physicians who have to act as the gatekeepers or coordinators of care. Perhaps they will get a call in the middle of the night from a patient, as Dr. Smith did, asking whether an emergency department visit was warranted. They'll think back, as Dr. Smith did, to their utilization parameters, think whether the case falls within the gray area or not. It's insidious. Many providers would state that the answer is simple. When clinically warranted, send the patient to the emergency department; when not, do not do so. If it were as easy as that we would not have the large number of cases based on faulty decisions concerning emergency department referrals. There is risk to the managed care organization as their liability continues to broaden and there is risk to the emergency department physician who is attempting to determine whether a patient should be seen, stabilized, or transferred in light of multiple managed care rules. This is one of the most explosive areas because it worries jurors. The emergency department is one place they thought they could go and get help, all the help they need, quickly, and without question. When they hear it is something different they get scared, especially in communities where there is just one or two emergency departments within large community hospitals. When they get scared they tend to send a message. That message, unfortunately, is usually in the form of a multi-million dollar verdict!

The answer in this area is multifaceted. Managed care organizations are making an effort to educate both their members and physicians on when emergency department care is appropriate, and when it is not. However, that should include letting patients know where those urgent, not yet emergent, problems, conditions, and questions should be taken and telling them how they can receive prompt care for those conditions. In the September 1997 issue of *Annals of Emergency Medicine*, the question of access to emergency care was reviewed in detail.[66] The study was to determine whether patients understood how to gain access to emergency care under TennCare which is a government mandated managed health care initiative designed to replace Medicaid in Tennessee. They found that improvement of communication of information such as the proper use of the system, the role of the primary care physician, the fact the patients needed to contact their primary care physician first, was necessary.[67] The primary care physician, when contacted, must follow-up more promptly. It wasn't that the information wasn't provided because it had been. However, in light of the study's findings it had not been provided effectively enough. More effective education is the key.

It doesn't make sense to give patients a laundry list of urgent problems that are painful, frightening, and bothersome to them and asking them not to go to the emergency department, unless they can get care for those problems easily and promptly elsewhere. Is there an urgent care center with which the managed care organization has a contract? Is there a family care center with 24-hour coverage in close proximity of the emergency department? Do their primary care physicians have 24-hour coverage and are they able to provide enough telephonic advice to get a patient through a problem, or be able to send a patient to a center with the appropriate level of services? More patient education is needed, and more importantly, plans for how to meet the patients' expectations in this regard.

It seems that the health care system has a need for a classic change of the "where." Shouldn't there be 24-hour triage available at the emergency department, so that patients who truly need emergency care can be treated promptly and others sent to a family care center more appropriate for their ailments? Many departments are using this very model. Setting aside the prospect of legislation to change the EMTALA, emergency departments and managed care organizations have to work together to set up joint guidelines and protocols to work through the examination and stabilization issues. Each has to be respectful of their legal and organizational responsibilities. Certainly, if more patients are informed and a different environment is provided, less difficult stabilization decisions will need to be made.

Emergency departments and primary care doctors will have to be thorough in their documentation, describing the findings that resulted in the triage decisions. These are where the suits arise. The patient, in retrospect, had symptoms that the family thought warranted an emergency department visit. However, the doctor heard a different story at the time it was happening, a story that would reasonably dictate that a trip to the primary care office the next day would have sufficed. Without clear documentation of those findings when the decision was made, it is a very difficult case, especially when society in general may believe that decisions were economically motivated. In fact, at a certain level they were, but appropriately so.

How to reduce the risks:

- Recognize that emergency department services are costly and that a large percentage of the visits can be better addressed in a different setting.
- Patient education as to what setting is appropriate for their emergent vs. urgent conditions is important and should be accomplished.
- Patient education about access to emergency treatment needs to improve.
- Physician promptness when calls are made needs to improve. This should be in the patient brochure and further or more effective education of the patients may be necessary.
- Patients should be given an understanding of how to engage the services needed for problems that they perceive as being either urgent or emergent. Receiving urgent care should be as easy or accessible as emergent care.

- Clear documentation is necessary by the primary care physician coordinator as to what level of care is being recommended and why, whether at home or at the office. It must clearly delineate the symptoms and findings, and why the level of care that was chosen was felt to be warranted. Again, a snap shot.
- Emergency department physicians also must document clearly the symptomatology before making any treatment decisions and must further document clearly any relevant directions by managed care organizations. Protocols and policies should be in place so that prompt decisions can be made.
- Emergency department and managed care organizations should work together on creating systems that respect both legal requirements and organizational goals.

Many of the same type of liabilities can occur when a consultant is making a decision as to whether or not admission is indicated from the emergency department. Often a call is made by the emergency department physician to the consultant. Documenting those symptoms so that your judgment as a consultant can be evaluated in retrospect, is critical. Testimony that you were at home and did not have the chart available will not hold up in court if a significant clinical decision is made over the telephone. Careful and complete notes on the emergency department chart and in your consultation note are necessary. This is not business as usual. This is a change, since your decision may be suspect and because utilization decisions about hospitalization are changing.

There are also changes in the "who" in the providing of health care. This actually may be one of the most profound changes and it will continue to evolve rapidly. It, of course, creates challenges as well as opportunities.

6. ADVANCED PRACTICE PROVIDERS

As described earlier, advanced practice providers, sometimes referred to as mid-level practitioners or allied health providers, have tremendous opportunities in the new health care environment. This is reflected by the number of physicians' assistants, increased 38% from 1991 to 1996, from approximately 25,000 to almost 35,000 individuals, according to the American Academy of Physicians' Assistants.[68] The number of education programs for physicians' assistants has also grown from 78 in 1996 to 96 in 1997. It has been recently reported that there are close to 60,000 clinical nurse specialists, 25,000 certified registered nurse anesthetists, and 6,000 certified nurse midwives.[69]

Managed care has embraced these providers. A program developed by Oxford Health Plans, Inc. of Newark, CT, and Columbia Presbyterian Medical Center, New York, allows for all plan members to choose a nurse practitioner instead of a doctor as their primary care provider. Mario Mundinger, Dean of Columbia University School of Nursing, stated in the *BNA Managed Care Reporter*, "we want to see whether patients would choose to go to a nurse practitioner and why."[70] Under their plan, approximately 20 nurse practitioners from the nursing school will act as primary care providers for plan members who choose that particular option. These nurses can exercise broad authority including the diagnosis and treatment of illnesses, prescribing medication, and admitting patients to Columbia Presbyterian Hospital. Of course state law must be considered carefully; in New York, nurse practitioners must maintain a formal consultative type of arrangement with a physician. In the same *BNA* report, Tom Readon, Chairman of the AMA Board of Trustees, voiced his concern saying, "they don't have the same level of expertise" and "I would be concerned that they would be put in a situation where the demands exceed their competency."[71]

There is also a plan under development at Kaiser Permanente. Kaiser has done some investigation and found that none of their members who were polled are dissatisfied seeing a nurse practitioner for some conditions. Kaiser sees it as a way to create value. They put together a team which includes a physician, physician assistant, nurse practitioner, social worker, and pharmacist who are exploring ways that these advanced practice providers can be incorporated into their practice.[72]

However, along with the opportunities that these advanced practice providers create, come challenges. In the case of a misdiagnosis, patients are quick to jump to the conclusion that "my doctor would have diagnosed this." Patients may also feel that they were shortchanged or that they were seen by the advanced practice provider simply to save costs for the managed care organization or the physician. At times, advanced practice providers are pushed to the limit and not given appropriate backup. This backup must be in the form of systems that assure careful compliance with regulatory requirements in their particular jurisdiction, and physician backup in a way that they will feel comfortable seeking advice or support. Too often there are subtle ways in which the supervising physician discourages questions, in all likelihood inadvertently, because of a busy or hectic schedule. This may generate reluctance on the part of the advanced practice provider to seek advice when, in the circumstances, it would be quite appropriate. This needs to be guarded against. Credentialing systems also need to be set up so these advanced practice providers are credentialed in the right fashion and their care is monitored; otherwise an organization or physician group can be liable to a corporate negligence claim.[73]

In the new health care setting, advanced practice providers can help soothe the tension that increased volumes bring. Dr. Smith could have benefited from an advanced practice provider to help him cope with the stress of seeing the increase in volume that he did. He could have made it make economic sense as well. Reimbursement rules are changing and becoming more economically favorable.

Too often, however, advanced practice providers are quickly brought in and plugged into a practice after there is a problem with no advanced planning, and neither staff nor physicians completely understand their role. There is no prior explanation to patients and they may see this individual as one who will block their encounter with a physician, and not as an extension of the health care team. Unfortunately, all too often they are treated like assistants and not as colleagues.

How to reduce the risks:

- Education is mandatory for physicians, staff, and patients to explain the role of the advanced practice providers.
- Credentialing criteria and monitoring methodology need to be developed before appointing an advanced practice provider.
- Compliance with the regulatory schemes in the particular jurisdiction must be maintained. This means that a statutory compliance check-off sheet should be developed and maintained by every organization that employs them.
- Coordination with human resource departments is necessary when advanced practice providers are being employed by a hospital or managed care organization.
- Ongoing peer review and monitoring is necessary for their own protection, as well as for the organization employing them, so as to prevent corporate negligence claims and to ensure ongoing improvement in the quality of care.
- Systems should be set up to develop a collaborative relationship between the physician and advanced practice provider and to assure it is an ongoing relationship.
- You may need to develop appropriate protocols and lines of communication.
- Advance practice providers must be treated as the professionals they are. If the physician doesn't demonstrate confidence, neither will the patient.
- Advanced practice providers need to document clearly and understand how to use the documentation systems in the office, including not only the chart, but telephonic encounters as well.

The next dilemma deals with another change in the "where." It is one of the fastest growing areas of health care delivery, which makes it even more important to address.

7. TELEMEDICINE

Telemedicine has been defined by the AMA's Council on Medical Education, Council on Medical Services as "the provision of health care consultation and education using telecommunication networks to communicate information" or "medical practice across distance via telecommunications and interactive video technology."[74] Telemedicine has been with us for over 30 years. In 1959 there was a project in Nebraska which allowed physicians and patients to interact over a closed circuit TV for psychiatry purposes.[75] There were similar projects in Alaska in the mid-1960s and several in the 1970s by the University of Washington.[76,77]

According to a national journal for telemedicine, *Telemedicine Today*, in their second annual review, there were 26 interactive telemedicine programs and 2,000 interactive patient-physician telemedicine consultations in North America in 1994. The number of telemedicine programs doubled in 1994 and then doubled again in 1995.[78] Telemedicine has particular significance to rural areas. In the "Exploring Evaluation of Rural Implication to Telemedicine Executive Summary," it was explained that by the end of 1996, 30% of rural hospitals used telemedicine and 68% of them used teleradiology.[79] Telemedicine has also seen significant growth in the area of cardiology, orthopedics, dermatology, and psychiatry. It has been boosted in the last several years with the development of digital technology and information highways.

The thought is that this type of technology can both be efficient and improve patient care. In rural areas it means that individuals can link up with a specialist at a tertiary care center. It does not take days to have an x-ray film read by a board certified radiologist, but a matter of minutes. It is also thought that telemedicine could be used significantly for home health care monitoring. Blood pressure and oxygen peak flow could be monitored and home care nursing could even be aided by two-way video.[80] Medical experts could be linked together to address difficult problems and interpret studies. Robot-type monitors are being developed for home health settings.

The American College of Radiology has already issued a technical clinical standard for a telemedicine protocol.[81] Also in place are services providing telecardiology to interpret diagnostic cardiac evaluative studies, such as a chest x-ray, EKG, or cardiac ultrasound; telepathology, which can allow a consulting pathologist to review a biopsy done in a rural hospital while the patient is still under anesthesia; telepsychiatry, which can allow interactive psychiatric interviews in evaluation of patients; and teledermatology, which can be performed by allowing the remote transmission of an image of a skin lesion for interpretation. Presently there is a great deal of research being done in this area, and the Department of Commerce, the Health Care Financing Administration (HCFA), and the Office of Rural Health Policy and Department of Defense have all funded telemedicine research and set up demonstration projects. By 1995 there were state and federally funded programs underway in at least the 40 states which were illustrating increasingly the effectiveness of telemedicine patient management.[82] In fact, recent information indicates that funding may well increase over the next several years.[81] Further, Medicare reimbursement may well begin to take place under certain circumstances for telemedicine services.[84]

One can certainly see how, in a managed care environment, telemedicine could have tremendous growth. First of all, it is touted to be a cost effective and efficient way to provide care. In many instances it can improve the quality of care or the level of care that a patient could receive. As use becomes even more widespread, costs can be reduced although clearly setting up the telemedicine network in itself is an expensive project. According to an article in *Family Practice Management*, Jane Preston, MD, President of the American Telemedicine Association, is quoted as estimating start-up costs of a bare bones system for a rural site as $50,000 in 1991, and $35,000 in 1993.[85] She further estimated that the transition costs for an interactive video system, which she bases on rates from telephone carriers in central Texas, to be between $1,400 and $2,000 per month. Over the years the cost of this technology has actually been reduced, but it is a significant initial start-up cost. With the objectives of improved care, particularly for rural residents, lower costs for treatment, less time between diagnosis and treatment, and expanded opportunities for continuing education for rural providers, clearly it is going to continue to garner interest.[86]

Like with many new opportunities, there are also significant legal and risk management issues in telemedicine. There are issues at multiple levels. There is a question as to whether physicians can practice over state lines and still be in compliance with licenser laws in each jurisdiction. Each state regulates the practice of medicine through individual laws which vary. The penalties for the unlicensed practice of medicine can be severe, including civil fines, suspension or revocation of medical licenses, or expulsion from participation in Medicare and Medicaid, so physicians need to ensure compliance. Some states such as Massachusetts have created exceptions to allow these types of consultations under limited circumstances.[87] Model legislation has been drafted, and in April of 1996, The House of Delegates of the Federation of State Medical Boards approved this proposed model litigation regarding licensure. There are still critics, but as of 1997 several states have legislation based on the act and 17 were going to consider it in 1998.[88]

There are also reimbursement issues. At the present time, HCFA requires that Medicare patients must have direct contact with the physician in order to receive reimbursement for a consultation.[89] However, with new legislation, this is beginning to change. The federal government does allow Medicaid agencies to establish their own coverage policies for telemedicine and there are exceptions for services that do not normally require face-to-face contact, such as radiology and pathology. More and more, private insurers are beginning to reimburse these services. Certainly as telemedicine services are seen to deliver cost effective services and can maintain quality, reimbursement will follow. Under the Balanced Budget Act of 1997, Public Law 105-33, the Medicare Program will probably begin reimbursement for telemedicine services by 1999.

There is also a confidentiality concern as well as privacy. Both state and federal legislative efforts are looking at this issue, which is similar to those raised by computerized medical records. Other legal issues concern whether a patient-physician relationship exists. Some commentators feel that if services are being rendered for the benefit of the patient, and the physician accepts that responsibility, a patient-physician relationship will have existed and liability could attach if negligence occurs.[90–92] Many other issues are not that clear. For instance, the pathologist who is reading a slide and rendering an interpretation to a requesting physician, would be responsible if the slide were interpreted negligently. However, there is a question whether the pathologist would be responsible if the physician requesting the interpretation did not provide the correct information. This analysis could also apply to a consultant radiologist who is reviewing a mammogram at a distant site at the request of a general radiologist. Although the reviewer of that mammogram would be responsible if it is interpreted in a negligent fashion, the reviewer does not have the same level of involvement as the initial general radiologist who, perhaps, did an examination or had interaction with the patient. The general radiologist would also be responsible for communicating the information to the patient and having systems in place to assure that took place.[93] Some have opined that the consultant at the distant site could, under some limited circumstances, be held liable for the action of the referring physicians who fail to perform their duty or that one who is asking for a teleconsult could be held responsible for the consultant if he or she is negligent. Does the consultant, since the patient-physician relationship has been formed at some level, have a responsibility to make sure that the referring physicians follow up? Could he/she potentially be sued on a theory of abandonment if not?[94,95] There are also issues relative to informed consent which would seem to be the responsibility of the referring physician to let the patient know of the limitation of telemedicine, including confidentiality concerns, technology concerns under some circumstances, and its relative experimental nature. California requires a written informed consent before delivering telemedical care.[96] You should check the laws regarding telemedicine in your jurisdiction.

There are also questions, when consultations are occurring across state lines, as to what type of malpractice coverage the physician would need. Would your professional liability insurance carrier cover such exchanges? If there is a malpractice claim, and given that laws vary among jurisdictions, which law would apply? An argument could be made that patients, who were allegedly injured because of telemedicine consultations, could sue in their particular jurisdiction, or perhaps in Federal Court, alleging diversity of citizenship to argue the necessary jurisdiction. Could that potentially mean that physicians could be drawn out of their own jurisdictions and need to defend cases in multiple states?

From a risk management point of view and considering implications of telemedicine in a managed care environment, physicians who are going to become involved in telemedicine need to cover certain legal groundwork. Licensing questions need to be raised and discussed if you are crossing state lines. Your professional liability insurer should be contacted to assure that you are going to be covered in the event there is a claim from a patient at a distant site. Your role must be clearly delineated and spelled out in any provider agreement or contract that's developed. These agreements will need careful legal review by someone experienced in telemedicine issues. Protocols should be set up as to how these telecommunication consultations are handled by both the referring physician and the consultant. Reimbursement issues should be carefully addressed prior to the start of the project. You should check the applicable laws in your jurisdiction to find out not only about licensure, but informed consent as it applies to telemedicine as well.

Telemedicine brings to light additional and more pragmatic dilemmas. Consider telemedicine not only in a high-tech fashion, but also as it is used in the consultations, some formal, others not so formal, that occur over the telephone every day. In a managed care setting, patients are calling their physicians for multiple reasons and the volume is increasing. Care has to be given to how those communications occur. There would be great liability exposure if the right level of practitioner were not handling those telephone calls and if they were not properly documented. Another concern are the telephone calls that go to the on-call physician who has to make decisions as to whether emergent care, urgent care, or care the next day is required. These types of decisions happen daily in a managed care setting. Having a protocol in place for how those decisions will take place and having a documentation system in place will reduce liability. There are many telephone calls to the office during the day from patients who are wondering whether care is needed in an emergent, urgent fashion, or whether a visit can be scheduled the next day. Often these telephone calls are taken by different levels of provider. An advanced practice provider or nurse can handle many of these calls, but should have some threshold questions to ask and appropriate physician backup. It is impractical for a physician to take all of these calls and therefore triage will be necessary. Often these are calls with questions about medications, postoperative complications, or rehabilitation. It is important to make sure that these calls go to the individual with the appropriate level of experience and that the information that is provided is well-documented. Too often, after a complication occurs, patients have a vivid recollection of information given to them by the provider, which may not be accurate. If the information, which was allegedly provided by you to the patient, has not been recorded somewhere, those assertions are hard to rebut.

How to reduce the risks:

- Before entering into a telemedicine arrangement that will require consultations across jurisdictional lines, consider licensing issues.
- Consider malpractice issues including: what standard of care will apply, technology limitations, and to what extent your responsibility extends to the patient.
- Consider reimbursement issues.
- Consider professional liability insurance issues and call insurance carrier to discuss coverage.
- Consider whether an informed consent must be obtained in your particular jurisdiction.
- Have your agreement carefully reviewed by legal counsel.
- Set up protocols both at your site and with referring physicians.
- For the telecommunication that occurs daily in your office, assure that the individual with the appropriate level of experience is handling the call.
- For the use of advanced practice providers, make sure protocols are in place and physician backup is available.
- Make sure that documentation systems are in place to document presenting symptoms and instructions or information provided.

REFERENCES

1. L. Kertesz, "What's Right, Wrong? California Task Force Taking a Close Look at Managed Care," *Modern Healthcare,* 11 August 1997, 70, 74
2. Kertesz, "What's Right, Wrong?"
3. J. Blum, "Achieving Quality in Managed Care: The Role of Law," *Monograph* 5 (Health Law Section of the American Bar Association, June 1997).
4. "Managed Care Docs Dissatisfied—Survey," *Modern Healthcare*, 10 March 1997, 22.
5. *The National Coalition of Healthcare, How Americans Perceive the Healthcare System* (January 1997). A report on a national survey conducted for the National Coalition of Healthcare by International Communications research.
6. D. Nather, "Growing Support Raises the Stakes in Congressional Debate," 5 BNA Healthcare Policy Reporter 9 @ D-5 (March 3, 1997).
7. G. Aston, "Regulating Care," *American Medical Association News* 40.11 (1997).
8. L.O. Prager, "Panel at Work on Patient Bill of Rights," *American Medical Association News* 40.21(1997): 1.
9. J.A. Jacob, *American Medical Association News* 40.46 (8 December 1997): 6.
10. E. Weissenstein, "The next reform fight," *Modern Healthcare* (26 January 1998): 6.
11. Kertesz, "What's Right, Wrong?" 70.
12. J.P. Kassirer, "Managing Managed Care's Tarnished Image," *New England Journal of Medicine*, (July 31, 1997): 338.
13. J.P. Kassirer, "Managing Managed Care's Tarnished Image," 338.
14. Aston, "Regulating Care," 40.11.
15. Aston, "Regulating Care," 40.11.
16. L. Kertesz, "Patient-protection Rift," *Modern Healthcare* (29 September 1997): 6.

17. L. Kertesz, "Patient-protection Rift," 13.
18. E. Roskey, *BNA Managed Care Reporter,* 4:4 (28 January 1998): 77.
19. L. Kertesz, "Patient-protection Rift," 13.
20. L. Kertesz, "Patient-protection Rift," 13.
21. L. Kertesz, "Patient-protection Rift," 13.
22. "Staff Model HMOs Fare Best in Minnesota Doc's Ratings of Plans," *BNA Managed Care Reporter,* 24 September 1997, 901.
23. "Where Have All the Nurses Gone?" *American Journal of Nursing* 96, 11 (November 1996).
24. L. Prager, "Can New Cost Data Save Fate of Liability Reform in Budget Bill?" *American Medical Association News*, 40.29, 27.
25. "Torture Alleged in Parent's Suit against Pacificare for Denial of Home Health Care (Calif. Super Ct.)," *BNA Managed Care Reporter* (25 June 1997): 619.
26. Interview with Mark Hiepler conducted in *Family Practice News* (Boston: Houghton Mifflin Co., 1996).
27. Telephone interview with Mark Hiepler, 25 October 1997.
28. G. Anders, *Health Against Wealth: HMOs and the Breakdown of Medical Trust* (Boston: Houghton Mifflin Co., 1997), Chapter 8.
29. D.C. McGraw, "Financial Incentive to Limit Services: Should Physicians be Required to Disclose These to Patients," 83 *Georgetown Law Journal* (1995): 1821.
30. See generally: Smith v. Yohey, 412 Pa. 94, 194 A2d 167 (1963).
31. Duckworth v. Bennett, 320 Pa. 47, 181 A.55 (1935).
32. Telephone interview by author with Robert E. Lee, Executive Director, Lancaster County Health Plan, 31 October 1997.
33. Wickline v. State of California and Wilson v. State of California; Sammarco, MD v. Anthem Insurance Companies, No. A9705591, Ohio, Pleas Hamilton County.
34. *BNA Managed Care Reporter* (24 September 1997): 901.
35. "Managing Managed Care," *American Medical Association News* (September 1996): 8.
36. Potvin v. Metropolitan Life Insurance Co., No. B10070 (Ca. Ct. App., 2nd Dist., April 30, 1997).
37. See: Mealy's Litigation Report: Managed Care, September 17, 1997. This is an excellent resource for such information, they may be contacted at (610)688–6566.
38. *BNA Managed Care Reporter* 3 (19 November 1997): 1092.
39. C. Lundy and J. Knox, "Managed Care Fundamentals: Implications for Healthcare Organizations and Healthcare Professionals," *The American Journal of Occupational Therapy* 50.6 (1996).
40. E. MacLaren, "Basics of Managed Care," *Nurse Week* 50.13 (1995): 10–11.
41. M. Lepler, "Managed Care Capitation and Change Raise Issues in Nursing Leadership," *Nurse Week* 8.21 (2 October 1995): 24–25.
42. G.P. Young, et al., "Ambulatory Visits to Hospital Emergency Departments: Patterns and Reasons for Use," 276 *Journal of the American Medical Association* (1996): 460.
43. L. McCraig, *National Hospital Ambulatory Care Survey* (National Center for Health Statistics, 1992).
44. R.W. Derlat, D. Kinser, L. Ray, B. Hamilton, and J. MacKenzie, "Prospective Identification and Triage of an Emergency Department: A Five-Year Study," *Annals of Emergency Medicine* 25 (1995): D15–23.
45. See also MacNamara, Witte, and Kanek, (1993).
46. See also Nadell, (1993).
47. See *Hospital and Health Networks* (5 March 1996): 12.
48. "Analysis of Emergency Room Use for Primary Care Needs," *Nursing Economics* 15 (Jan–Feb 1997).

49. "Emergency Room Misuse by Medical Assistance Patients in a Family Practice Residency," *Journal of Family Practice* 8.2 (1979): 341–345.
50. "Alteration of Emergency Room in a Family Practice Residency Program," *Journal of Family Practice* 15.6 (1982): 1135–1139.
51. 42 U.S.C.A. Section 1395dd (West 1992).
52. Anders, *Health Against Wealth,* 139.
53. Anders, *Health Against Wealth,* 139.
54. Anders, *Health Against Wealth,* 139.
55. L.C. Baker and L. S. Baker, "Excess Cost Emergency Department Visits for Nonurgent Care," *Health Affairs* 162 (1994).
56. "Redefining the Emergency Department: Five Strategies for Reducing Unnecessary Care," *Health Care Advisory Board* (1993).
57. K.C. Elam, et al., "How Emergency Physicians Approach Low Back Pain: Choosing Costly Options," *Journal of Emergency Medicine* 13 (1994): 143.
58. R. Brook, et al., "Effectiveness of Nonemergency Care via an Emergency Room," *Annals of Internal Medicine* 78 (1973): 33.
59. Also see G.P. Young and D. Sklar, "Healthcare Reform in Emergency Medicine," *Annals of Internal Medicine* 25 (1995): 666.
60. Matter of Baby K, 16 F.3d 59 (4th Cir. 1994) cert. den., 115 S. Ct. 91, 130, L.Ed. 2d 42 (1994).
61. Business Bulletin, *Wall Street Journal* (8 August 1996).
62. Also see generally, Hyman, "Consumer Protection and Managed Care," ABA Health Law Section, Monograph, 5 June 1997.
63. Hyman, "Consumer Protection and Managed Care."
64. Hyman, "Consumer Protection and Managed Care."
65. Hyman, "Consumer Protection and Managed Care," 68.
66. "Access to Emergency Care Under TennCare: Do Patients Understand the System?" *Annals of Emergency Medicine* (September 1997): 281.
67. "Access to Emergency Care," 281.
68. *Physician Assistants: Statistics and Trends, 1991–1996* (American Academy of Physician Assistants).
69. "Primary Care Nurse," *AMA News.*
70. *BNA Managed Care Reporter* 3.33 (13 August 1977).
71. *BNA Managed Care Reporter* 3.33 (13 August 1977).
72. *BNA Managed Care Reporter* 3.33 (13 August 1977).
73. See generally: Thompson v. Hospital, 57 Pa. 330, 591 A.2d 703 (1991).
74. "Joint Report of the Council of Medical Education and Council of Medical Services of the American Medical Association," released at the AMA Annual Meeting, Chicago, Illinois, June, 1994.
75. C.L. Wittson, D.C. Afflack, and B. Johnson, *The Use of Two Way Television in Group Therapy* (Omaha, Nebraska: Psychiatric Institute, University of Nebraska College of Medicine, 1961).
76. The Anchorage Public Health Hospital, "Using A Satellite Link to Rural Parts of Alaska to Perform Patient Consultations," (1976).
77. The Washington, Alaska, Montana, and Idaho project conducted by the University of Washington, 1974 for distance education and clinical consultation.
78. R. Carlson, "Can Telemedicine Deliver What It Promises?" *Family Practice Management* (March 1996): 138.
79. Health Resources and Services Administration (HRSA), "Exploration and Evaluation of Rural Applications of Telemedicine Executive Summary," (Internet presentation, available at http://www.nrsa.dhhs.gov/news.htm)(3 April 1997).

80. Serafini and M. Weber, "High Tech House Calls," *The National Journal*, 3 February 1996, 258.
81. American College of Radiology Standard for Teleradiology, American College of Radiology, Weston, Virginia, 1994.
82. M.D. Perednia, and D.A. Allen, "Telemedicine Technology and Clinical Application," *Journal of the American Medical Association* 273, 6 (1995): 483–488.
83. *Modern Health Care*, August, 1997.
84. See generally: A.S. Goldberg, Health Lawyers Association Health Law Update on Telemedicine and the Law, June, 1997, presented at the NHLA/AAHA Managed Care Institute in Chicago, Illinois in December, 1997.
85. R. Carlson, "Can Telemedicine Deliver What it Promises?" 36–45.
86. See generally "Telemedicine: An Overview of Applications and Barriers," produced by the Physicians Insurer Association of America, 1996.
87. Mass. Gen L. c.112 Section 7.
88. See generally: Outline by Allan S. Goldberg, Esquire, prepared for the NHLA/AAHA Managed Care Law Institute, December 8–10, 1997, Chicago, Illinois.
89. J. Grisby, "Lack of Coverage for Telemedicine Services: A Barrier to Implementation of Telemedicine," Background Paper to Western Governors' Association, Telemedicine Action Report, June 1995.
90. Bienz v. Central Suffolk Hospital 557 NY 2d 139 (N.Y. App. Div. 1990).
91. See Dougherty v. Gifford 826 S.W. 2d 668 (Tex. Ct. App. 1992).
92. P.F. Granada, "Medical Malpractice Issues Related to the use of Telemedicine: An Analysis of the Ways in which Telecommunications Affects the Principles of Medical Malpractice," 73 N.Q.L. Rev.65, 69 (1997).
93. See generally P. Granada, "Malpractice Issues Affecting the Implementation of Telemedicine," Western Governors' Association, Telemedicine Action Report, June 1995.
94. K. E. Brooten, Jr. and S. Chapman, *Malpractice: A Guide To Avoidance in Treatment* (New York: Groton, Stratton, Inc., 1987): 1.
95. Also see: L.A. Herscha, "Note, Is there a Doctor in the House? Licensing and Malpractice Issues Involved in Telemedicine," *B.V. Sci. Tech.* 8, 37 (1996).
96. Cal. Bus. & Prof. Code Section 2290.5.

Chapter 11

The Joy of Practice

"Work is love made visible. And if you cannot work with love but only with distaste, it is better that you should leave your work and sit at the gate of the temple and take alms of those who work with joy."

Kahlil Gibran, 1883 – 1931

PHYSICIAN SATISFACTION?

Patient satisfaction has been a major theme in this book and a constant goal of managed care organizations, and rightly so. We know that lawsuits are filed by dissatisfied, or irate, patients, or their families, so one of the most effective malpractice deterrents to malpractice suits is patient satisfaction. We have also shown that patient satisfaction is directly dependent on good communication and the opportunity to be active participants in their own health care. This, and documentation, comprise the major solution to the problem of malpractice prevention. However, there is another essential and often ignored ingredient—physician satisfaction.

Comparatively little has been written about physician satisfaction, or about the influence of a doctor's attitude or frame of mind, in precipitating lawsuits. It is a difficult area to investigate, but nevertheless, it does seem obvious, a veritable *res ipsa loquitur*, that an unhappy doctor is at greater risk for a malpractice action.

The major causes of malpractice actions are actual medical negligence, failure to communicate effectively, unsatisfactory patient-physician relationships, and inadequate documentation. All of these are, in large part, doctor responsibilities. They are more likely to occur if the physician is impaired, and impairment may be due to frustration with the present system, distraction by multiple stressors, or confusion with the required procedures. The feelings generated may be hidden from patients for a time, but as physicians get to know their patients, the patients also learn to know their physicians. Some patients actually study their physicians and discuss them with their friends, and their observations are sometimes disturbingly accurate. As patients perceive their doctor's negative feelings, they begin to generate their own, adding to the possibility that an already tense milieu may become dismal, and a breeding place for malpractice claims.

Patient satisfaction is a major goal of managed care, partly on principle, partly as a real malpractice deterrent, and partly because of competition and the need to show a profit. This profit comes from capturing marketshare through patient satisfaction surveys. Physician satisfaction needs to be viewed with the same priority, and for exactly the same reasons.

What do most physicians want in order to experience the joy of practice, or at the very least, feel satisfied in their work?

- Sense of accomplishment, doing something worthwhile, making a difference. "Am I helping my patients to better health, am I pleasing them?"
- Patient-physician relationships: "Do I enjoy my patients as individuals?" This is especially important in continuing care as in the primary care specialties.
- Ethical practice: for most professionals it is essential to know that the work they are doing meets the highest ethical standards.
- Compensation: this must be perceived as adequate, of course, and must always be going up, not down, and is rarely considered to be entirely satisfactory. (One faculty member pointed out that an adequate income could be defined as 15% above present income, so as to match expenses.)
- Autonomy: the practice of medicine in the past, before managed care, was usually characterized by remarkable autonomy. Physicians could generally choose their fields of interest, where they wanted to practice, which patients they wanted to see, whether to practice alone or with a group, and, to a large extent their hours and days of work.

With that freedom as an enticement, it is probable that many chose dentistry or medicine, at least in part, for that reason. It certainly seemed to typify Dr. Smith, who tried desperately to retain his prized autonomy. Would he have chosen to go to medical school in this environment?

The answer was clearly, "No!" The Smiths' daughter, Phoebe, was in her third year of a liberal arts college when her father's practice problems began to overwhelm him. She was still undecided about a career, but began talking seriously about medical school. She loved people, was willing to work hard, had excellent grades, and wanted to do something "meaningful." Dr. Smith noted all this with pride, partly because it sounded so much like him. But he did not want her to suffer the same disillusionment he was enduring. He knew that she was very close to decision time, and spoke with her often.

Dr. Smith's message to his daughter was always the same, but phrased in different ways:

> "Don't go to medical school! The practice of medicine is no longer any fun. You can't even control your own schedule, like I used to do.

There are always pressures to do more, someone is always looking over your shoulder and telling you what you should do and what they think you have done wrong. You can't even choose your own colleagues, and sometimes not even your own staff. If Gladys was still working, I probably couldn't even work with her; someone else would make the assignments. A lot of the patients I loved most have been lured elsewhere, all for a few dollars saved. I seem to have a choice," he grumbled, "between being capitated or decapitated!"

"And I've had two lawsuits, and I never had any before in all my years of practice. That was awful. I hope you never hear the terrible things they said about me. Now, with every patient I see I keep wondering, 'Are you going to sue me too?'"

PHYSICIAN SATISFACTION STUDIES

Although the research on physician satisfaction is sparse, there have been some investigations which have been helpful in understanding some of physicians' requirements for enjoying their practices.

Baker and Cantor analyzed data from a very large collection of interviews with young physicians.[1] Their goal was to determine the relationship between practicing medicine under managed care, and the levels of perceived professional autonomy, practice satisfaction, and career satisfaction.

The interviews were conducted during a seven-month period in 1991. The sample was designed to be representative of practicing physicians, but restricted to those who were under 45 years of age and had been in practice from two to nine years. Only physicians who were involved in direct clinical care were included. These interviews were conducted by telephone and lasted about 45 minutes. There were 4,257 successfully completed interviews.

The sample was divided into six groups: 1) solo and group practices without managed care affiliations; 2) solo and group practices with managed care affiliations; 3) HMOs; 4) government agencies; 5) other employers without managed care affiliations; and 6) other employers with managed care affiliation. The physicians were asked a series of questions relating to autonomy, including the ability to control their own schedules, spend sufficient time with their patients, freedom to hospitalize or to order tests and procedures, and to keep patients in the hospital as long as they thought necessary.

The results were mixed. Generalist physicians who were self-employed, or employed without managed care affiliation, most often responded affirmatively, but those who were in HMOs were less likely to do so. Specialists, on the other hand, who were in managed care, were more likely to respond affirmatively than those who were employed otherwise.

As might be expected, most (85%) of self-employed physicians felt able to control their own schedules, while only 64% of employees of other employers, and 39% of HMO employees felt they were able to do so.

When asked about their ability to treat patients who cannot pay, only 71% of HMO physicians felt free to do so, but 90% of others did have this freedom. On the other hand, managed care physicians actually felt more free to hospitalize patients, keep them as long as they thought necessary, and to order tests and procedures, than other physicians. This was true for both generalists and specialists.

Physicians were asked about their satisfaction with their current practices. In the self-employed and the "other employer" groups, there was no difference between those who were and those who were not involved in managed care. Those who were HMO employees were about as satisfied as those with other employers, but less so than the self-employed.

When asked about their satisfaction with their career in medicine, almost two-thirds of all physicians said they would go to medical school if they had it to do over again. About three-fourths of the self-employed and those affiliated with managed care, said that the opportunity to practice quality medicine meets or exceeds their expectations. Only half, in all categories, said that the degree of professional autonomy meets or exceeds their expectations.

The authors of the study conclude that, while it had been expected that HMO physicians would feel a much limited autonomy, that is not always the case, although generalists feel less autonomy than specialists. They also noted that there was little difference in the responses of those employed by HMOs, or affiliated with managed care as self-employed or as employees of "other employers."

Their final conclusion was that, "these results do hold out the hope that a large scale move toward managed care might not cause the damage to physicians' morale that some observers have expected."[2]

It is disturbing to note that in this large group of young physicians, new in practice, a third would not go to medical school if they had it to do over again. It is clear that not only managed care, but our society, needs to consider physician satisfaction. We certainly do not want our young, bright students to be dissuaded from entering the profession which could have profound long-term implications.

There has been much speculation that practicing in a managed care organization would lead to great job dissatisfaction, especially in primary care. In the previously cited study, this was not found to be the case with most physicians. That investigation, however, was restricted to physicians under 45 years of age with two to nine years of practice experience. They entered practice knowing that managed care was a present and growing practice style.

In another study, involving the majority of physicians in Dane County, WI, there was no age restriction, and 47% of the respondents were 47 years of age or older. Dane County, which includes Madison, the state capitol, was chosen for the survey because at the time, 40% of the population was receiving their care through one of six HMOs.[3]

There were 850 physicians practicing in Dane County, most of whom were in group practices, part of the staff of an HMO, or on the medical school faculty. Questionnaires were sent to all of them, and there were 543 respondents, 75 of whom were hospital based, 152 in primary care practices, and 316 in referral based practices. The physicians were asked about six different components of job satisfaction: income received from practice, status within the profession, current work satisfaction, satisfaction with resources available to them, autonomy, and professional relations.

In overall satisfaction, 68% said that they were either satisfied or very satisfied with their jobs. (These were the two top ratings on the scale.) Only 8% of the 543 physicians expressed some degree of dissatisfaction. The remaining 24% were either moderately satisfied or neutral.

Psychiatry was the only specialty in which fewer than half of the respondents were satisfied with their work situation. Except in this field, the effects of specialty on job satisfaction were not significant. Psychiatrists were significantly less satisfied than surgeons in terms of income, autonomy, and overall career.

Hospital-based physicians were less satisfied in regard to resources, status, and professional relations in comparison with surgeons. Internists in subspecialties were also significantly less satisfied with respect to professional status in comparison with surgeons. Medical school faculty members, both volunteer and full time, were especially satisfied with their status within the profession.

Another notable finding was that there was a positive coefficient for age. The investigators speculated that this might be due to an appreciation of the advances in technology and expansion of resources during their years in practice. Women were significantly less satisfied than men with their status in the profession, but not in any other category.

The authors of the study note that previous surveys in Dane County indicated that physicians' expectations of managed care were found to be more negative than their actual experience. The findings of this study suggest that the previously expressed fears were unfounded. It is of special interest to note, however, that in Dane County, the six HMOs were organized and controlled by physicians. The authors also believe that their study suggests, "the specific organization and its management and success are very important to physicians' satisfaction."[4]

Both of these studies, by Baker and Cantor and by Schultze, et al., were conducted more than six years ago. In this rapidly evolving field of managed care, more recent studies could indicate change, or at least trends. Kerr, et al., published a physician satisfaction study in July, 1997, with some interesting and different results.[5] This investigation included only primary care physicians in California, in partially capitated medical groups.

The authors report that on a national basis, 80% of primary care physicians are involved in at least one managed care arrangement, and that 45% are managed care employees, and about half are at least partially reimbursed through capitation. In California the effect of capitated care is even greater, with about 60% of physicians under capitation contracts.

Along with these major changes in how primary care physicians are paid, they have accepted a basic change in responsibilities. They are expected to treat patients for a wider variety of ills, both acute and chronic, in ambulatory settings, and must do so cost effectively. They have become "gatekeepers," controlling patient access to testing and imaging procedures, and to most consultants. The "gatekeeping" role has at least the potential to alter their patient-physician relationship, since their traditional role of patient advocate has been expanded to become, in addition, the patient's warden.

The purpose of this study was to address two key questions:

> "1) Do these primary care physicians report different levels of satisfaction with their overall practice than with their care of patients for whom their groups receive capitated payments, especially in the areas of quality of care, autonomy, and relationships with patients?
>
> 2) Does satisfaction with capitated care differ among physicians in different practice arrangements and under different reimbursement mechanisms?"[6]

The investigators began their study by interviewing physicians and meeting with focus groups. From this preliminary work, they found that primary care physicians were quite cognizant of differences in their practice style between the capitated and the non-capitated patients. A questionnaire was developed addressing the issue of satisfaction with quality of care, using four groups of questions concerning their relationship with patients, their own perception of the quality of care they were able to provide, their freedom to treat patients according to their clinical judgment, and their ability to arrange for referral to other specialists when needed.

Questionnaires were sent to 1,138 physicians in 89 medical practice groups. In all of these groups physicians continued to see both capitated and non-capitated patients, with a variety of other forms of insurance. The questionnaires were returned by 910 physicians, representing an 80% response rate.

An analysis of the results of this survey showed that there was a marked difference in the level of physician satisfaction in all four parameters of quality of care, between the capitated and the non-capitated patients. In their relationship with patients, 88% were very or somewhat satisfied with their overall practice (i.e., non-capitated), but only 71% with their capitated patients. As far as the perceived quality of care they were able to provide, 88% again were satisfied in regard to their non-capitated patients, but only 64% with capitated patients. In ability to treat with their best judgment, 79% were satisfied with their overall practice, in contrast to 51% in the other group. In the ability to obtain specialty referral, for unexplained reasons, there was far less satisfaction in either group; 59% for the former, and 50% for the latter.

Some differences were also noted, depending on the actual ratio of capitated to non-capitated patients. Those physicians whose practices were 75% or more capitated were more satisfied in all four categories than those who had a smaller percent of capitated patients. The authors suggest several possible reasons for this finding. Physicians with higher numbers of capitated patients may have developed systems that make their practice easier and more efficient, or they may have chosen to do more capitated work because they enjoy it and are good at it. It also shows the difficulty a physician has when going through the transition to managed care or, more specifically, capitation from fee-for-services.

These findings are disturbing. This investigation involved a large number of physicians, was well focused, and is quite current. Are physicians now delivering different levels of care depending on how they are paid? The investigators point out that these results are all based on the practicing physicians' perceptions. The next level of research needs to address the harder question of whether their perceptions do translate into actual technical quality of care provided.

This information is important, but we also need to know whether the patients in capitated care perceive that their care is of lower quality, or delivered less compassionately, and whether they feel they are fully involved in their own health care decisions.

An even more recent study was published by Bell, et al., in September, 1997.[7] The purpose of this investigation was to identify some of the components of physicians' attitudes toward managed care. They also wanted to design a tool to measure these aspects. They were able to identify five areas of thought which contributed significantly to physicians' attitudes toward managed care:

- perceived quality of care
- need to adapt to managed care
- perceived cost containment effectiveness
- personal knowledge of managed care
- inevitability of managed care.

Primary care physicians, probably because of their role as "gatekeepers," had a greater understanding of how managed care works than did the consultants, were more likely to have confidence in the quality of care, and were more convinced of the inevitable dominance of managed care.

Before their study, Bell, et al., thought that they might find that physicians had a global attitude toward managed care, not discriminating by its several components, or might have an attitude focused on one particularly annoying managed care tool. They found the opposite to be true; physicians had distinct feelings about each of the various mechanisms used by managed care. They also found a distinct link between physicians' attitudes and behavioral intentions. For example, positive responses on three of the five scales—quality, need to adapt, and cost containment effectiveness—correlated with the physicians' intentions of reducing medical costs.

Bell, et al., concluded, "The link we found between attitudes and behavioral intentions reaffirms the importance of procuring physicians' support of managed care reforms. The physicians who were most supportive in their attitudes were most inclined to reduce unnecessary tests and modify their referral patterns.... This pattern of results accentuates the critical role that physicians' sentiments play in the ultimate outcomes of managed care reforms."[8]

Since it is our premise in this book that physician satisfaction is an essential ingredient in a malpractice prevention strategy, the reasons for physician dissatisfaction ought to be sought out and, where possible, remedied. It drives home the point that involving physicians in the creation of systems or in the development of new pathways of care is critical.

These four studies were published over a period of approximately six years, and involved nearly 6,000 physicians, in a full array of clinical specialties. The groups surveyed, and the methods employed, were different, but there are some overall inferences that can be drawn. While the general interpretation of the survey instruments could be considered to imply the question, "Tell us what is wrong with managed care," nevertheless, in all the studies, there were more positive than negative statements about managed care. It is also interesting to note, however, that the two earlier studies had, in general, more positive views of managed care than the more recent surveys. This could, of course, be a result of the methods used or the groups studied, but it should be considered as a possible early warning. It could also be a time trend indicating a response to the tightening of managed care restrictions, or a growing disillusionment by physicians, or their failure to adapt. Several of the investigations clearly implied that physician involvement in decision-making was an important factor in physician satisfaction.

All of this demonstrates a remarkably parallel phenomenon. The greatest deterrents to filing malpractice claims are patient satisfaction, close patient-physician communication, including informed consent, and active patient participation in the health care process. Physicians seem to be reflecting these same needs, not to keep them from suing their managed care organizations, but to enlist their enthusiastic support. Physicians want to understand managed care, and its goals, to have an active part in decision-making related to themselves or their patients, and to be partners, not antagonists, of managed care. Physicians want to help promote and cultivate the good about managed care and to reduce or diffuse the perceived abuses or problem areas.

BUT IS IT RIGHT?

Most physicians cannot experience the joy of practice, or even feel comfortable in their practice, unless they have a strong sense that what they are doing meets their own standards of medical ethics. Organizational standards, such as the AMA's Code of Medical Ethics, are helpful, but not definitive for an individual. For example, The Code at one time strongly prohibited physicians from advertising. Now, with certain restrictions, it is considered acceptable, or ethical. Nevertheless, each physician must decide with what actions she or he is comfortable.

The Hippocratic Oath has been generally accepted as a worthy, almost sacred, standard, and many medical students still choose to take this oath at the time of their graduation. There have, however, been appropriate modifications such as in "not cutting for the stone." This was, no doubt, a valuable admonishment for those practicing medicine in Hippocrates' era, but does not necessarily fit with our current understanding of urology. But do we now need to modify the Oath further, in view of our current understanding of economics? Instead of swearing by Apollo, the physician, should we swear by Adam Smith, the economist?* "I will use my ability to treat the sick, but within my utilization norms." "Whatever. . .I see or hear in the life of men, which ought not to be spoken of abroad, I will not divulge, as reckoning that all such should be kept secret, except as required for the medical records, accessible only to the office staff, the hospital staff, all members of the healing profession, and plaintiff's attorneys."

The American Medical News in August, 1997, reported on a yet-to-be-published study that addressed this issue directly.[9] A group of practicing physicians was convened by The Integrated Healthcare Association of Pleasanton, CA, and asked to re-examine the key Hippocratic principles as applied to managed care.

The group identified three Hippocratic principles which they considered to be key: patient advocacy, integrity of motive, and spirit of inquiry. Patient advocacy was said to mean promoting the welfare of patients based on their individual needs, and practicing good medicine founded on sound scientific principles. Advocacy today may mean distinguishing between what a patient wants and what a patient needs. It also means, "doing the very best thing for the patient, at the best time, by the right provider."[10]

---

*"It is not from the benevolence of the butcher, the brewer, or the baker that we expect our dinner, but from their regard for their own interest. We address ourselves, not to their humanity, but to their self-love." Adam Smith (1723–1790).

The second principle, integrity of motive and process, is the one most under attack by the public, and reflected by actions in the legislatures. The participants in the study group believe that this issue will not be resolved until there are outcome studies proving what is the best care under any given set of circumstances.

The authors of this book are less pessimistic. Developing such standards for every ill, or even just the most prevalent, will require many years, compounded by the fact that all of the basic factors required to make those determinations are continually changing. In addition to defining the "Right Treatment," it would still be necessary to inform and convince the patients. Prevailing distrust can gradually be displaced through exercise of the same basic skills required for malpractice prevention. Close patient-doctor relationships need to be built and maintained. Communication needs to be a continuing focus, in all of its aspects, listening, speaking the same language, using written, oral, and palpable (healing environment) vehicles.

Patients seem to be saying that they distrust the new system because it gives the physicians monetary incentives to influence their decisions. They do not yet seem to realize that this is not a change. Surgeons have always known that there is a major ethical component to many of their decisions. For example, recommend surgery for cholelithiasis, for which they get paid, or watchful waiting, for which they don't? Do we circumcise newborn boys because it is in their best interest, or because it increases our fee? To what extent does that consideration influence our clinical judgment? Patients have always known this, too, but at a lower level of awareness, not often discussed openly. Now there is a third party involved, an impersonal one whom they have not yet found reason to trust. They feel outnumbered, two to one. Of course, we are talking about potentially undertreating and not overtreating, which also had dangers. This distrust can be dispelled, in time, through frank and open discussion, and by truly inviting patients to be partners in their care. It is also going to take much additional dialogue between managed care plans and physicians to reduce the dilemmas discussed in Chapter 10.

The third Hippocratic principle identified by the physician group was the spirit of life long inquiry. This was recognized as a gray area, where managed care organizations need to find a balance between continuing education and research on the one hand, and maintaining a competitive edge on the other.

The group concluded that, "the core principles of ethical physician conduct are the same in a fee-for-service and a managed care environment." "Ethical physicians can practice ethical medicine in any system."[11]

Not everyone shares the confident view of this group of California clinicians. In the same article in *The American Medical News*, Jerome P. Kassirer, MD, editor-in-chief of the *New England Journal of Medicine,* is quoted as saying, "The situation can be more threatening to professionalism because the physician is given the responsibility to keep costs at a minimum. The concern that I have is that responsibility may lead them to go too far in restricting services that shouldn't be restricted."[12]

The criticism of managed care seems to be that it has shoved physicians into a position requiring difficult ethical decisions. We share the confidence of the California group that "ethical physicians will make ethical decisions." However, recognize the tremendous challenge that will need to take place. Perhaps the greatest difficulty for practitioners is that there is no one BIG decision, no "one decision fits all." The same issues arise many times each day, each in different circumstances, requiring individual consideration, requiring many ethics-based decisions.

From a malpractice prevention viewpoint, the requirements are quite clear; communicate openly with the patient, discuss your decision, and document the fact that you have explained it to your patient, along with your reasoning for that decision. You are not liable for making an error in clinical judgment. You may be sued by any patient who is angry or does not understand the situation. You may be considered culpable and that your decision was made strictly for pecuniary reasons, if you have not documented your real reasons.

Practicing medicine in an ethical way is an essential part of physician satisfaction, of the joy of practice, and was recognized since the time of Hippocrates. "I will follow that system of regimen which, according to my ability and judgment, I consider for the welfare of my patients, and abstain from whatever is deleterious and mischievous... While I continue to keep this Oath unviolated, may it be granted to me to enjoy life and the practice of the art, respected by all men, in all times!"

THE DRS. SMITH

Dr. Wright sat down at his desk and glanced at the document in front of him, another application for admission to the panel. The name, Dr. Smith, caught his eye, and he thought back to that very painful day when he had to tell Dr. Smith that he was being terminated from the panel. He knew the good doctor had really tried, but his efforts were erratic and inadequate—he just did not understand. Although Dr. Wright knew that the termination was necessary, and had never regretted the decision, he still hated the process. Now he wondered on what grounds Dr. Smith could possibly be reapplying. He turned quickly to the page asking the question, "Why do you wish to be a member of the panel?" The answer he read astounded him. Here was a doctor who really understood what managed care meant, understood the goals and accepted them, and recognized the potential benefits to patients of being members of the health care plan, and was very eager to participate. How could this be the same Dr. Smith? It wasn't.

As he turned to the last page, Dr. Wright saw that it was signed, Phoebe Smith, MD, Dr. Smith's daughter.

Membership on the panel was all that Phoebe expected it to be. Her practice developed quickly, and with her simple but frank explanations, her patients seemed to understand the system they had joined. She enjoyed having colleagues available for discussion of clinical problems, and felt that she was able to keep on learning because of the continuous peer review system. She liked having the support of the organization in developing and maintaining all the systems she needed for a smooth running practice, scheduling, telephone triage, patient education, recall for health maintenance, billing, and follow-up. She recognized the need for all of these, but was glad to share the responsibility with someone else. The more time she had to spend with her patients, the better she liked it. With these systems in place, the continuing peer review, and the backup of a large organization, she felt secure from the threat of malpractice.

Phoebe had encountered several occasions in which she disagreed with the utilization review board on specific issues. She quickly learned, however, to present a forceful case on behalf of her patient. She did not always win these discussions, but she also learned that by asserting herself she could become a part of the policy-making committee, with the possibility of revising those policies with which she disagreed.

On one occasion she encountered a situation which clearly raised an ethical issue. While it was quite clear that the issue was an ethical one, it was not at all clear what was the best resolution. Phoebe called for a hearing before the Ethics Committee, and was most gratified that her dilemma was taken seriously and pondered carefully and compassionately. It was not as timely as she had hoped and she had to be tenacious, yet not vicious.

As she tried to explain to her father, no, she did not have complete control of her own schedule, and yes, there were differences about utilization, and no, she did not really have complete control over her own practice, but these were just trade-offs. They were, on balance, far outweighed by the benefits of belonging to the plan, both for her patients and for her. Her practice was a great joy to her. "All I wanted to do, Dad, was take good care of my patients."

Source: Copyright © 1997, SC Saxton.

REFERENCES

1. L.C. Baker and J.C. Cantor, "Patient Satisfaction Under Managed Care," *Health Affairs* (Supplement 1993).
2. Baker and Cantor, *Health Affairs*, 270.
3. R. Schultze, et al., "Physician Satisfaction in a Managed Care Environment," *Journal of Family Practice* 34.3 (1992): 299.
4. Schultze, et al., *Family Practice*, 303.
5. E.A. Kerr, et al., "Primary Care Physicians' Satisfaction With Quality of Care in California Capitated Medical Groups," *Journal of the American Medical Association* 278, no. 4 (July 1997): 308–312.
6. Kerr, et al., "Primary Care Physicians' Satisfaction With Quality of Care in California Capitated Medical Groups," 309.
7. R.A. Bell, et al., "Physicians' Attitudes Toward Managed Care: Assessment and Potential Effects on Practice Behaviors," *American Journal of Managed Care* 3.9 (1997): 1297–1304.
8. "Can the Hippocratic Oath Apply to Managed Care?" *American Medical News* (18 August 1997).
9. "Can the Hippocratic Oath Apply to Managed Care?"
10. "Can the Hippocratic Oath Apply to Managed Care?"
11. L.O. Prager, "Physicians Leery About PRO Changes," *American Medical News* (18 August 1997).
12. Prager, "Physicians Leery About PRO Changes."

About the Authors

James W. Saxton is a partner in the Pennsylvania law firm of Stevens and Lee, where he is also Chairman of the Health Care Litigation Group and a senior member of their health law group. He is a graduate of Shippensburg State University and Duquesne University School of Law. For the past sixteen years, he has been representing health care providers in the courtroom in health care litigation and advising providers and managed care organizations on practice and risk management and other related health care issues. He has written several books on the subject of risk management for providers, as well as on the litigation process generally. He has authored numerous articles and has been an invited lecturer across the country on health care litigation related issues and on managed care. Mr. Saxton sits on several editorial boards including *The Medical Practice Communicator, The Doctor's Office,* and a new publication entitled *Managed Health and You.* He is a member of the Lancaster Bar Association, Pennsylvania Bar Association and the National Health Lawyers Association/American Academy of Health Care Attorneys. He also chaired the American Academy of Health Care Attorneys' Committee on revising their managed care manual and is now one of the Vice Chairs of the Managed Care and Integrated Delivery System Committee, with specific responsibility for managed care liability. He is also the President of the W. Hensel Brown Inn of Court, a chapter of the National Inns of Court.

Thomas L. Leaman, MD is Professor Emeritus of Family and Community Medicine of the Milton S. Hershey Medical Center of The Pennsylvania State University. He is a family physician, first certified by the American Board of Family Practice in 1970, and recertified three times thereafter. He practiced in the same small town, Hershey, Pennsylvania, for forty years, at first in solo practice, and then as the founding chairman of the first academic department of Family Medicine in the United States. He served as the president of The Society of Teachers of Family Medicine in 1983–84, and was also elected president of The Association of Academic Departments of Family Medicine. He served on the Editorial Board of *The Journal of Family Practice* for ten years, and as Editor of *The Female Patient* for three years. He has published numerous articles and chapters, and several books. Dr. Leaman has also served as an expert witness in many malpractice cases, both for the defense and for plaintiffs. He retired from the University and from practice, and has continued as a medical writer and in making educational presentations. He is a member of The Society of Teachers of Family Medicine, The American Academy of Family Physicians and The American Medical Association. Dr. Leaman lives in Hershey with his wife, Jeanne.

INDEX